Toward a Christian Clinical Psychology

THE CONTRIBUTIONS OF H. NEWTON MALONY

Louis Hoffman, PhD, Editor

WIPF & STOCK · Eugene, Oregon

Wipf and Stock Publishers
199 W 8th Ave, Suite 3
Eugene, OR 97401

Toward a Christian Clinical Psychology
The Contributions of H. Newton Malony
By Hoffman, Louis
Copyright©2010 by Hoffman, Louis
ISBN 13: 978-1-4982-2585-4
Publication date 10/1/2015
Previously published by Fuller Seminary Press, 2010

TABLE OF CONTENTS

FOREWORD

I count it a privilege to be asked to write the forward to this book, published as a tribute to my long-time colleague and close friend Dr. Newton Malony. The articles, addresses, presentations and sermons of Newton's are gathered together in this volume to honor him and his dedicated professional life. They speak volumes! And the title of this book "Toward A Christian Psychology" says it all. Newton's whole career as a scholar has been focused on one primary theme: integrating a Christian theology with the best that psychology had to offer. It captures the soul of his life's commitment: to help psychology find its way back to its origin in the heart of God. He also served the profession of psychology with distinction, including participation in Division 36 of APA, the California Psychological association, the Society for the Study of Religion, and several accrediting boards.

While the content of this book superbly reflects the scholarly and professional life of Newt (as he is affectionately known) my focus here is mainly on the man behind this book. Newton arrived on Fuller's campus in 1969 when the fledgling Graduate School of Psychology was barely four years old. Lee Edward Travis, our distinguished founding Dean, told once told me that of the entire faculty he recruited at the beginning, Newton had impressed him the most. It was not just his training as a clinical psychologist, but he had a theology degree from Yale and had served for a few years in ministry before turning to psychology. This "dual" training would serve the school well. More importantly, he was impressed with his character. At Travis' invitation I came to the Graduate School of Psychology at Fuller as a "post-doctoral Fellow" in 1971. I was immediately impressed by the character of Newton. So, when I was invited to join that group of pioneering faculty I jumped at the opportunity, gave up my career on the other side of the globe, packed up my wife and three young girls, and immigrated to Fuller. It was my privilege later to serve as Dean and to work alongside Newton while he served as Director of our programs in integration.

What a joy it was to work alongside him. He could differ with you without being offensive; disagree without any sign of malice. He was generous in his praise, always honest to the core in his feedback, and quite notably, champion of the underdog. If a student was in any sort of trouble, it was Prof. Malony they would run to. He and I would often "have it out" over some student's poor performance or failure. I am sure there are many graduates out there who are thankful to God for his intervention and wise counsel in how to solve a problem or two.

He also served, unofficially, as our school historian. In collaboration with

Dr. Hendrika Vande Kemp, he recorded the history of the school's phenomenal experiment in linking psychology and theology. In the book "Psychology and the Cross" he provides a sensitive, detailed account of the school's origin and development up to the year 1995. And while the book details the lives of all who helped develop the school, in typical Malony style he sells himself somewhat short. His description of himself as the third "Travis Boy," meaning that he was the third faculty member to be recruited by founding Dean Lee Travis, doesn't do justice to his enormous contribution. I can personally attest that he faithfully defended the importance of solid theological training for our students right from the outset, often having to badger the faculty not to reduce the theology curriculum. He instigated the involvement of both a psychology and theology professor in all integration courses, and fostered interfaculty integrative dialog throughout the seminary. I doubt very much if we would have been the same without him.

And that is the man he was and still is. This tribute to his superb scholarly ability is well deserved. But it only reveals half of the man he really is. It is my honor to call him "my dear friend."

Archibald D. Hart, PhD, FPPR.
Senior Professor of Psychology and Dean Emeritus
School of Psychology
Fuller Theological Seminary

Bringing Depth and Soul to the Psychology of Religion

LOUIS HOFFMAN, PhD

My first prominent memory of H. Newton Malony was during my years as a student at Fuller Seminary's Graduate School of Psychology. Along with others in my cohort, I was sitting in Travis Auditorium watching Dr. Malony walk back and forth across the stage asking questions and suggesting some difficult ideas for us to consider. As the discussion grew more intense, Malony smiled and laughed, enjoying the development of ideas. Some were frustrated that we were not always given clear answers on the integration of psychology and religion, which was the focus of the class, but no one could deny that we were thinking about integration on a deeper level.

As I went through the program, researching and writing many papers, I frequently was astounded that for seemingly every topic I researched, Malony had a paper for that. In our History and Systems class, our professor told us that Malony had published over 300 papers, book chapters, and books in his career – and that was over 20 years ago! His contribution to the professional literature is prolific. Yet, when you sat with the man, Newt Malony, he would not speak of such things. A few years ago, in speaking with James Nelson, a contemporary leader in the psychology of religion, he noted that Malony never drew attention to himself. Because of this, Nelson said, many who had contributed and accomplished much less, but were willing to clamor and draw attention to their work, received more attention. For Malony, it was about the work. He often seemed to delight more in the accomplishments of his students than in his own.

As I am drawn to Malony's work now, having been active in the field for 10-years, I again return to the idea of depth. His greatest contribution as a teacher has been helping people think more deeply about the psychology of religion and the integration of psychology and religion. He has taken on controversial issues, such as homosexuality, with openness and honesty. His book, *Pastoral Care and Counseling in Sexual Diversity*, addressed one of the more controversial issues of our time with great sensitivity and a balanced perspective. In his book *A Christian Existential Psychology: The Contributions of John G. Finch,* Malony recognized the contributions of Finch to the often misunderstood relationship between existential psychology and religion. Many other examples could be noted of his unique contributions.

From the beginning of my career until more recently, Newt Malony has been an important influence on my professional career. His contributions can be broken down to his contributions as a teacher/mentor, an academic, a clinical psychologist, and a person.

Newt Malony: The Teacher/Mentor

Malony had a gift for getting people to engage with psychology whether they liked it or not. As the illustration above demonstrates, Malony enjoyed getting the class to discuss the various sides of important issues while he stood back, watching the conversation develop. Along the way, he would gently guide the class to include certain ideas or topics. But the class did much of the thinking and the work. Unfortunately, graduate education today has too often become about the accumulation of knowledge. For Malony, this was never good enough. He did not want his students to just acquire knowledge; he wanted them to be able to apply this knowledge and to understand it in a personal way.

We applied his teaching to our lives, our families, and our clients. This was not because Malony told us to, but because he helped his students engage the material in a manner that made it relevant. This helped turned abstract ideas into something practical, something useful. He guided us to carefully consider the knowledge we acquired as it was acquired.

Malony's influence as a teacher went well beyond the classroom. I imagine I was not always an easy student. I was not interested in just following the path of what I was told to learn through graduate school. I maxed out the number of independent studies I could take, brought my own ideas for dissertation, and often followed a non-linear path. I imagine many advisors would not have allowed for me to do this; however, Malony was always ready to work with me. Other professors, I could tell, were not so appreciative of my desire to make my education my own. But this was his concern, too: to make education personalized and relevant.

I could tell that Malony cared about me, and all of his students, deeply. He invited us into his home, he spoke with us about our lives, and he stuck with us through our program. After having taught in numerous graduate programs over the last 10-years, it is evident that few, if any, of my many teachers have influenced my approach to being a professor more than Newt Malony. It was this personal care and commitment, in particular, that influenced me.

Newt Malony: The Academic

Preparing to write this introduction, I reviewed many of Malony's papers, articles, books, and book chapters. I was again astonished not just at the number of contributions, but the breadth of topics covered. The vast majority of these contributions dealt with the psychology of religion or integration of psychology and religion. Topics include psychodynamic therapy, behaviorism, existential psychology, transpersonal psychology, transactional analysis, religious freedom, ethics, sexual orientation, brainwashing, clergy assessment, the psychology of religion for ministry, diagnostic issues with religious clients, religious diagnosis, conversion, conflict resolution, John Wesley's relevance to psychology, prayer, religious maturity, the history of psychology, and many more. While most prolific academics focus on one or two areas of specialization, Malony was able to demonstrate expertise across a wide range of topics.

In addition to professional writing, Malony served in many professional roles, including being president of Division 36 of the American Psychological Association (then called Psychologists Interested in Religious Issues) and the

Christian Association of Psychological Studies International. He served on editorial boards for 9 journals and served as a visiting scholar at several colleges and universities. Malony is also a fellow of 5 divisions of the American Psychological Association as well as being a fellow of the American Psychological Society. Awards from numerous organizations, including the Templeton Foundation and Christian Association of Psychological Studies, have recognized these accomplishments. Few scholars, indeed, could boast of such a diverse breadth of achievements.

Newt Malony: The Practitioner

Malony was not just an academic; he also spent many years practicing psychology outside of and in addition to his academic roles even after beginning teaching. In addition to seeing therapy clients, Newt was also involved in other practice roles. Malony's therapeutic approach was fairly unique, being an integrative approach drawing strongly on Transactional Analysis, which has been largely subsumed into other practice orientations today. He was also involved in clergy career assessment as one of the early pioneers. Later, with Richard A. Hunt and John E. Hinkle, he wrote one of the few books focusing specifically on assessing clergy: *Clergy Assessment and Career Development* (Hunt, Hinkle, & Malony, 1990).

One of Malony's notable roles was serving as a professional witness on cases of religious freedom. I remember talking with Malony about this as graduate student. He maintained that standing for one's own religious freedom required us to also stand for the religious freedom of others. As someone who grew up in a very conservative church that was not always tolerant of differences, this had a deep and lasting influence upon me. While many devoutly religious individuals examine religion primarily from their own religious beliefs and values, Malony demonstrated the importance of being able to understand the dynamics of religion and politics of religion from beyond one's immediate context.

Newt Malony: The Person

Before I arrived at Fuller Seminary's Graduate School of Psychology, I read a great deal about the integration of psychology and faith/religion. Although much of this was good academic work, I always sensed that something was missing. When taking Malony's Introduction to Integration course, it became evident what was missing: the *personal integration* emphasis that Malony added.

My experience with professional psychology up to that point of my education was that it was something that one did from 9:00 to 5:00 and then left at work. Even more, it was often emphasized that this is what one ought to do. One had poor boundaries if they continued to care for clients beyond the 50-minute hour and one was unethical to bring their professional knowledge and skill into their personal life, especially with family and friends. This never made sense to me. If psychology, and the integration of psychology and faith, were such great things, why must we keep them separate from our personal life? Obviously, it is not wise to *do* therapy, *do* assessment, or *do* professional psychology on our friends and family members, but what we do professionally is very personal and many aspects of the wisdom of psychology can and should be applied in our own lives.

Malony's personal level of integration filled what was an important gap for me. But more than that, this was something that Malony lived and role modeled. His life was informed by psychology, faith, and their integration. Also, his professional practice was informed by who he was as a person.

Overview

Toward a Christian Clinical Psychology: The Contributions of H. Newton Malony is divided into 3 sections: Christian Clinical Psychology, Psychology of Religion, and Personhood. The idea of a Christian clinical psychology signifies the integration of psychology and religion, which is different, but related to, the psychology *of* religion. Ideally, these two distinct but related fields draw upon each other in their advancement and ideas; however, they reflect a different methodology. The psychology *of* religion applies the methodology of psychology to religion in order to better understand religion. Conversely, a Christian clinical psychology intends to integrate psychology with religion.

The psychology of religion relies primarily on a psychological epistemology and is not necessarily concerned with the reality of the metaphysical and theological assumptions of religion. Rather, it focuses on the psychological and, to a degree, sociological reality of religion. The psychology of religion could be a legitimate field of study even if religion is nothing more than a human creation; the belief in religion still could have a lived reality.

A Christian clinical psychology, however, assumes that Christianity is also a valid way of knowing. This requires a more complex epistemology and methodology when approaching religion as it adds another way of knowing that needs to be integrated or negotiated with the psychological epistemology and methodology.

While in many ways these represent radically different approaches to understanding religion, ideally they interact with and inform each other. For example, the psychology of religion, through attempts to take a more objective approach to religion, can illuminate realities that may be hidden to a Christian clinical psychology. This is illustrated well in chapter 6, "Brainwashing and Religion: The Influence Process Revisited." Malony, informed by his psychological understanding of religion, is able to take a non-defensive approach to this topic. When reading this chapter, one quickly notes that is quite different in tone than many of the more defensive responses religious groups make when accused of using coercion to convert people. Similarly, there is not the attacking or negative tone often present when accusing a religious group of brainwashing. Instead, there is a balanced approach to this topic.

A Christian clinical psychology also has much to offer the psychology of religion. For instance, several chapters in Section 2 (Psychology of Religion) use theologians, such as John Wesley, as a starting point for identifying and looking at issues in the psychology of religion. Malony shows how some theologians, even though rooted in a Christian belief foundation, were able to make legitimate contributions to the psychology of religion. Similarly, in Chapter 15, Malony examines an important change in the language used by religious individuals. As he discusses the change from "religious" to "spiritual" that is popular in American culture, he looks at the psychological and spiritual significance of this transition.

Section 3, Personhood, provides a different and much more personal approach. Those who know Newt Malony are aware that he is someone who approached psychology in a personal and applied manner; it was part of who he was. In this last section, the chapters reflect the personal integration of Malony's psychological and religious beliefs with his life. They reveal in an intimate and vulnerable manner how the psychology of religion and integration of psychology with religion influenced his personhood.

Section 1: Christian Clinical Psychology

Chapter 1, "Hope is What I am Doing," provides a brief overview to Malony's approach to psychology. In particular, it addresses what he considers the foundation of his approach, which is rooted in the philosophy, theory, and science of psychology. However, he also addresses the role hope plays in all that he does as a clinical psychologist. In many ways, this provides an interpretive frame for the rest of the book.

Chapter 3 tackles the popular topic of mindfulness from a Christian perspective. Mindfulness, most frequently associated with Buddhist thought, has swept across the field of psychology as one of the most popular contemporary topics. Christians, however, have shied away from it, probably largely because of its Buddhist associations. Yet, Malony shows that Christianity has been dealing with some akin to mindfulness, albeit in a different language, for some time.

Chapter 5 addresses the idea of religious diagnosis. Although the *Diagnostic and Statistical Manual of Mental Disorders, Fourth Edition, Text Revision* (DSM-IV, TR; American Psychological Association, 2000) has a generic diagnosis, or rather a V-code (i.e., problems in living), for religious and spiritual issues, this is still given only tertiary consideration by the majority of professional psychology. Malony shows why a more thorough consideration of this issue is important from religious, spiritual, and psychological perspectives.

Chapter 6 introduces one of Malony's more important, but most neglected, contributions: brainwashing and religion. While a student at Fuller, I remember encouraging Malony to write and publish more about this topic. He has, to some degree, done this; however, it has not been given the recognition it deserves. Hopefully, this chapter will help introduce his ideas on this important topic to a broader audience.

Section 1 closes with a chapter on why the integration schools (i.e., schools integrating religion and psychology as part of their training) need the American Psychological Association (APA). There is a long and difficult history between the religious schools focusing on integration and APA. The debate centers on religious freedom and the ability to use religious beliefs and standards as criteria for admission. While I may personally disagree with many of the religious schools on their use of these standards, Malony does a nice job in this chapter elucidating why it is important for the integration schools to continue to seek APA accreditation and involvement with APA. Yet, many of these schools and many religious individuals retain a negative feeling toward APA because of this difficult history and feelings of ongoing bias against the religious schools, values, and ideas. Fuller Seminary's Graduate School of Psychology, where Malony taught for years, has been the most important and influential player in establishing a place for religious schools to be accredited by the APA. Furthermore, Malony along with many of Fuller's faculty members, remained involved with APA, including serving in leadership positions.

Section 2: The Psychology of Religion

Section 2 shifts to focusing on the psychology of religion. Several chapters

(11, 19, and 20) focus on the history of psychology of religion. Chapter 11, in particular, discusses the often neglected and forgotten role of Clark University in the psychology of religion's history. Similarly, chapter 20 highlights the important role of Gordon Allport. Chapter 18 is a bit different. It draws, in part, on the well-known writings of Freud on religion. However, it provides an important twist by focusing on Freud's dialog with Oskar Pfister, a minister, who was one of the few people who disagreed strongly with Freud yet maintained a close relationship with him.

Two chapters (15 and 17) deal with important contemporary challenges. Chapter 15, as discussed briefly earlier, examines the significance of the transition from discussing religion to discussing spirituality in the professional psychological literature. Chapter 17 focuses on another topic I had long hoped Malony would address more in his published works. In this chapter, he draws a comparison between the psychology of religion and what he calls "the religion of psychology." He draws a comparison between how religion functions and how psychology functions. It is too often believed that psychology has attained an objective method beyond values. However, this is a dangerous misnomer. In reality, psychology espouses a strong values system; however, it often remains at the implicit level because of the resistance to acknowledging that these values exist. Even within professional psychology, many diverse values systems can be deduced from the various theoretical orientations and specialties. Malony begins to expose this reality in this chapter.

Section 3: Personhood

Section 3 is very different than the first two sections with a significant shift in tone, style, and theme. These are much more personal chapters. The first chapter in this section, chapter 23, offers very personal reflections on death and the role it played in Malony's personal development, beginning with his father's death at age 6. Chapter 24 provides the beginnings of a confession of faith. The last chapter offers a reflection on the vocation of being a counselor or psychotherapist as a ministry. This idea, too, had a profound impact upon me when in graduate school. It helped me see my career as a calling with a deep spiritual significance. Although my faith has transitioned greatly since that time, I never lost sight of the sacredness of the profession I chose to enter.

CONCLUSION

The process of pulling these papers together has been deeply meaningful to me. Prior to this project, I was quite aware that Newt significantly influenced my professional development, but I did not recognize the depth and breadth of his influence upon me personally and professionally. I am left feeling this project was as much a gift to me as a professional project. I hope many other students of Malony will be reminded of his influence on their life. For those not blessed to be one of his students, I hope this will help them benefit from the wisdom of this great man.

REFERENCES

American Psychiatric Association (2000). *Diagnostic and statistical manual of mental disorders* (4th ed., Text Rev.). Washington, DC: Author.

Hunt, R. A., Hinkle, J. A. & Malony, H. N. (1990). *Clergy assessment and career development.* Nashville, TN: Abingdon Press.

Malony, H. N. (Ed.). (1980). *A Christian existential psychology: The contributions of John G. Finch.* Lanham, MD: University Press of America.

Malony, H. N. (Ed.). (2002). *Pastoral care and counseling the sexually diverse.* New York, NY: Routledge.

EDITOR BIO

Louis Hoffman, PhD, is a faculty member at Saybrook University in Oakland, CA and has been an adjunct faculty member at Fuller Theological Seminary's Graduate School of Psychology. He is author of seven books including The God Image Handbook for Spiritual Counseling and Psychotherapy, Existential Psychology East-West, Spirituality and Psychological Health, *and* Capturing Shadows: Poetic Encounters Along the Path of Grief and Loss. *He has authored numerous articles, book chapters, and conferences papers on existential psychology, the psychology of religion/spirituality, and multicultural issues. Dr. Hoffman also regularly travels to China to participate in dialogs and give trainings on topics relevant to the psychology of religion and existential psychology. More information is available about Dr. Hoffman's professional work at www.louis-hoffman.com.*

Toward
a Christian
Clinical
Psychology

SECTION ONE

Christian
Clinical
Psychology

ONE

"Hope" Is
What I'm Doing

I am a clinical psychologist. Like others of my colleagues, however, I am a psychologist first and clinician next. This means several things to me. The history of psychology, the philosophy of science, general theories of personality, perception, motivation and learning, and particularly research in social psychology all interest me. My task as clinician (i.e. consultant, psychotherapist, diagnostician) is guided by these issues. Further, my daily tasks are clinical only in part. I retain active interest in many of the above fields through teaching and research. As a professor, I conduct classes in social psychology or related areas such as group processes and social change. In addition, I supervise research pertaining to a variety of basic psychological processes.

Nevertheless, much of my professional life is related to the clinical task that I define as that of "intentional intervention into the lives of persons, families and groups so as to enhance their adjustment and their fulfillment through the use of psychological methods." I am an action-oriented psychotherapist in the sense that I encourage risk behavior which might lead to a more positive self perception. I agree with those who say that insight follows behavior rather than vice versa. I utilize the methods of Gestalt psychology, role playing and behavior modification to help persons achieve their goals. I make psychoanalytic assumptions about developmental processes and find the jargon of Transactional Analysis especially helpful in helping persons understand themselves. In addition to work with individuals, I conduct weekly group therapy sessions and direct periodic classes, marathon encounter groups, psychodrama sessions and week-long personal growth training events. I supervise several students who are in training and attempt to share my skills through interaction with them.

In the institution where I teach I have responsibility for training students in community consultation, which we consider to be a prime skill of the contemporary clinical psychologist. Society needs the skills of the psychologist in such areas as community planning, conflict management, leadership training and organizational development. Thus, the psychologist's skills in working with individuals must be supplemented by expertise in working with groups. Most of my clinical teaching is directed toward meeting these larger needs of society.

Turning to some comments on my Christian faith, I consider myself to be a theological man in spite of the fact that I do not consider myself to be a theologian. Better said, I am a faithing person. For me, the persistent question is "What am I doing?" And the answers I give to this are intentionally those I derive from my Christian faith. I perceive myself to be a growing, open, and seeking person. I persist in exploring my self-understanding as a forgiven sinner who is nevertheless created in the image of God.

Prior to detailing my present struggle with the "What am I doing?" question or noting several of the practical ways I express my faith in my practice, a word of personal history seems appropriate. I came to psychology through the ministry of the United Methodist Church. After seminary I served as pastor of local churches and as the chaplain of a mental hospital. I entered graduate school with the thought of someday teaching in a seminary. However, my general interest in psychology grew as I pursued graduate training and I began no longer to see myself as primarily concerned with pastoral counseling. My years as professor in a Methodist college allowed me to broaden these learnings. There my faith expressed itself through a growing interest in the study of the psychology of religion.

My present role as Associate Professor[1] in the Graduate School of Psychology of Fuller Theological Seminary is an optimal combination of my training and interest. A description of some of my present tasks is, at least, a structure for expressing my faith in my profession. Herein, I engage in the excitement of preparing Christian psychologists. I retain my role as academic psychologist (not pastoral counselor) but I do so within a context where persons are also studying theology and attempting to relate this to psychology. Periodically, I teach an "integration seminar" with one of the professors in the School of Theology. In these endeavors I have the chance to theoretically relate such concerns as the nature of man and the development of religious constructs in persons. I also teach courses in the psychology of religion from time to time. I conduct research on the psychological correlates of religious experience and the dynamics of religious leadership. I abstract several journals for Religious and Theological Abstracts.[2]

In a very practical way, I relate my faith and my profession through consultation with religious organizations. In our consultation we are primarily concerned with the church as an institution which has been relatively untouched by psychology. We direct much of our training toward equipping our students to consult with the church. We consider it to be one of the more important tasks in which a Christian psychologist can become engaged. I direct our school's Church Consultation Service. We have assisted churches in establishing counseling centers, training lay counselors, managing conflict within their fellowships, upgrading their leadership skills, and providing their members with growth and enrichment. I also do the psychological screening for the San Gabriel Valley Presbytery of the Presbyterian Church, U.S.A. and the United Methodist Church in Southern California. A final way I relate my faith and my profession is by directing a counseling center in my own local church.

As I suggested earlier, my persistent question to myself has been"What am I doing?" Above I have given the structural answer to this question by describing my activities. The more important answer, however, is a dynamic one. In the midst of these activities "What am I really doing?" My present answer to this follows. I take some comfort in knowing these thoughts need not be final answers. If there is one characteristic of myself in which I take pride it is a quality of flux and openness. I am "in process." I hope to remain sensitive to God's ongoing revelation to me of what it means to live as a Christian.

The "What" of my activity is my concern at two levels. The first is my need to ground my own actions in the context of Christian Discipleship. The second is my need to understand my interventions into the lives of others within the context of the Christian Hope.

Simply stated, I value persons in whatever context I experience them, i.e. as individuals or in groups such as families or churches. I yearn for fulfillment for them. While I usually construe this as self-fulfillment, I am aware of the limitations of such an idea apart from a Christian view of persons. Therefore, I trust that the new self affirmation toward which I lead them will be completed by their affirmation of themselves as completely understood, treasured and needed by God as we know him in Christ. To me this is the larger context in which I work. I do not do the task well. I remain in tension, not about the value of the task, but about the means toward the end. I continue to be concerned about when the task is done and I remain somewhat self-conscious about the explicit use of religious language in my day to day activities. Nevertheless, to me it is not a matter of *whether* but of *how* the good news I know in Christ is to be utilized as an intervention procedure in my work as a psychologist.

Two of the latest influences in my thinking have been Thomas Oden (1967) and Rueben Alves (1969). Oden has compared the psychotheraputic conditions of client centered therapy to the attitudes of God toward man revealed in Christ. In therapy the conditions of acceptance, understanding, and honesty enable the person to become free to be himself. I commit myself to providing these conditions. Oden (1967) suggests these are the ways God in Christ relates to persons. This is the good news from God that frees persons to live to God's glory. I agree with Oden that as a psychologist I share in this gospel task.

Just as the acceptance of the love of God frees persons from sin for life that is life indeed, so in therapy do the attitudes I convey enable persons to become free to be themselves, i.e. that person they were intended to be.

The weakness of this position is that it assumes God's attitude toward humans is communicated implicitly, i.e. without intentional identification of these human behaviors as Christian. Further, it assumes the communication is the same as if it came from Christ. I have managed this dilemma for myself by admitting the inadequacy of my efforts along with all human efforts toward good or Godly action. Nevertheless, I acknowledge the image of God in myself and affirm that, in fact, I am capable of behavior that is accepted as good by God. It would seem to me that I do communicate the love and acceptance of God even though it be done only partially and implicitly.

Turning to another issue, I have affirmed for some time one aspect of "hope", i.e. that both my efforts and the growth of persons I work with are within the context of a fulfillment promised and yet to come. It is not that I can be less intent or can work casually but that God is not entirely dependent on my skills or the other person's motivation. He has a power to fulfill lives that is apart from my efforts. I often think of this in terms of the eschaton, i.e. the end of time at which God will fulfill His plan and make all things new. More typically, I experience the press of the end back onto my time and perceive Him capable of creating novelty and fulfillment within the situation which supercedes all my skills. In fact, I believe some persons get better in spite of me rather than because of me. To be sure, "The whole is more than the sum of the parts", as the Gestalt psychologists are prone to say. This is one way I live in Christian hope!

Another contribution to my thinking about hope has been Reuben Alves' emphasis on the hope of the dispossessed. Although he emphasizes the dilemma of minority races and undeveloped nations, his ideas could as easily be applied to individuals who are caught in the throes of intra-personal anxiety or interpersonal conflict. And these are the persons with whom I work.

Alves suggests that the dispossessed of the world will not find freedom by accomodating themselves to the economic patterns of the work ethic or the customs of the majority races. To adjust to what is to be subjected to further servitude. Freedom is found only in the struggle to be true to oneself. Dispossessed persons need not know the end toward which they are moving but they do need to hope and to exert their power. Creativity, or new life, comes both in the struggle to free oneself from domination and in the strain toward a future which is uncertain.

This structure is very akin to the relationships in which I function. The persons and groups with whom I work are struggling to be free. They do not know what the future holds or the end toward which they are moving. Like the dispossessed, they are demeaned and enslaved if I encourage them simply to adjust to their society so they can manipulate the world more effectively. They will likewise be dehumanized if I mechanically impose my values on them even if those values be the Christian message. It is their struggle for freedom in which I am privileged to be a part. I should not ursurp their initiative. The great danger is that I will inadvertently do what psychologists are prone to do—, i.e. unintentionally but methodically teach my own values. As one writer (Fields, 1970 has suggested, "we (psychologists) have been justly charged with turning out..."oreos" (those black on the outside, white on the inside); "coconuts" (brown on the outside, white on the inside); "bananas" (yellow on the outside, white on the inside); and "apples" (red on the outside, white on the inside)." We have solved too many persons's struggles with our solutions. Thus, we have often created puppets who are alienated from their fellows with whom they must live. I feel I am called to fulfill the ethical demand of objectivity as espoused by the code of ethics of the American Psychological Association and that, in part, this is Christian respect for the worth of each person.

One might say that these strictures leave me with nothing to say. Silence is certainly an option. Another option is to risk myself, in-trust myself to them, participate in their struggle, have faith in the process and hope that new life will come. The character of this new life may surprise and, yea, change even me— the therapist. The critical issue here is a willingness to ally myself with their struggle and to trust the process of self-fulfillment.

Understanding this stance within the Christian Hope is not easy. It is not easy because it affirms a post-reformation view of man as one who can use his power for good and who does not automatically approach God in a dependent position. It further calls for faith in the process of struggle rather than in the prior acceptance of the truth that we are to live to the glory of God. I acknowledge this dilemma yet I trust it is possible for me, a faithing Christian, to stand with others in their struggle to be free without arbitrarily imposing on them my answers to their quest.

The reader will probably find the above dissatisfying because it makes little reference to the method wherein my own faith is expressed in consultation and therapy. To say I have hope in the process is probably insufficient. It thrusts me back onto the weaknesses of Oden's implicit communication. I want to resist, however, any mechanical formulation of the communication issue. I am involved in a process of mutual struggle and exploration that cannot be reduced to a lecturer-student relationship.

Both the dangers of implicit and mechanical communication were illustrated in my doctoral dissertation wherein fourteen ministers interviewed the same woman (an actress playing the role of a parishioner with a problem). She presented the same problem to each man. She reported that her husband was becoming distant and was not coming to church with her anymore. One minister asked if her husband played ping-pong. He was convinced that they could get her husband to Christ and the church through the Wednesday evening men's recreational fellowship. At the opposite extreme, another minister paid no attention to her husband's problem but told her that he had been "up and down the streets of life and seen many problems just like her's." What she needed, said he, was "the Lord Jesus Christ." Surely the expression of faith cannot be intrusted to ping pong or one-to-one preaching.

Nevertheless, silence is not an option. I recognize this both as a psychologist and as a Christian. The American Psychological Association ethical code calls me to integrity as well as objectivity. Christian discipleship includes sharing my hope in a present and future which has been made new by the act of God in Christ. Integrity and discipleship are felt obligations for me. Thus, as stated before, it is not whether but how this faith shall be expressed.

Methodologically, Sellers (1961) *The Outsider and the Word of God* and Jourard (1964) *Self Disclosure* have been instructive for me.

Sellers suggests the way to persons is through their anxieties. This is similar to the Tillichian principle of correlational theology. Faith comes as answers to the questions persons ask. Faith meets needs, although it often does so by posing the questions in a new form and by positing answers that were long considered no answers. Certainly the very structure in which I work, counseling and consulting, is one in where persons have needs which are expressed in anxieties. They are looking for answers which brings me to Jourard (1968).

Jourard suggests that the deepest level of communication is that of mutual self-disclosure. I have found that sharing or disclosing myself to others in the midst of their struggling has been a most productive means of change in them and in me. The what of what I share in the Christian faith and hope. But sharing is much more than content. Most important, I share myself as a faithing person, i.e. a person with commitment yet with tentative answers, i.e. a person who himself is in the process. I share myself as a person who self consciously stands in the long tradition of those who have accepted the meaning of their life and destiny as coming from God in Christ. I share myself as one who remains open to further elaboration of this faith as it comes from those who also struggle to find themselves.

Thus, this is my story. It takes its place with others who are also in the midst of the struggle to find meaning in their profession. As directors of Psychodrama often say, "Now here is another possibility. Just because its the last does not mean it is of more value than the others. Its just another way of looking at the role. Accept it if you like. Use it if you find it helpful."

ENDNOTES

1. Subsequent to essay Malony was promoted to Professor and is presently Senior Professor in Fuller Seminary's School of Psychology where he has been for more than 36 years.

2. Subsequently Malony has become part of the editorial boards of a number of journals plus was one of two founding editors of the *International Journal for the Psychology of Religion.*

REFERENCES

Alves, R. *A Theology of Human Hope,* Washington, D.C.: Corpus Books, 1969.

Fields, Rona M. Is it Moral to Teach Psychology? *Teaching of Psychology* Newsletter, Dec. 1971, 1-2, 12.

Jouard, S. *The Transparent Self,* Princeton, N. J.: Van Nostrand, 1968»-

Oden, T. C. *Contemporary Theology and Psychotherapy,* Philadelphia: Westminister Press, 1967.

Sellers, J. E. *The Outsider and the Word of God,* New York: Abingdon Press, 1961.

TWO

Counseling
Body/Soul Persons

This article considers the implications of nonreductive physicalism for counseling. A discussion of the secular and religious meanings of "soul" in contemporary culture is followed by several critiques of the assertion that human nature should be understood from a unified, monistic, psychosomatic point of view. After proposing definitions for spiritual capacity, religion, and faith, a model for embodied spiritual counseling that includes a place for soul is suggested. Nonreductive physicalism need not polarize counselors into those who contend, on the one hand, that only physical remedies or medication will help troubled people and those, on the other hand, who contend that appeal to a spiritual substance called soul is needed.

It is in such acts of help-giving as counseling where convictions about human nature are directly applied to daily living. Counseling is always undertaken against a background of basic assumptions about what it means to be a person. Thus, changing from viewing persons as being body and soul dualities to being body/soul unities will significantly impact the way that counseling is done.

After commenting on current thinking about soul in the culture at large, I consider reactions to the notion that body and soul are a unity, not a duality. Taking the position that human beings have a capacity for soulishness or spirituality, I conclude with a discussion of how counseling can become more spiritual at the same time that it does not deny human physicality.

SOUL IN CONTEMPORARY CULTURE

In traditional churches, not much is heard about soul anymore, especially when the word is used in the classical sense of referring to some nonphysical, but substantive, component of the human being. Likely, most mainline Christians will hear the word used in this sense only on Memorial Days when preachers speak about the memory of the departed, whose souls are with God and who we, if we are faithful, will someday join in life that will never end. Soul may also be

heard at gravesides when a minister might intone the following words of com-
mittal:

> *Forasmuch as almighty God hath received unto himself the soul of*
> *our departed sister, we therefore tenderly commit her body to the*
> *ground, in the blessed hope that as she hath borne the image of the*
> *earthly so also she shall bear the image of the heavenly.*

For centuries many Christians have assumed that they have souls as well
as bodies—even if they do not talk about this much anymore. During the
Inquisition it was thought that burning heretics at the stake was a pastoral act,
because the devil would flee from fire and, although the body would die, the
soul would still be saved. The prison chaplain in the recent film *Dead Man*
Walking expressed this same conviction in modern terms by advising Sister
Helen that her main task in dealing with a condemned man was to save his eternal soul by leading him to confess his sin to God and asking for forgiveness
before he died.

Although rarely referred to in everyday religious parlance, *soul* as used
in funerals and on death beds is grounded in the commonly accepted Platonic
assumption that, at the time of creation, the body is joined to a preexistent soul
that is composed of spiritual substance that cannot be destroyed at death. Such
a view has comforted countless persons through the ages when death occurs.
Mormons have incorporated this view into their belief that humans have an
obligation to provide bodies for souls, which are on a trajectory of pre-mortal,
mortal, and post-mortal existence.

This view can be seen in the growing influence of New Age thinking.
These ideas are grounded in Hindu convictions about reincarnation and the
transmigration of souls. Even Edgar Cayce, the late Presbyterian photographer
turned psychic reader, incorporated past-life readings into his uncanny sessions
of diagnosing and treating physical illnesses (Drummond, 1978). Cayce died in
1945, but the Association for Research and Enlightenment in Virginia Beach,
Virginia, still carries on an active program of education and training.

Moreover, the streets of most cities are replete with marquees announc-
ing the services of psychics, and national television now offers several psychic
hotlines replete with testimonies from satisfied customers who are convinced
that they have touched base with the souls of those who have died or have
experienced contact with their own spiritual nature deep inside their bodies.

In addition, the yellow pages of most metropolitan areas include spiritualist churches, which offer similar services. The Agasha Temple of Wisdom in
Los Angeles is but one example. Until his death, Agasha Pastor Fred Zenor
gave private consultations and led weekly worship during which he spoke, in
seance, with the voices of several deceased persons. Undoubtedly, those who

were ministered to by Zenor felt that they were in contact with the souls of their loved ones (Miller & Malony, 1978).

Alongside this cultural ferment, western society has cultivated a unique type of music called "soul" that combines religious convictions with secular hype. Soul music is a popular expression of the yearning to retain a semblance of transcendent experience in daily life. Each year televised awards are given to vocalists who enthusiastically exude a type of improvisational, yet stylized, lyrics and melodies that are common in African American worship services. This kind of music reflects the a-rational depths of human experience. It is spontaneous and explosive. It is free-floating and cannot be reduced to rigid strictures of time and tone. As Winston Gooden suggested, soul is the "essential sense of being that pulsates in the life of the black community ... it is the ability to express feelings in deeply creative ways ... it contains spontaneity, emotion, and rhythm" (Gooden, 1990, pp. 1203).

All of this is to say that although soul may not be a frequent preoccupation of mainline religion, this is not the case in the wider culture—both religious and secular. The late Swiss psychiatrist Carl Jung, although rejecting the classical theological understanding of the term, still retained the concept of soul in his psychology. He spoke for many in the modern world who want to claim that there is a "non-reductive reality and mystery" in psychic life and who protest against the rationalism and materialism of modern psychology that would reduce human life to less than people knew it to be (Muller, 1990).

Even contemporary psychology has embraced some of these ideas. Under the label of "higher mental processes," humanistic counselors, among others, have advocated therapy that included out-of-body or near-death experiences—either induced by meditation or reported after mortal illnesses (Goleman, 1977; Ring, 1980). They have asserted that attention should be paid to a spiritual reality in life or therapy is not complete, although it is never clear whether these counselors are referring to a type of metaphysical material or a cognitive capacity. Terms like spirit, self, mind, ego, and the unconscious have become contemporary synonyms for soul in a way that makes this distinction difficult to apprehend.

However, the distinction between dualist and monist views of persons is not difficult to ascertain in two extant and contradictory approaches to counseling—the rational/emotive and the nouthethic. The rational/emotive approach has been epitomized by the theorizing of Albert Ellis (1965, 1980) and the nouthetic approach by Jay Adams (1970, 1979). According to Ellis, belief in a transcendent power, such as God, is antithetical to mental health. Humans are physical beings whose primary role is to adjust to their environment. Any presumption that they have some spiritual part of themselves that can, or should, relate to transcendent reality is "irrational" thinking. Such fanciful preoccupation will confound humans' ability to function, according to Ellis. Adams, on the other hand, contends that much of what Ellis advocates is erroneous. He takes a dualistic point of view and contends that humans are composed of two realities, both substantive in different ways. Nouthetic or spiritual counseling contends that mental health results from following the rules for living contained in the Bible—rules that pertain primarily to the soul and its eternal destiny rather than the body and its day-to-day existence. Adams's approach has led some, such as Bobgan and Bobgan (1979, 1987), to reject such psychological counseling entirely. Their strong emphasis on the soul, combined with a rejection of the mind, has resulted in their contention that mental illness is caused either by disease in the body or a sinful rejection of spiritual reality. They contend that other kinds of counseling are harmful.

REACTIONS TO THE NEW IDEAS ABOUT SOULS AND BODIES

The question remains: How do conclusions about persons being body/soul unities—that is, embodied states of consciousness who exist within physical limitations—relate to these continuing manifestations of, and debates about, the reality of a transcendent, substantive, spiritual dimension to human life called *soul*? Moreover, how does this challenge of modern science to traditional religious faith relate to such comfort as might be given by clergy in the face of death, or, for that matter, the advice given by various counselors to more mundane existential problems such as phase of life changes, situational anxiety, or interpersonal conflict? Have the advances in the physical and neurological sciences taken away the basic assurance afforded persons by counselors who affirmed a substantive spiritual reality to which one could retreat in the face of the stress and strain of life? Will wider culture's presumption that humans are material bodies inhabited by spiritual phantasms become a passing fantasy? Have the somewhat dated positions of Ellis (1965, 1980), Adams (1970, 1979), and Bobgan and Bobgan (1979, 1987) been superseded in any way that would allow for an alternative view that perceives no threat in a monistic view that sees human beings as body/soul unities? Can this view, labeled *nonreductive physicalism*, become the foundation for a type of counseling that honors, rather than discounts, the uniqueness of persons?

Some are convinced that, unlike Freud's (1927, 1961) prediction about religion, the conclusions of the sciences about human physicality are valid and will not pass away. In fact, these commentators contend that the body has always been the central fact of existence and that embodiment is the way life is experienced by the average erage person. They further contend that modern science's conclusions that the soul cannot be separated from the body is not a new idea but is as old as the Hebrew scriptures. A bodily base for human existence has been established once and for all by modern science, according to such scholars as Richard Hutch (1991) and James Nelson (1978).

In an essay entitled "Mortal Body, Studying Lives: Restoring Eros to the Psychology of Religion," Hutch (1991) asserted that much postmodern scholarship has given in to relativism—the contention that human nature differs qualitatively from culture to culture. He challenged this viewpoint by asserting a foundational truth that every human being is created a physical organism whose life is basically determined by "needs" and "actions."

To a degree, Hutch's (1991) position is a restatement of Reinhold Niebuhr's (1941, 1943, 1949) belief that the primary fact of human existence is the awareness of finitude, that is, the limits of power and knowledge coupled with the realization that one will die. However, Hutch is more physical and less cognitive than Niebuhr. Hutch conceived of the "laws of the moral body" as thanatos and eros—the succession of the generations through life that leads to death and gender complementarity, which leads to reproduction. As he stated, "Sexuality is located within mortality" (Hutch, 1991, p. 198). He was far less concerned than was Niebuhr with the anxiety this awareness engenders and more with the actions that result from basic human propensities.

Hutch (1991) was convinced that psychology has put too much emphasis on cultural differences and too little emphasis on these universal bodily needs and the acts that result from them. According to Hutch, life is unavoidably based on the perceptions that arise out of masculinity or femininity as well as the realization that one will ultimately die. The foundational facts that unify human nature wherever it is found are primarily physical and only secondarily mental. Although Hutch was not so naive as to deny the validity of thought and cognition, as early behaviorists did (Watson, 1913)[1], he stated that the accounts of human behavior, dramatically portrayed in biographies, are where reality can best be seen. He was impatient with the deconstructionist preoccupation of modern psychology that analyzes human behavior into attitudes, values, expectations, and so on. In such studies, "the living body vanishes" (Hutch, 1991, p. 195).

Nelson (1978) agreed with Hutch (1991). In his seminal volume, *Embodiment*, Nelson asserted that "our sexuality, in its fullest and richest sense, is both the physiological and psychological grounding of our capacity to love" (pp. 14-15). In a fascinating comment on John 1:14, "And the Word became flesh and dwelt among us," Nelson stated, "Christian faith ought to take embodiment seriously ... The embodiment of God in Jesus Christ is, in faith's perception, God's decisive and crucial self-disclosure ... The Word *still* becomes flesh. We as body-selves ... are affirmed because of that" (p. 8).

It should come as no surprise that Hutch (1991) would prefer the reading of biography to the study of beliefs, the substance of religion. Nor should it be unexpected that Nelson (1978) recommended beginning with sexuality in self-understanding. These preferences align Hutch and Nelson with the current trend toward "story theology," in which life stories (read *physical experience*) are used as the prime indicator of God's presence (McClendon, 1974). In this model for understanding human beings, reflections on the meaning of events after they occur replace contemporary psychology's concern for prediction of behavior on the basis of perception and intention. Both Nelson and Hutch would applaud an emphasis on the physical basis for spirituality and an understanding of human beings as body/soul unities, with an emphasis on the body.

Others are not as optimistic about the future of a view of human nature that depends so heavily on bodily experiences. Psychologist Phyliss Watts (1996) represents the point of view that something will be lost if the body's needs and actions are overemphasized in counseling. Commenting on the current health care environment in which she, and all counselors, increasingly are having to work, she warned that an overemphasis on bodily health and its corollary, overt actions, will result in a type of help-giving that neglects the spiritual realities that make human beings unique. The title of her essay is "Are We Becoming a Soulless Profession?" Her question about the loss of the soulful dimension is directed to all counselors, be they pastoral or secular.[2] Her conclusion is that the trend toward hyper-physicalism is already dominating the mental health field in a way that Hutch would find commendable with his emphasis on basic needs and observable actions. To think that this type of thinking would last, alarms Watt.

If such an environment continues to flourish, society will fall into the trap of defining all illness as bodily disease. Health will be depicted as a return to daily activity—situations that Nelson and Hutch might applaud. For Watts 1996), these definitions ignore the cognitive/perceptual/spiritual dimension of life that she, and many other counselors, depend on in their understandings of illness and health. She questioned whether the human capacity to transcend physical reality can be broached in the current social environment where so much emphasis is placed on the physical body and where cost-cutting concerns limit treatment outcomes to observable behavior.

Watts's (1996) reasoning is suggestive for a consideration of how counselors should react to non-reductive physicalism. She is a social and clinical psychologist who spends most of her time in organizational consultation and long-term, intensive psychotherapy—tasks that might seem conflictual but that, to her, are twin foci of her concerns to relate spirituality to therapy and to reassert soul into the postmodern social environment. Her prime concern is peoples' behavior out in the social/organizational world. She would agree in part with Hutch. Both personal healing and social involvement are the prime goals that counseling espouses. One without the other is insufficient. However, she would understand personal healing less in recounting the chronological events of biography, a la Hutch, and more in terms of the insight that comes from extended self-reflection—a type of self-reflection that she feels is grounded in the awareness of an essential spiritual dimension to life.

In cautioning against the loss of deep spiritual reflection and insight, Watts (1996) joined a chorus of voices from early to late in this century who have decried psychology's tendency to become a science without a soul. She would almost accuse Hutch and Nelson of joining this trend. The chorus of those who would caution psychology against becoming too physiological began as early as 1911 with Gruender's *Psychology Without a Soul: A Criticism* and have continued as recently as 1996 with Vande Kemp's assertion that she refuses to join "philosophers of science in rejecting an anthropology that takes spirit or soul an essential component of the person" (p. 163).

Watts's (1996) argument is as follows: She is convinced that it will be tragic to allow managed care[3] and the *Diagnostic and Statistical Manual of Mental Disorders* (4th ed. [DSM-IV]; American Psychiatric Association, 1990) to delimit counselors' roles to the kind of short-term treatment that is directed solely to helping "patients" readjust to adequate "social role functioning"—be that at work, at home, or at play. She called for counselors to reassert their claim to be that profession that conceives that "it is a central part of our task to facilitate for our clients a movement toward wholeness and the fullness of who one is" (Watts, 1996, p. 15). I have no doubt that, for Watts, this "fullness of who one is" includes a spiritual dimension or soul. She feels that this "fullness of who one is" can only be achieved in long-term counseling and can never be measured solely by whether one is able to return to work—whatever that "work" may be (Worthington, 1995).[4]

A Comment On Watts, Hutch, And Nelson

I agree more with Watts (1996) than Hutch (1991) or Nelson (1978). I affirm the goal of retaining a place for soul in counseling, but I disagree with her method. Although long-term counseling may be reassuring to counselors that their "spiritual" objectives have been reached, I do not believe that the number of sessions is the key to such insights. In fact, I believe that long-term care may run the danger of resulting in self-centered insights that do not lead necessarily to interpersonal effectiveness—a goal I share with managed care as well as with Watts. The possible narcissism that might result from such counseling may not result in socially responsible living, particularly among the financially well endowed. Thinking that soul is something that only comes after many sessions may reflect an imbalance in what Watts hopes to achieve by her mutual involvement in psychotherapy and organizational consultation. Her distrust of short-term contact may have blinded her to the kind of good social functioning that she encourages by her involvement with organizations.

However, I do think that Watts's (1996) caution about the loss of "soul-ness" is well taken. There is danger here, but it may be due more to the potential imbalance that might come from overemphasis on either the body or the mind. I do not think that Watts would be much concerned about whether soul referred to a substantive reality alongside the physical. I imagine she would follow much of 20th-century psychology, however, in bracketing the metaphysical question (Vande Kemp, 1986/1995) and preferring to talk, instead, of experiential spiritual realities—regardless of whether these "soul-filled" experiences could ever be proven to have corporeal counterparts or not. In fact, I sense that Watts would prefer to talk of "soulness" rather than "a soul," as if there were an essential spiritual dimension to human experience that managed care and the *DSM-IV* were in dire danger of ignoring, and, thus, losing.

Managed care (see end note 2) is the term for the trend to bring counseling under the same controls that are being exercised for physical treatment. It is well known that in the United States the private practice of counseling, in which clients pay for many sessions over long periods of time, may be ending. Increasingly, counselors will become part of large group practices in which financial cost-cutting will be of prime concern. This has already happened to physicians by a 3-2 margin (Coleman, 1996). The day of even physicians offering private fee for service to individuals may be ending. Counselors of all stripes—pastoral, family, psychological—are rushing to join these groups. In these HMOs, to which most physicians now belong, counseling will be limited to less than 20 sessions and the treatment effect will be measured in terms of whether the client can return to adequate social functioning.

It is this managed care structure for health care that worried Watts (1996), because she perceived that the individual exploration into the spiritual meaning of life will be severely curtailed. She seems to assume that spiritual issues will be addressed only after the symptoms of emotional disturbance have been quelled by medication. Watts reflects a model many of us have espoused in the past. I used to claim that I counseled persons toward wholeness first and holiness second—an approach that would support Watts's concern about the dangers of short-term treatment (Malony, 1995a). As will be seen, such a delay in addressing spiritual issues may not be necessary.

Watts's (1996) other concern is the growing importance of the *DSM-IV*, on which many counselors depend for reaching diagnoses. She bemoaned the fact that the *DSM-IV* describes psychopathologies in purely behavioral terms and, until recently, provided no means by which religious and spiritual issues could be discussed in counseling without their being considered part of the pathology rather than its amelioration (American Psychiatric Association, 1990, p. 687). She is partially right. Even though the *DSM-IV* includes, for the first time, religious and spiritual issues among its V-Codes, the focus is still on the way in which these types of issues may, or may not, be associated with other existing pathologies. And although references to religion have been omitted from illustrative descriptors of dissociative disorders, the *DSM-IV* is singularly bereft of references to the health-giving effect of religious involvement or spiritual commitment. This is a foreboding trend, according to Watts.

There is the possibility, however, that Watts (1996) may have misperceived the nature of the *DSM-IV*. It is a descriptive, rather than an etiological or ameliorative, treatise. It only provides depictions of symptoms that combine into syndromes. It does not offer explanations of how these psychopathologies arise, nor does it suggest treatments. Thus, no mention is made of family cohesion, identity formation, social skills, or self-esteem as processes counselors might utilize in treatment. Religion and spirituality are not alone in not appearing in its pages. The *DSM-IV* poses no challenge to the contention that humans have a spiritual capacity, in my opinion.

Nevertheless, I agree that there is an essential spiritual capacity in human behavior and experience. I think this capacity, or spiritual propensity, can be affirmed in spite of the fact that many counselors have followed the practice of bracketing the question of whether there is such a substantive entity as the soul, or even the self, or the mind. This assumption has long guided humanistic counseling (Lukoff, Turner, & Lu, 1992).

Most counselors have tended to deal in functions, rather than substances. At best, soul or spirit has stood for a dimension of experience rather than a metaphysical reality. Persons behave in ways that reveal a search for meaning in the tragedies, the enigmas, and the mysteries of life. This is spirituality. This is soulness. Soulness can be reported and observed. It is a significant mediating variable that leads to observable behavior. Typically, counselors have asserted a "psycho/physical parallelism" (Misiak & Sexton, 1966, p. 14-16), whether they knew it by that name or not. This approach admits to a timely correlation between behavior and underlying physiology, yet affirms a significant distinction between the "I" (the individual) and "0" (the organism) stories," as MacKay (1967) was wont to label them. Although admittedly this implies, at best, a soft interactive dualism, it allows causative reasoning to be top-down as well as bottom-up.

This understanding of a parallel between physical and psychological events is crucial where soulness or spiritual capacity is considered. As McDougall, the social psychologist, stated in his autobiography almost 60 years ago, "the secrets of human behavior should be approached from two sides, from below upwards by way of physiology and neurology, and from above downwards by way of psychology, philosophy, and the various human sciences" (Misiak & Sexton, 1966, p. ft61). Human beings can best be understood by attributing to them propensities stemming from their search for meaning, their spiritual side, alongside those propensities stemming from their physical experiences.

The "I" story, centered introspectively and reflectively in the human function labeled "the mind," always supersedes any absolute determinism of physical state or brain matter for most counselors, be they religious or secular. The "I" story is delimited, but not constrained, by physical existence. Soulness, that capacity of experience that relates humans to transempirical realities and purposes, is no exception to this truth. But the function is drastically different.

It is from this point of view that I affirm Watts's (1996) more pivotal point that there is, indeed, a spiritual capacity in human functioning that must not be ignored in counseling. I have used the word *capacity*, rather than *need*, because I do not believe that every counseling experience results in an experience of spirituality, such as the word *need* might imply.

It is at this point that I disagree most with Hutch (1991). He implied that humans can be understood on the basis of how they satisfy their basic needs. There does seem to be a basic need to propagate the race through heterosexual interaction, but I question whether there is anything essentially spiritual or soulful about this act. Without question, propagation and intercourse can be blessed with a spiritual interpretation. Most Christian groups have done so. But the fact remains that such convictions are deductions from more basic theological understandings; they are not inductions rising out of sexual needs or acts themselves.

Some might claim, however, that there is a difference between spirituality and religion that might still allow for the assertion that there is a basic "soul need" in the human being. This may be the basis of the distinction made in the *DSM-IV* V-Codes between *spiritual* and *religious* (Lukoff, Lu, & Turner, 1992).5 One theologian put it this way: He claimed that every person had an "ultimate concern" (Tillich, 1967, pp. 12-14). From this point of view, being ultimately concerned was what it meant to be spiritual. Accordingly, the content of the ultimate concern mattered less than the all-consuming passion with which one embraced it. This would make everybody religious, regardless of whether their ultimate concern happened to be Buddha, English literature, Jesus Christ, out-of-body experiences, the St. Louis Rams, or existential philosophy.

Personally, I think this might confuse the issue of soulness. It could cause apologists to ascribe spirituality to persons who would vehemently reject the label. That is the reason I prefer the word *capacity* to *need* in thinking about these issues.

It is best to think of spirituality as a latent capacity or a potential dimension of human behavior that many, but not all, persons express or actualize. Being spiritual or soulful is grounded in a basic human capacity. Being spiritual expresses itself in a search for a deeper, trans-empirical dimension to life. More often than not this spirit-based behavior expresses itself religiously, in some new or old religious group.

Although it might seem reductionistic to those of us who value and encourage the exercise of persons' spiritual capacity, it is probably best to understand religion as an "interest" (Malony, 1995d) that reflects an expression of this spiritual capacity. Like all interests, spirituality has specific content; it presumes selection and discrimination. The spiritual behavior we observe is never the direct result of some biological need. It is a result of individual or cultural perception—a cognitive process, not a biological compulsion. No one is interested in everything; not everyone expresses an interest in spirituality, even though they have a capacity for doing so. As an interest, spirituality refers to some, but not all, persons' search for the meaning in life (Fowler, 1981).[6] Although somewhat offensive to insiders, it is important to remember that, like La Place when asked what place God had in his theories of planetary motion, many have "no need for that hypothesis!" Not all persons admit to their spiritual capacity; some of them even deny it.

However, spirituality is more than a synonym for enthusiasm, obsession, passion, or fixation. James (1902/1985) noted this uniqueness when he defined religion as "whatever men do in relation to that which they consider divine" (p.42)., What makes soulness, spirituality, and religion unique is its object—that which people consider "divine," in James's terms. Divine means that which is trans-empirical; that which is supra-natural; that which goes beyond the kinds of reality that can be understood and explained by the five senses. Although religion has similarities to many other psychological processes, its object is different. A passion for English literature may resemble a passion for God, but one is spiritual and the other is not, from my point of view. Nor can spirituality be made synonymous with consciousness, as Daniel Helminiak implies in his discussion of the theorizing of Bernard Lonergan, the Catholic philosophical theologian (Helminiak, 1996). I recognize that I am implying that the expression of human's spiritual capacities can be clearly identified and is not just another term for a sense of beauty or a passion for justice.

Yinger (1970) identified the unique expressions of spirituality as threefold when he claimed that religion was the way that people handled the enigmas, the tragedies, and the mysteries of life. *Enigmas* pertain to fate or circumstance; *tragedies* pertain to disrupted plans or unexpected losses; *mysteries* pertain to ultimate meaning and purpose. Not one of the three is susceptible to being finally assuaged by empirical means, although they can be staved off for a time by hyperactivity or over-investment in tangible reality. Although tragedies and enigmas appear as frustrations of living, mysteries can come early and late in life. Thus, religion is more than an afterthought to failed problem solving; it is a thrust into life that makes existence more than animalistic pragmatism.

However, it should be reiterated that some people can live without attention to their spiritual propensity being expressed at all. Jesus illustrated this possibility of delaying attention to matters of mystery, of fate, and of tragedy in his contention that it was easier for a camel to crawl through the eye of a needle than for a rich man to enter into the kingdom of heaven (Matthew 19:24). Riches have a way of shielding persons from asking themselves the questions to which religious faith, or spirituality, can be an answer. Jesus was aware that there were some persons whose life circumstance was so comfortable that they never experienced a desire to actualize their spiritual, or soul, capacity. At another point, Jesus told the rich young ruler what he needed to do to inherit eternal life, but "when the young man heard this word, he went away grieving, for he had many possessions" (Matthew 19:22, NRSV). Jesus clearly distinguished between the type of misplaced frantic concern to amass money and the ultimate concern of spirituality. Apart from that which many, including Jesus, might contend is a universal need persons have for actualizing their spirituality, the truth remains that not everybody wants to be spiritual or soulful.[8] The phenomenal reality is that many are not, and never become, spiritual. They live as if they were "soulless." Watts was correct in her caution about counseling that focused on function, although she may not have expressed it in these terms.

"SOUL-FILLED" COUNSELING

Turning to the question of what soul-filled counseling is. this caution of Watts (1996) should be not be forgotten. She expressed concern that psychotherapy might function in a managed-care, *DSM-IV* environment in a manner that facilitated a suppression of spiritual experience. I agree with her concern that awakening persons' souls—their spiritual capacity to find meaning and wholeness—should be an integral part of counseling. I am as concerned as she about the possibility that counseling would become so culturally constrained that it would become a handmaiden of societal concerns to cut costs or create conformist automatons.

However, although I acknowledge her insight and concern, I am not as discouraged as Watts (1996) about the future of counseling, nor am I as pessimistic about the ultimate behavioral goal of stimulating adequate social functioning as it might seem. I believe counselors can infuse short-term treatment with spiritual breadth and depth. I believe that psychotherapists can counsel in a manner that provokes the likelihood that persons acknowledge and use their soulness in the midst of their relationships with other people.[9] I do not believe that contending that persons are body/soul unities handicaps this goal to any degree.

In this regard, counselors are not helpless pawns of societal pressures that limit the number of their sessions or define proof of their effectiveness in purely functional terms, as Watts's (1996) presumptions might imply. They are skilled professionals who, like Watts, are mandated by culture to exercise their best judgment about what true health is. They can enhance spirituality in their clients, if they will. They have the capacity to shape culture as well as respond to it. They can help society identify its need to be more than a rationalistic machine of functioning parts that have no insight or values. They can define mental health as an increasing awareness to respond to life in spiritual terms. My explanation of this therapeutic possibility follows. Not all the functions of counselors are restorative. They can function as guides, reconcilers, and sustainers, as well as healers. In fact, the very definition of healing should encompass all these goals.

Further, we should leave open the possibility that a given mental disorder might have spiritual, as well as physical, mental, or social causes, as Jay Adams keeps ascertaining. It is always necessary to go beneath the symptoms that coalesce into any *DSM-IV* diagnosis to ask the question, "What caused this to happen?"—a question that the *DSM-IV* does not even attempt to answer. Counseling is, in the final analysis, interested far less in describing symptoms than it is in correcting causes. It is here that soul issues or spirituality becomes as viable as any other cause. In an essay entitled "Diseased, Deluded, Deranged, and Demonized: Options in Diagnosis for Christian Mental Health Professionals" (Malony, 1995b), I suggested a taxonomy for determining causation. I think this taxonomy can be used by all counselors whether they are religious or not.

The term *demonized* is meant to include a place for evil as a cause for the problems brought to counselors. May (1950) called this the *demonic*. The demonic includes all those choices people make that violate ultimate reality as they deal with the major imponderable issues of life—fate, tragedy, meaning, mystery, morals, and relationships. Although demonized can refer to the possibility of becoming consumed by active evil, I have little, or no, investment in asserting the substantive reality of demons who exist outside persons and take possession of them. In all but very rare circumstances, there is enough evil within human beings to take care of the great majority of their problems. I do believe strongly in evil, therefore, understood as the human proclivity for self-enhancement at the expense of others. I am convinced that some mental disturbance is based in a process whereby individuals become seduced by immoral, selfish impulses that go far beyond the laws of societal customs. There. is evil; there is wickedness. And it is grounded less in deviation from societal norms than in a decision to flaunt the moral structure of the universe.

There are those who refuse to identify with that which Kant (1950) called "the moral imperative." Mowrer (1961) included this tendency toward human evil, or sin, in his moral theory of psychopathology. Mowrer contended that many symptoms were based on real, rather than fantasized, guilt. I agree with this possibility.

More to the point, however, I affirm the likelihood that a lack of resolution of the spiritual problems inherent in finding a purpose for living in the face of fate and tragedy and mystery might underlie a number of *DSM-IV* diagnoses. In a sense, I acknowledge this viewpoint comes close to conceiving evil in an Augustinian manner as the absence of good. I also acknowledge that in doing so I have left the descriptive approach of psychology and am suggesting a metaphysical, structural reality to life that comes out of my Christian faith. I do believe that there is a divine intent written into the fabric of the universe that, if violated or not acknowledged in faith, will result in life lived at less than its best. Not to face this possibility would be a monumental error that counselors could blame on no one but themselves. It is here that I think the Bobgans and Adams are right. I do not think that taking a nonreductive physicalist approach to the body/soul question compromises this insight in the least, however. As the 18th-century divine, John Wesley (asserted, affirming this spiritual dimension to life can become a growing, life-long project that is not only possible but desirable.

It is now widely recognized that all counseling involves diagnosis of the causes of problems brought to the counselor. Counseling is not a process of passively letting things happen. It is a healing endeavor based on active listening and the giving of counsel (Bergin, 1980; Malony, 1995c). All counselors are directive, and the guidance they provide is grounded in their diagnostic judgments about what has gone wrong. To be so truncated that one ignores the possibility of the demonized options would be a travesty of psychotherapy. And it is out of the judgment that there is a spiritual problem that the possibility of a soul-filled remedy becomes possible. Although this might sound as if I am advocating a deliverance-type solution, such as might be seen in exorcism, I am thinking of a much broader solution that might, for example, be seen in the renewal and reactivation of religious faith.

It is a truism that most human behavior is due to multiple causation, and emotional disturbance is no exception to this rule. In discriminating among the diseased (organic), deluded (cognitive/emotional), deranged (social abberational), or demonized (spiritual/religious) options, it is, therefore, best to approach diagnosis from a "both/and" rather than an "either/or" or "nothing/but" mind-set. Although many therapists would be hesitant to slavishly follow the contention of Tillich or Fowler that there were spiritual dimensions to every emotional disturbance, every counselor would do well to always consider the possibility of spiritual, soulful, or demonic involvement. Failure to adequately deal spiritually with finite human existence may well confound most of the other determinants of human problems.

Having considered the spiritual dimensions of the diagnostic tasks, I now turn to the issues of treatment in counseling. Some years ago Maslow (1964) proposed a model for spiritual or "peak experiences" with which I think Watts might agree but which I think causes her to despair about how such experiences might be incorporated into short-term, managed-care treatment. Maslow contended that people prioritized their behavior along a "hierarchy of needs." This meant that they only had spiritual experiences after they met their survival, physical, and relational needs. He identified spiritual experiences with self-actualization. If psychotherapists adopt Maslow's model, it should come as no surprise to contend that short-term treatment directed toward a return to social functioning would never get to the soul dimensions of life. The Maslovian approach identifies spirituality with altered states of consciousness or mystical peak experiences that can impact life only after all other needs have been met. This is a dualistic, false, elitist, very constricted understanding of soulness. Like Maslow, I too, believed that spirituality was like icing on the cake; something that topped off life after all other needs had been met. As noted earlier, I contended that "holiness," my word for spirituality, could only become a part of treatment after issues of "wholeness," my word for mental health, had been achieved.

This point of view needs to be corrected by a more robust understanding of soulness. Soulness, or spirituality, is not something that has to be relegated to the end of therapy, as with those upper-middle-class, successful citizens who have the leisure to become "more spiritual." As noted in the discussion of diagnosis, the concerns of the demonized (spiritual) option can be ever-present in the midst of persons' efforts to deal with their physical, mental, and social realities. If, as Yinger (1970) proposed, religion is the way people deal with the enigmas (fate), the tragedies, and the mysteries of life, it is foolish to think that these concerns do not underlie what they are experiencing every day of their lives in almost every circumstance. Expressing one's soul or becoming more spiritual is not something one does off to the side of life; it is enmeshed in the daily struggle to survive. A nonreductive, physicalist solution to the body/soul issue is supportive of this approach.

McMinn (1996), in a recent book entitled *Psychology, Theology, and Spirituality and Christian Counseling*, makes the same mistake as Watts (1996) in assuming that religious faith is something added to life rather than a total approach to existence. This makes his approach artificial. He highly recommended adding spirituality to the counseling task but missed entirely the point that spirituality is a practical, earthy, event-enmeshed process, not just a delightful option to add to the cake of life. One gets the feeling that spirituality for McMinn would be similar to a knowledge of Shakespeare—something one might like to have but that was only tangentially related to daily living. Surely spirituality has a more robust meaning than that.

My hope would be that instead of relegating spirituality to the end of long-term treatment, counselors could make it a part of any and all sessions in the time-limited, managed-care environment. It is problematic to base psychotherapeutic treatment on a stair-step model, such as Maslow's (1964) or on an icing-on-the-cake model like McMinn's (1996). Better to conceive of the task in a table-top, part-of-the-basic-recipe model in which all concerns coexist and are equally relevant. Likewise, it is a mistake that pastoral counselors only deal with spiritual matters or that secular counselors only deal with mundane issues. Both deal with both.

Human beings face, at every crossroad, the ultimate questions of life. It has been suggested that humans are those organisms that are "sense making" and "meaning seeking" (Malony, 1995e). In attempting to make sense out of life, people experience neurotic anxiety. In attempting to deal with fate, tragedy, and mystery, people experience basic anxiety. According to Tillich (1967), at its core, neurotic anxiety is essentially basic anxiety. Thus, his contention: "Life poses the questions to which faith is the answer" (p(13).13

Spirituality, soulness, religion, and faith all stand for that human problem-solving capacity that goes beyond empirical reality and reaches for assurance based on trans-empirical, supra-natural reality. The behavior that can be observed and that indicates clearly that spiritual capacities are an essential part of humanness is the courage of faith. And faith is that easily observed, tenacious, sensitive, spiritual behavior that counselors can observe, encourage, and support. As Hutch and Nelson contended, life is, indeed, experienced through the body, but there is an inborn spiritual capacity that can make life more than digestion and sexuality.

The practice of the spiritual courage that faith brings is based on four cognitive/perceptual processes. They are the ways in which soulness is expressed and developed. As James noted, these processes are not unique. They are part of the physical capacities of the brain. They differ from other capacities only in the object of their focus: transempirical reality. This is what make these behaviors spiritual. These cognitive/perceptual processes are: insights, understandings, feelings, and actions. They have special meanings when exercised in a spiritual manner.[10]

Insights are those basic transformations of outlook that imply one has reconceived the basic meaning of existence in terms of trans-empirical reality. This "seeing-into" the ultimate purpose of existence changes persons' total outlook in a manner described by James (1902/1985) under the rubric of "conversions." They can be theistic, as in the Jewish and Christian sense of the providence and grace of God, or non-theistic, as in Buddhist enlightenment about the transitoriness of life.

Understandings are the applications of insights to the ongoing events of life. These are the meanings attached to experience, as basic spiritual insights assist persons in re-perceiving and gaining new perspectives on both their day-to-day stresses and opportunities as well as their movements through the changes that occur during the phases of their lives.

Feelings are the emotions people experience as they approach life events with the understandings that derive from the insights of faith. Feelings predispose persons to sense that they can respond courageously and altruistically to stresses and opportunities. The spiritual emotions give them the willingness to enter into life with confidence and expectation.

Actions are the actual movements and actions people engage in that are based on their courageous feelings that, in turn, result from their understandings that are grounded in their spiritual insights. These are the works that can be seen and that have effect. They are those behaviors that exude soul or spirituality. They include choices of associations, as in religious institutions to which they might belong, as well as styles of relating, which others experience and observe.

These four processes—insights, understandings, feelings, and actions—are the evidence of "soul-filled " living. They can become a part of psychotherapy in a managed-care, short-term, *DSM-IV* environment. They do not have to be relegated to the last stages of long-term psychotherapy. They eventuate in actions—behavior with which many of the authors discussed in this article would agree. *Newsweek*, in reporting the death of Cardinal Joseph Bernardin, quoted from the Cardinal's forthcoming memoirs The Gift of Peace (1996), vividly illustrating this truth. His words about living the last 3 years of his life under the threat of terminal cancer are poignant of this fourfold process of soulfulness or "expressed spirituality." Bernardin stated: "I have tried to live my life openly and honestly with a deep commitment to the Lord, the Church, and the human community. The past three years ... have challenged me like never before to hold firm to my beliefs and trust in the Lord. But my main point has been to put my faith into action, to live out the principles that guide my life" A better statement of the spiritual meaning of embodiment would be difficult to find.

What seems to be neglected by both Hutch and Nelson is the impact of culture or tradition on these processes. The basic insight that may well be provoked by the facing of the dilemmas of embodied finitude is colored and shaped by the cultural paradigms that are available. And the content supplied by the culture becomes the essential perceptual framework of the experience. For example, Bernadin's spirituality was shaped by the Christian religion. This was the insight that led to the understandings, the feelings, and the actions of his whole life. This shaped his spiritual development.

Psychologically, this basic insight, regardless of its cultural content, could be understood as conversion. At some point in time or at some life phase, the conversion or insight occurs. This is followed by a lifelong series of applications of this basic insight to the events of life." The process could be called *spiritual development*. Practicing the presence of God, as Brother Lawrence termed it, is what could be seen in the actions of Cardinal Bernardin's life. As John Wesley described it, this is "going on to perfection." Wesley felt that all Christians should take as a life-goal being perfect at least "five minutes before death" (Williams, 1960, p. 169).

Social Adjustment—The Goal Of Counseling

I turn finally to the social adjustment goals of counseling in a managed-care, *DSM-IV* environment. Spirituality should impact daily problem solving. It should not just be an elite but impractical body of knowledge that leaves one smug but essentially unchanged. If it is true that the Christian faith is uniquely transactional, interpersonal, and historical (Malony, 1989), then the goal of any therapeutic endeavor, especially counseling, cannot be better expressed than in adequate social functioning.

The great councils of the first 600 years of the church established as heretical any presumption that spirituality or soulness was something one did off to the side of relations with other persons. The Apostles' Creed states that God is the "Maker of heaven and earth." And the primary way Christians show the Lordship of Christ in their lives is in the ways they deal with other people. As the theologian Ray Anderson concluded, to be a person is to be in relationships (Anderson & Guernsey, 1985).

Maybe the HMOs that assert that managed-care treatment goals pertain to social functioning are more spiritual than those counselors who would prefer more inside-the-person, potentially narcissistic insights that have no necessary interpersonal relevance. Maybe returning to social functioning is the optimal goal for counseling, whether in today's or in yesterday's environment.

Counselors need not be discouraged about the exercise of their professionalism in a postmodern world. Nor should they be troubled by a monistic approach to the human being. Understanding the human being as a unity of body and soul makes spirituality a more integrated and wholesome option than a dualistic approach can do. Opportunities for bringing "soul" back into counseling exist if counselors will take advantage of them. Timidness should not be the rule. Good counseling will include spiritual dimensions, and the techniques are available for all who would use them.

Conclusion

Although some, like Watts (1996), are bemoaning the cultural environment in which counselors must work and others, like Hutch (1991) and Nelson (1978), are applauding the new bodily emphasis in views of human nature, neither group has assessed the situation accurately. Contrary to Watts's concern, there is no need for counselors to panic at the time-limited, role-functioning threats of managed care. Nor do counselors need to become physiologists and give in to an implicit determinism that makes mental insights epiphenomenal, as Hutch and Nelson might imply. Counselors can accept the renewed understanding of the importance of the physical body at the same time that they affirm a spiritual capacity in human beings that can be evoked and nurtured by their ministrations. Humans are indeed embodied, but they can transcend their finitude through cognitive/perceptual capacities inherent in the brain. Religious faith, understood as the expression of humans' spiritual capacity, will continue to be the prime way in which persons can utilize their soulfulness in meeting the challenge of life's enigmas, life's tragedies, and life's meaning. Encouraging persons to face the spiritual dimensions of daily life will continue to be a viable procedure for all help-givers--early as well as late in counseling (Malony, 1983). And a monistic understanding of human beings will assist them in these endeavors.

Endnotes

1. In regard to Watson, it is interesting to note that his behaviorism would be radically physicalist. Thought, to Watson. was epiphenomenal. It was only the side effect of muscular movements in the throat. Only instinctive, physical adjustment was real. Thus, he would be just as suspicious of Ellis's emphasis on cognition as he would be of Adams' emphasis on the reality of the soul.

2. In regard to the comment that the question of soul is a general question for all counselors, it is interesting to note that the program for the 1996 Centers and Training Conference of the American Association of Pastoral Counselors announced that Professor Homer U. Ashby of McCormick Theological Seminary would deliver a major address entitled "Reclaiming the Soul for the Cure of Souls." This indicates

that the question of what shall be the place of the soul in counseling is a question all types of counselors are asking.

Pastoral counseling has always been considered under this rubric of "soul-care" as can be seen by McNeill's classic volume *A History of the Cure of Souls* (1951/1977).

3. *Managed care* is the term given to grouping all health specialties under umbrella groups called *health maintenance organizations* (HMOs), which take care of the total health needs of individuals. In many states these HMOs have become the primary providers of service. It is thought that this type of managed care will result in reduction of costs and greater effectiveness.

4. In his presentation. Worthington (1995) noted that the three influences on how counseling functions in U.S. society have drastically changed in the last quarter-century. In the 1970s. patients and their counselors determined when counseling was needed and when it should end. Society. in the form of insurance companies, typically went along with this and paid the bill. Today, society, through HMOs and managed care, determines when counseling is needed and how long it should last. Patients and their counselors have far less influence on treatment than before.

5. In their article, the authors make the distinction that appeared later in the V-Codes of the *DSM-IV*, namely that problems brought to counselors pertaining to doubt or anxiety in regard to beliefs or experiences with institutional religions should be labeled religion, but that problems of a general nature (such as vision, numinous experiences), related to no institutional religion, should be labeled spiritual.

6. It seems to me that Fowler makes the mistake of assuming every human being searches for meaning. Unless one implies by this that meaning can come from a variety of sources that change frequently, I do not believe it to be so. I do not deny that finding an overarching sense of meaning can bring purpose and unity to life. Meaning functions positively in life. In fact, this is the prime result of attending to the soulful dimensions of life, and I am convinced that such a search is best served by traditional faith—long tried, historical transcendent, metaphysical faiths. But I am uncomfortable with reasoning backward and attributing behaviors seen in some people to a basic need for everyone. This is like an automobile dealer saying everyone needs a car when it is obvious that many individuals can live their lives very comfortably without owning one.

7. The word given by the theologian Paul Tillich to these frantic efforts to handle the questions of life without reference to the answers of faith is *heteronomy*. Heteronomy refers to placing one's confidence in matters that are varied and unstable. Heteronomy is different from *autonomy*. which refers to anxious attempts to avoid life's dilemmas. It also differs from *theonomy*, which pertains to intrustment of oneself to God (see Tillich, 1967, pp. 83-86).

8.'This distinction between needs and wants has been a cardinal tenet of Gestalt therapy. Perk (1969) contended that one of the basic sources of emotional disturbance is confusing what one wants in life with what one really needs.

9. It is here that I strongly affirm the observation that one of the essential and basic propensities of human beings is "relatedness." One of the major developments of

psychoanalysis since Freud has been that of the ego psychologists who have contended that much of human behavior is "conflict free" and is based on a natural tendency of persons to relate to, not simply use, one another. An extension of this observation could be to assume that social functioning within a culture (be that at work, at home, or at play) is an explicit expression of this relational propensity. For those who are spiritual in the classical Christian manner, it is but a short step to affirm that this relating to others in service, justice, and love is the central intent of Almighty God for human life.

10. The discussion to follow is a paraphrase of a description of these cognitive processes in Malony and Hunt's (1991) *The Psychology of Clergy* (pp. 111 ff.).

11. For a more complete discussion of the processes of conversion and spiritual development see Malony (1985, 1996).

REFERENCES

Adams. J. (1970). *Competent to counsel*. Grand Rapids, MI: Baker Book House.

Adams, J. (1979). *More than redemption: A theology of Christian counseling*. Phillipsburg, NJ: Presbyterian and Reformed Publishing.

American Psychiatric Association. (1990). *The diagnostic and statistical manual of mental disorders* (4th ed.). Washington, DC: Author.

Anderson, R., & Guernsey, D. (1985). *On becoming family*. Grand Rapids, MI: Eerdmans.

Bergin, A. E. (1980). Psychotherapy and religious values. *Journal of Consulting and Clinical Psychology*, 48, 95-105.

Bernardin, J. (1996). *The gift of peace*. Chicago: Loyola Press.

Bobgan, M., & Bobgan, D. (1979). *The psychological way/the spiritual way*. Minneapolis, MN: Bethany Fellowship.

Bobgan, M., & Bobgan, D. (1987). *Psychoheresy: The psychological seduction of Christianity*. Santa Barbara, CA: Eastgate.

Coleman. B. C. (1996. August 21). Majority of physicians no longer self-employed. *Pasadena Star News*. p. B6.

Drummond. R. H. (1978). *Unto the churches: Jesus Christ, Christianity, and the Edgar Cayce readings*. Virginia Beach. VA: A.R.E. Press.

Ellis, A. (1965). *The case against religion*. New York: Center for Rational/Emotional Psychotherapy. Ellis, A. (1980). Psychotherapy and atheistic values. *Journal of Consulting and Clinical Psychology*, 48, 635-639.

Fowler, J. W. (1981). *Stages of faith: The psychology of human development and the search for meaning*. San Francisco: Harper & Row.

Goleman, D. (1977). *The varieties of meditative experience*. New York: Dutton.

Gooden, W. E. (1990). Soul (Black Church). In R. Hunter, L. 0. Mills, H. N. Malony, & J. Patton (Eds.), *Dictionary of pastoral care and counseling* (p. 1203). Nashville, TN: Abingdon.

Gruender. H. (1911). *Psychology without a soul: A criticism*. St. Louis, MO: Joseph Gummesbach. Helminiak. D. (1996). *The human core of spirituality: Mind as psyche and spirit*. Albany: State University of New York Press.

Hutch, R. A. (1991). Mortal body, studying lives: Restoring eras to the psychology of religion. *International Journal for the Psychology of Religion*, I, 193-210.

James, W. (1985). *The varieties of religious experience: A study inhuman nature*. Cambridge, MA: Harvard University Press. (Original work published 1902)

Kant, I. (1950). *A critique of pure reason*. New York: Universities Press.

Longergan, B. F. (1957). *Insight: A study of human understanding*. New York: Philosophical Library.

Lukoff, D., Lu, F., & Turner, R. (1992). Toward a more culturally sensitive DSM-IV: Psychoreligious and psychospiritual problems. *The Journal of Nervous and Mental Diseases, 180,* 673-682.

Lukoff, D., Turner, R., & Lu, F. (1992). Transpersonal psychology research review: Psychospiritual dimensions of healing. *The Journal of Transpersonal Psychology, 25,* 11-28,30.

MacKay, D. M. (1967). *Freedom of action in a mechanistic universe*. London: Cambridge University Press.

Malony, H. N. (1983). God-talk in psychotherapy. In H. N. Malony (Ed.), *Wholeness and holiness: Readings in the psychology/theology of mental health* (pp. 269-280). Grand Rapids, MI: Baker Book House.

Malony, H. N. (1985). An S-O-R model of religious experience. In L. B. Brown (Ed.), *Advances in the psychology of religion* (pp. 113-126). New York: Pergamon.

Malony, H. N. (1989). The uses of religious assessment in counseling. In L. B. Brown (Ed.), *Current psychology of religion* (pp. 3-18). New York: Springer-Verlag.

Malony, H. N. (1995a). The ALABAMA model of integrative psychotherapy. In *Integration musings: Thoughts on being a Christian professional* (Rev. ed., pp. 127-142). Pasadena, CA: Integration Press.

Malony, H. N. (I 995b). Diseased, deluded, demonized: Options in diagnosis for Christian mental health professionals. In *Integration musings: Thoughts on being a Christian professional* (Rev. ed., pp. 99-106). Pasadena, CA: Integration Press.

Malony, H. N. (1995c). A psychotherapist's confession of faith: Part 1. In *Integration musings: Thoughts on being a Christian professional* (Rev. ed., pp. 121-126). Pasadena, CA: Integration Press.

Malony, H. N. (1995d, April). *Religion as interest rather than instinct or why religions seem to have such little impact on behavior*. Paper presented at the annual meeting of the Christian Association for Psychological Studies, Virginia Beach, VA.

Malony, H. N. (1995e). Theology, philosophy, social/behavioral and natural science: Who studies what and how? In *Integration musings: Thoughts on being a Christian professional* (Rev. ed., pp. 29-38). Pasadena, CA: Integration Press.

Malony, H. N. (1996, January). *Brainwashing and religion: Implications for counseling and evangelism.* Paper presented at the annual meeting of the Integration Symposium for Fuller Theological Seminary Graduate School of Psychology, Pasadena, CA.

Malony, H. N., & Hunt (1991). *The psychology of clergy.* Harrisburg, PA: Morehouse.

Maslow, A. H. (1964). *Religion, values, and peak experiences.* Columbus: Ohio State University Press. May, R. (1950). *The meaning of anxiety.* New York: Ronald.

McClendon, J. W. (1974). *Biography as theology: How life stories can remake today's theology.* Nashville, TN: Abingdon.

McMinn, M. (1996). *Psychology, theology and spirituality and Christian counseling.* Deerfield, IL: Tyndale.

McNeill, J. T. (1977). *A history of the cure of souls.* New York: Harper & Row. (Original work published 1951)

Miller, R., & Malony, H. N. (1978). The Agasha Temple of Wisdom: Modern spiritualism revisited. *Journal of Altered States of Consciousness, 4,* 277-290.

Misiak, H., & Sexton, V. (1966). *History of psychology: An overview* (pp.14-17)New York: Grime & Stratton.

Mowrer, 0. H. (1961). *The crisis in psychiatry and religion.* New York: Van Nostrand.

Muller, R. A. (1990). Soul. In R. Hunter, L. 0. Mills, H. N. Malony, & J. Patton (Eds.), *Dictionary of pastoral care and counseling* (p. 1202). Nashville, TN: Abingdon.

Nelson, J. B. (1978). *Embodiment: An approach to sexuality and Christian theology* (pp. 8-15). New York: Pilgrim.

Niebuhr, R. (1941, 1943, 1949). *The nature and destiny of man: A Christian interpretation.* New York: Scribner's.

Perls, F. (1969). *In and out of the garbage pail.* Moab, UT: Real People.

Ring, K. (1980). *Life at death: A scientific investigation of near death experience.* New York: Coward, McCann, & Geoghenan.

Tillich, P. (1967). *Systematic theology: Three volumes in one* (pp. 12-14). Chicago: University of Chicago Press.

Vande Kemp, H. (1995). The dangers of psychologism. In H. N. Malony (Ed.). *Psychology of religion: Personalities, problems, possibilities* (pp. 64-83). Pasadena, CA: Integration Press. (Reprinted from *Journal of Psychology and Theology,* IS, 97-109, 1986.)

Vande Kemp, H. (1996). Psychology and Christian spirituality: Explorations of the inner world. *Journal of Psychology and Christianity, 15,* 161-174.

Watson, J. B. (1913). Psychologist as the behaviorist views it. *Psychological Review, 20,* 158-177.

Wartts, P. (1996). Are we becoming a "soulless" profession? *The California Psychologist, 29,* 115-167.

Williams, C. (1960). *John Wesley's theology today.* Nashville, TN: Abingdon.

Worthington, E. (1995, April). *New directions in helping marriages and families.* Paper presented, at the annual meeting of the Christian Association for Psychological Studies, Virginia Beach, VA.

Yinger, J. M. (1970). *The scientific study of religion.* New York: Macmillan.

THREE

Mindfullness

" **S**hift happens." Now I know that you will think I mis-pronounced the word *shift* and that I really meant a four letter word that leaves out the next to the last letter in the word shift. But I made no mistake, When I said shift, I meant shift.

Shift happens—If there is one thing that is as sure as death and taxes it is change. Things shift. Shift happens. This is rule that you can count on. It is the one constant in life. Shift is a maxim as old as Democritus who proclaimed "You never step in the same river twice." Shift is a truth as recent as Hegel who proclaimed that all of history goes through repeated cycles of thesis, antithesis, and synthesis. Shift is an axiom as current as Thomas Kuhn who proclaimed that science, like history, follows a recurrent pattern of paradigm shifts that defy any straight line predictions of development. Shift happens—If there is one thing we can count on it is that change will occur. And the 21ˢᵗ century term for change is *psychology*.

Psychology—the study of human behavior. Psychology—the attempt to understand, explain, and influence behavior—and behavior shifts, it changes.

In many, many, ways the psychology of today, is not the psychology of yesterday. Nor will the psychology of today be the psychology of tomorrow. Norms change, new paradigms appear, rivers flow, syntheses evolve, behavior changes—shift happens. Psychology is the mirror that reflects each shifting turn in the road. Shift is the game, and psychology is its name!

In my graduate training in psychology I never heard of attachment theory, cognitive/behavioral therapy, attention deficit disorder, object relations, wounded healers, pastoral psychotherapy, family of origin, neuroscience, sexual orientation, or dissociative disorder, to mention only a few of the behavioral concepts of today that will fade away in the psychology of tomorrow. Of course, we can ignore or deny that shift occurs. We all remember professors reading from well-worn, yellow sheets of paper that reflected lectures they had prepared many decades before. They were oblivious to the changes that had occurred since they first prepared those lectures. This may have been acceptable if the topic was the history of 10ᵗʰ century England, but it was abominable if the subject was psychology.

Some years ago Candid Camera used a tree that moved as a metaphor for peoples' reactions to a changing environment. As people walked along a given street, an artificial tree on their right moved with them. Seven out of ten persons either ignored the moving tree entirely or sped up to get past it. Two people adjusted their cadence to match the moving tree. Only one person turned to the tree and shook it. What should we do with the shifting trees to our right or left around us? More specifically, what are we who bear the name *Christian* psychologists to do in the face of the obvious fact that the environment in which we live and the environment in which we function is as unstable as the shifting sand dunes of the Sahara Desert?

Tertullian, the third century Christian theologian, posed one solution to the dilemma when he asked the rhetorical question "What has Jerusalem to do with Athens?" "What have the *timeless* truths of faith, Jerusalem, to do with the *timely* truths of science, Athens?" "What has faith to do with reason?" "What has Christianity to do with Psychology?" The implied answer of Tertullian was "none."

The late Swiss theologian Karl Barth agreed. If you want to understand human beings don't look to the social/behavioral sciences, don't look to psychology. If you want to study human behavior look to theology; pay only passing attention to psychology. All psychology can do is take surveys and come up with cutesy labels for its descriptions of what it finds—fashions, modes, averages. If you want to know the true essence and the real possibility of human life, look at Jesus, the Son of God and all that He has taught and revealed. Psychology is epi-phenomena, appearance; theology is phenomena, true reality. Psychology is like icing on top of a cake, theology is the cake itself.

An ancient saying in the Talmud affirms Barth's contention clearly: "Cursed is the man who tends swine and teaches his son Greek wisdom." And psychology is Greek wisdom. You may remember the incident in James Michener's book *The Source,* where the curse of teaching Greek wisdom led to murder. A rabbi's son had become a wrestler in the gymnasium built by the Greek governor of the Palestinian town where he lived. Although the wrestlers wore clothes at home, when they went to the Greek Empire games, they wrestled in the nude. Upon returning home, they gave a demonstration of their skills—in the nude, behavior declared an abomination by the Old Testament. When the rabbi saw his son nude in public he climbed into the ring and stabbed his son to death.

What has Jerusalem to do with Athens? None. None. Of course, if we choose this answer to the question, there would be very little need for Trinity College of Graduate Studies which states its purpose to be "Integrating Christian Spirituality with Psychology." Integrating! Integrating! Integrating, indeed! Karl Barth must be gyrating in his grave. Nein! No!—Barth would say.

But Trinity Graduate School does exist. And the integration of Christian Sprituality, faith, with Psychology, the shifting norms of human behavior, is its goal. I'd like to suggest two integrative options for you graduates to consider as you depart-these scholarly halls and attempt to put into practice what you have learned. I am indebted to my former student, the late outstanding psychologist Randy Sorenson, for proposing these alternatives in his recent book *Minding Spirituality* (2004). They are the basis for my title for these remarks "Mindfulness" — a title that probably elicited few feelings of excitement and many six-letter responses of "boring." The two options are "Mind the Gap," and "Mind the Store."

MIND THE GAP

Those of you who have been to London have heard the constant, repetitive admonition to "Mind the gap" as one boards subway trains. Mind the gap; take care that you do not fall into the empty space between the platform and the subway car; watch your step; look down; do not assume that the platform butts right up against the door of the car; there is a space there; mind the gap. Assume for the moment that the platform is theology (faith, spirituality, religion) and the subway car is psychology (behavioral norms, psychodynamic theories, treatment options). Even when the subway car stops and for a moment spirituality and psychology are at the same place — don't presume that there is no space between them. Mind the gap-Christian spirituality and psychology are not the same. For example, don't presume that everybody has a faith, or an ultimate concern, as the late theologian Paul Tillich contended or that everybody has some system of meaning upon which they build their life as James Fowler implies. Persons come to you for help because they never had or lost their sense of meaning.

Tillich's assertion that *everyone* has an ultimate concern (his title for faith) leads to the cryptic proclamation that "some live for God, some for country, some for Yale." The only problem with this is that those who live for country or for Yale will never call their devotion to either one similar to "living for God." Nor is becoming deeply involved with the LA Lakers, English literature, classical music, antique autos, Rotary International, or a thousand other interests the same thing as "religious faith" or "living for God." There is a difference. Mind the gap!

Fuller Seminary's late president, David Hubbard, was the most knowledgeable LA Dodger fan I have ever known. He knew a multitude of Dodger facts including the batting averages for the past ten years plus noteworthy Dodgers at the top of every statistic for many decades. Some got the feeling that he knew as much about the LA Dodgers as he did about the Old Testament –

his chosen field of scholarly expertise. But David Hubbard would never, never admit that he put his *faith* in the Dodgers. Mind the gap.

Further, don't presume that theology is just an example of aesthetics or imagination. Mind the gap. Bejamin Belt Hallahmi (1986), professor at the University of Haifa, wrote a seminal article some years ago entitled "Religion as art and identity." He noted that, from a psychological point of view, both aesthetic appreciation and religious experience entail imagination—the use of fantasy—a kind of contact with extra-empirical, transcendent, mystical reality. However, he further observed that there was a critical difference in the experience. Artists do not ascribe independent reality to the subject of their experience, religionists do – at least in Christianity, Judaism, and Islam. They believe God exists. Artists know their art is fantasy. Both artists and religionists assert they have experienced transcendent reality but religionists assert they have been in contact with the living God while artists only contend they have experienced their own higher selves. There is a critical, significant, qualitative difference. Mind the gap.

This leads me to offer for your consideration three definitions:

Spirituality could be defined as *the human capacity to experience transcendent reality.*

Faith could be defined as *the conclusion that a given spiritual experience can be understood through certain concepts and re-experienced through certain behaviors.*

Religion could be defined as *the shared agreement of two or more persons about a given set of concepts and behaviors that provide understanding as well as enhancement of spiritual experience.*

Briefly note several aspects of these definitions. God is not synonymous with or necessarily implied in the term "transcendent reality." Beit-Hallahmi was right. Spirituality is a generic, underlying, dynamic term that applies to aesthetic appreciation, nature mysticism, extra-sensory perception as well as a sense one has been in contact with Almighty God. Note also that Spirituality is defined as a *human capacity.* Spirituality is not an *instinct*—else all human beings would be spiritual. And they are not. Because not everybody is spiritual, not everybody is religious. Spirituality is not a *basic drive*—it is a capacity, a possibility, a potential, an ability waiting to be expressed. Note further that *faith* is defined as *concepts* and *behaviors.* The actions of our bodies follow the conceptions of our minds. Words (or concepts) follow from experience. They help us understand what has happened. And behaviors are based on concepts. They position us to re-experience events. As the Christian scriptures ask "What, then, shall we say to (about) these things?" (Romans 8:31). The putting of "words" to experience and the designing of behaviors to repeat experience is a human compulsion essential to faith.

Finally, religion is defined as shared agreements about concepts and behaviors. Religion is creeds (concepts) and rituals (behaviors). While we often hear, "I'm spiritual but I am not religious," I think this only applies to "lone wolf spirituality." The moment when two people reach consensus with each other, a religion is born – quite apart from whether that results in attendance at a Yoga session, a nature hike, a book-club reading of Matthew Fox, Scientology auditing, Transcendental Meditation, Psychic readings, sharing over a coffee cup, a Roman Mass or Sunday worship at the Crystal Cathedral.

It may seem as if my definitions blur the difference between psychology and spirituality. This may be so with regard to spirituality in general. The crucial difference lies, as Belt Hallahmi observed, in the words and behaviors that are put to the experience. There will always be a distinctive set of words that can be seen in the statements Christians make that their experience of transcendent reality has been with the God of Abraham, Issac, Jacob, Isaiah, and Jesus the Christ who has redeemed them from sin and who wants to be in relationship with them throughout all the days of their life. So, in summary, my first suggestion is *mind the gap*. I turn now to *mind the store*.

MIND THE STORE

Pretend with me for the moment that *the store* is you and folk who come to you for counseling are customers who are seeking the goods that you have to offer. You are a *store keeper* who has a product to sell. Minding the store means advertising, supplying, selling, and guaranteeing the product. Mind the store. The product you have to sell is "the integration of Christian spirituality and psychology." Integration is what you've got to sell. When you *mind the store* you choose which aspects of the integration of Christian spirituality and of psychology you will bring into the treatment at a given time. Just like a good store keeper, you will bring out a given product that meets the needs of a particular customer at a specific time. This is the essence of applied integration.

Mind the Store. Begin by never forgetting for a moment that you are the principal tool in all counseling. You are the passageway, the tube, the canal through which the integration product is delivered. My wife would say, "Any fool knows that." That is true. We all know that there are good sales clerks and poor sales clerks.

However, in your case, the issue is more basic than that. Beyond all your classes in integrating Christian spirituality with psychology, beyond all the unique ideas and methods of integration you have learned, you have put it all together in a unique and highly personal fashion. Unlike a garage door salesman who might not own a car, much less a garage, you are the embodiment of integration — in your own life you have found personal, private meaning in the very product you are selling. And you have put it all together in a very unique way that affects and determines what you do when there is nothing but space between you and another person and nothing going on but the sound of your voice. As Carl Jung reportedly said, "People not only have their Gods, they make their Gods" — and this is true of you, no less than your client.

Periodically remind yourself that your substance as well as your style of integrative counsel is in many ways like no other and probably includes a basketful of heresies. Mind the store by being mindful of your own biases in integration. Next Mind the Store by recognizing that the day of browsing has passed. *Browsing* is my name for non-directive, client centered counseling. Counseling means the giving of counsel. No one thinks anymore that clients heal themselves simply by free association and insight. Not even Freud believed this, according to a recent biography (Breger, 2000). He was a classic dogmatic interpreter.

To be sure, compassionate listening builds a sense of empathy and trust. But the time comes in counseling when help is needed – listening gives way to the giving of counsel. Mind the store means to engage in analysis, interpretation, recommendation, contracting, and monitoring – all within the framework of "integrating Christian spirituality with psychology."

I once chaired the diplomate examination of a child psychologist. As part of the exam, we observed her consulting with a nursery school teacher about an unruly child. After listening to the teacher describe the behavior of the child in detail, the psychologist replied, "My goodness that is a terrible situation. I don't know what I would do in that situation." We failed her. Psychologists are not paid to say "I don't know what I would do" and neither are you. Like a good store keeper, you should be ready to say "Here are some products that I think might meet your need." "Let's do some thinking together about your dilemma. I'd like to suggest some options. See what you think. Try on these ideas."

A fascinating dialogue has been going on in Division 12 of the American Psychological Association over what kinds of suggestions counselors should make. For many years the ideal of training for clinical psychologists has been known as the "scientist/professional" model. Scientist/Professional was the rubric under which I was trained and Scientist/Professional has guided Fuller School of Psychology curriculum throughout the years I have taught there. Recently, some in the field of clinical psychology have suggested that a true *scientist/professional psychologist* will only use treatment methods that have been demonstrated to be empirically valid in published research studies. The ideal under this recommendation would be for counselors to not interpret and/or recommend alternatives to problems presented to them by clients until they have searched the research literature and found treatments that had been demonstrated to be effective. However, to make this a mandate has been heavily resisted by the members of Division 12. To date, they have passed no such resolution. I agree. That is just not how therapists function. It is unrealistic and naively idealistic. In fact, psychotherapy may always be more an art than a science.

Nevertheless, any mandate to ground all counseling in empirical research may be especially pertinent for you who would integrate psychology and Christianity spirituality. Integration is probably much more a theoretical, intuitive than it is an experimental, empirical task. While I have had the privilege of chairing over 100 doctoral dissertations in psychology, many of which have been experimental, I have to confess that few, if any, of them have impacted what I did as a counselor. I suspect the same is, or will be of my students as it is probably true of you. Give yourself the privilege of theory not based on experiment realizing that much of what we do in integration can never be reduced to means, standard deviations, multivariate analysis, or probability tests—as intriguing as these may be.

This does not mean that minding the integrative store should not be concerned with behavior. Results are important and never forget *insight doesn't heal*. There may be no healing without insight, but insight by itself does not heal. Behavior is important. Never think that you have done a good job if all your clients take away is insight. Life is lived out of intentions, actions, change. I think the Cognitive/Behaviorists have it right. Cognition (understanding, insight) has to be followed by Behavior (decision, actions, behaviors).

Mind the store. Choose what you do with behavior in mind at the same time that you confess that what you recommend may never have been proven to be valid in some research study. Mind the Gap, mind the Store. Two possible options for Integrating Christian Spirituality with Psychology.

I end where I began. Shift happens, change occurs. Mindfulness is your task. Never forget the words of St. Paul, "Do not be conformed to this world, but be transformed by the renewing of your minds, so that you may discern what is the will of God—what is good and acceptable and perfect" (Romans 12:2)

References

Beit-Hallahmi, B. j(1986). Religion as art and identity. *Religion, 16,* 1-17.

Berger, L. (2000). *Freud: Darkness in the midst of vision.* New York: John Wiley & Sons.

Sorenson, R. L. (2004). *Minding spirituality.* Hillsdale, NJ: The Analytic Press.

FOUR

Psychological Soteriology

The scientism of the past several centuries has brought into question the need of human beings for a God who saves (Soteriology). This essay considers the manner in which six 20th century psychologists have dealt with this issue. Their positions are as follows: neo-orthodox liberalism (G. Stanley Hall), pragmatic functionalism (William James), radical reductionism (James H. Leuba), ethical transvaluationalism (O. Hobart Mowrer), negative cynicism (Albert Ellis), and optimistic self actualism (Gordon W. Allport). Their points of view are compared to theories of the atonement in Christian theology.

Since early in this century individuals' need for a saving God has been a topic of popular conversation. Without doubt, this has been in large part a function of the immense appeal of Freudian ideas. Yet Freud's challenge to a magical, wish fulfilling, morally blind Christianity was but the best heard in a chorus of voices. All were questioning the classical formula of a weak, sinful, helpless human in need of a strong, forgiving, all powerful God. Freud spoke for the scientific Zeitgeist that became loud and vocal in the writing of Hegel and Feuerbach in the late 19th century. They, too, were products of their time for these ideas had long been fermenting in the minds of social theorists such as Comte and Marx. With the increasing mastery of the physical world and the possibility of international Utopias, the sense of sin and powerlessness which pervaded the medieval world was fading. Even Christian theology itself was changing. The Liberalism of the turn of the century, with its great emphasis on social justice, was grounded in a rejection of human frailty and an affirmation of human strength. Implicitly, the Augustinian/Reformation view of humans as unable to do good deeds had been replaced by a renewed emphasis on the ability of humans to join with God in creating a perfect world. The Liberal hope to "win the world for Christ in one generation" was a call for persons to acknowledge their innate Christlikeness and to join with others in making a just world. It was not a call to admission of powerlessness and a confession of sin. Further, it unequivocally suggested that the job of convincing everyone of this need could be accomplished in a single generation.

Suffice it to say, Freud was not alone. He was part of a cultural milieu that was questioning tradition and was optimistic about human power. However, he was the most vocal in attacking religious practices and in insisting that magical sanctions for sin without guilt or recompense were more than benign pastimes. They were, in fact, means of maintaining the status quo and of promoting social injustice. Further, such religion was regressive behavior unworthy of humans in the 20th century. Persons should know better than to engage in wish fulfillment or fantasies of magical healing.

For Freud, this was regression—not unlike that seen in individual neurosis. In fact, religion was, for Freud, a mass neurosis. It was perhaps, more benign than individual neurosis but certainly a less adequate adjustment than was possible. However, Freud was optimistic about the progress of science and the ability of persons to live by its dictums. He, like Comte, envisioned the day when religion would have passed away and persons would assume responsibility for their behavior and would no longer ask for cheap forgiveness from an all-powerful God. Freud felt there was no "future" for the illusion of religion. It was destined to pass away.[1] Suffice it to say, Freud saw no need for a saving God. He perceived such needs as regressive and pathological.

The question to which this essay is addressed is "How have others in the twentieth century treated this subject?" While Freud, without doubt, has been the dominant voice in psychiatry/psychology during these decades, have other thinkers affirmed his point of view? In an effort to answer this question six theorists are herein considered. All are psychologists, not psychiatrists. Each of them has been part of main-stream psychology in this century. Every one has been a member of the American Psychological Association and several have served as its president. It is noteworthy that while religious issues have not been a main focus in American psychology, each of these has attended to the subject in a significant manner. The writers to be considered are: G. Stanley Hall, William James, James H. Leuba, O. Hobart Mowrer, Albert Ellis, and Gordon Allport. They will be considered in approximate chronological order.

In an effort to typify their position on the role of a "saving God" in human experience I have attached the following labels to the aforementioned psychologists:

G. Stanley Hall—Neo-orthodox Liberal
William James—Pragmatic Functionalist
James S. Leuba—Radical Reductionist
O. Hobart Mowrer—Ethical Transvaluationist
Albert Ellis—Negative Cynic
Gordon Allport—Optimistic Self Actualist

Prior to a discussion of each of these in detail a delimiting of the idea of a saving God is appropriate. The usual term for this is Soteriology.

WHAT IS SOTERIOLOGY?

In Christian theology, Soteriology is usually combined with Christology in a doctrine of the Incarnation. Incarnation refers to an understanding of who Jesus of Nazareth was and what happened when he appeared on earth. Representative of the classical viewpoint are the words of the Apostles' Creed which state,

I believe in God the Father, Almighty, Maker of Heaven and of Earth. And in Jesus Christ, His only Son, Our Lord, who was conceived of the Holy Spirit, born of the Virgin Mary, suffered under Pontius Pilate, was crucified dead and buried; the third day He rose from the dead, from which He shall come to judge the quick and the dead.

This has been the traditional view of the Incarnation. Jesus of Nazareth was viewed as the Son of God who came to earth and by his life, death, and resurrection redeemed human beings from their sin. Christology is the term usually applied to who Jesus was. Soteriology is the term usually applied to what Jesus did. Both are integral to the doctrine of the Incarnation (i.e. the meaning of God indwelling in human life).

Obviously for Incarnation (Christology plus Soteriology) to make sense a view of persons as sinful has to be accepted. The Biblical view of humans is that they were created in innocence, but that through rebellion they have deviated from God's intent for life. Humans have a proclivity for trying to make their own destinies rather than following the plan God has for them. This is sin.

The classical Christian view is persons are sinful almost from the beginning and are powerless to stop sinning. Therefore a Saviour is needed to bring persons back to God. God sent his message to humans through the centuries in the form of teachers and prophets. However, humans did not heed God's message. Finally, God sent His son, Jesus to save persons from their sin. Thus these are the presumptions of the traditional views of Soteriology. The major positions which have been espoused through the centuries are described below.

The first is known as the Ransom theory. In this position there is the assumption that God once owned humans but that the devil has seduced them away from God. Therefore to win human beings back God must pay a price to the devil. The price which God and the devil decide upon is the life of God's only son, Jesus. The life of Jesus is the ransom paid to the devil. After Jesus dies the devil frees humans thinking the bargain a good one. However, God tricks the devil by bringing Jesus back to life again.

The second is known as the Victory theory. This is a variety of the

Ransom theory except here the powers of evil are thought to be in greater combat with God for the life of human beings. They are almost victorious in that they engineer the death of God's Son but God overpowers them by resurrecting Jesus on the third day. God wins and claims humans for Himself.

The third position is termed the Satisfaction theory. It emphasizes the sin of humans and the moral demands of God. Humans cannot redeem themselves because God demands perfect obedience and thus even a perfect life could not atone for the past. On the other hand, God could not change or forgive humans for less than perfect obedience because he was God. God was in a dilemma. Only He could change the situation. So God sent His Son, Jesus, to die. Jesus' perfect life would not satisfy. Only the death of Jesus, which was undeserved, would allow God to love man and yet be honest with Himself. God sent Jesus, who was both man and God, to pay the debt. Satisfaction resulted.

The fourth point of view is called the Illustration theory. In contrast to the Satisfaction theory, it does not perceive God as having a problem. He could forgive if He wanted to—and He does. The only problem is humans do not know it nor can they conceive of it. Humans think God is angry and ready to punish. God, therefore, in order to get the attention of human beings and to demonstrate His love, sends Jesus to suffer and die. Thereby, God's love is made manifest and humans see it and repent. Fellowship is restored. Jesus' work is to illustrate the love of God.

The fifth viewpoint is called the Union theory. Herein the way to reinstating humans' relationship with God is shown by the suffering and sacrificial death of Jesus. The reunion of God and human beings comes through denial of the world and by giving up of oneself to the way of the cross. By suppressing the temptation to save one's life and to seek worldly success each human being is brought back into fellowship with God. The death of Jesus points the way that persons must go. It accomplishes something in their hearts if they would be one with God. They do not know the way until they see it pointed out in the life and sacrificial death of Jesus.

Finally there is a position called the Example theory. This has two variations. One emphasizes Jesus' death, while the other focuses on His life. In the former, Jesus's death is an example of suffering love. Humans, if they are to return to fellowship with God, must follow the example of Jesus and give their lives as a sacrifice for others. In the latter, Jesus' life is an example of just and ethical passion for the sake of the downtrodden and mistreated. Humans, if they are to be reunited with God must follow Jesus' example and become primarily concerned with helping the poor and downtrodden. In both variations Jesus is the example of how people ought to live.

Thus these several alternatives have been proposed for Soteriology within the Christian tradition. All pertain to the means by which the problem of mankind is solved. In each case persons are brought back into a positive relationship with God through God's action in Jesus Christ. God is seen as ransoming humans from the devil, winning a victory over evil forces, sacrificing His own demands for justice, manifesting His love in order to capture attention, providing a sacrificial means for reunion with people, and/or setting an example of love and justice for others to follow.

The psychologists we will next consider espouse one of more of these positions if they look favorably on the idea of people needing a saving God. Or they deny the validity of one or more of these viewpoints if they conceive people do not need a God who saves. They will be discussed in chronological order.

G. STANLEY HALL

G. Stanley Hall could be termed a neo-orthodox liberal in the sense that he combines the neo-orthodox insistence on the inevitable need of sinful human beings for divine salvation with a liberal interpretation of the dynamic effect of the Christ event. His thesis was that only through acceptance of such a radical idea that God loved humankind enough to die in its behalf was it possible for persons to be wrenched from their deep seated egotism and be "saved" for love and altruism -the true aims of life.

It is well known that Hall originally trained for the Christian ministry. It is of interest that with all his later education in psychology and philosophy he held onto a traditional interpretation of the atonement. This is even more noteworthy in light of the fact that the theological training to which he was exposed was heavily influenced by a neo-Kantian concern for Jesus as the representative of the moral law (cf. J. Kitsch) rather than a sacrificial expiation grounded in God's love.

Although Hall agreed with most scholars of his day in feeling pessimistic about knowing the true facts of Jesus' life, he, nevertheless, did not depreciate the cross-resurrection events, as others were prone to do. Thus, it was not the historicity of Jesus' death but its symbolic meaning that was important in Hall's thinking. The deep issues of life remained untouched by examples (such, as Jesus' life) or by culture. These depths could only be touched symbolically.

The racial soul was thought by Hall to be that deep-seated reality wherein true human nature resides. Although a symbol, it was nevertheless, unquestionably real. The racial soul included the real meaning of life—love and altruism. Culture had suppressed these to the point that most persons' lives were characterized by egotism and selfishness. Hall felt that there was no way short of confrontation by the symbol of the cross of Christ to make contact with the racial soul. It was symbol-making contact with symbol, truly real with truly real, depth with depth.

According to Hall's (1917) developmental and pedagogical theories, ado-lescence was the ideal time for the symbol of Christ's death-resurrection to be presented. At this point in life individuals are seeking the meaning of life as at no other time. During adolescence, the presentation of Jesus can overcome the egotistic inertia of persons and awaken them to their racial souls, i.e. their potential to love each other.

They dynamically followed this process: Once a person had been awestruck by the idea that God loved them enough to die for them, then he/she could cease being preoccupied with self -preservation and turn attention to the example of Love which Jesus set in His life. By patterning one's life after Jesus, the individual comes to know that love and altruism are the true goals for which they were created. Thus, the potential in the racial soul is brought to life again. Hall was optimistic enough to believe that if psychology would take as its primary task the guidance of educators in presenting of the profoundly transforming meaning of Jesus, then there would be a radical re-evolution and reconstruction of the world.

Thus did G. Stanley Hall combine a neo-orthodox interpretation of the importance of the death and resurrection of Jesus with a liberal interpretation of the importance of Jesus' example of love. His viewpoint resembles the Illustration theory of the atonement. God, in Christ, demonstrates His love and thereby gets man's attention.

WILLIAM JAMES

William James could be termed a pragmatic functionalist in regard to his view of Soteriology. Unlike Hall, James was unconvinced of the value of one type of religious stimulus over another. James was more concerned with individual dif-ferences than with a preconceived single avenue into the racial soul as was Hall. He was even equivocal about an ideal time for conversion even though he had Starbuck's data at hand and knew that adolescence was the time at which the majority of such events occurred. He simply stated that for some people con-version occurred during the teen years in response to a conviction that Christ died for their sins and for some people it did not. In this sense, he thought descriptively rather than prescriptively. He described what was rather than pre-scribing what should be, as did Hall. He was a pragmatist, not an idealist.

A diagram of the implicit views of God's saving work in Christ as it applies to James' categories of "once born" and "twice born" is as follows. The once born individual, as described by James, looks to Jesus as an example, feels good about the world, attributes strength and goodness to him/herself, and optimistically attempts to live the Christ-like life. The twice born individual, as described by James, looks to Jesus as Saviour, feels suspicious of the world,

DIAGRAM 4-1

Christian Theories of Atonement as related to once born and
twice born religionists

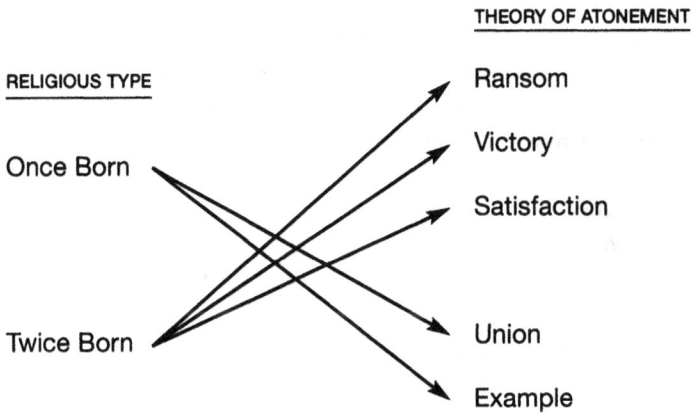

THEORY OF ATONEMENT

RELIGIOUS TYPE

Once Born

Twice Born

Ransom

Victory

Satisfaction

Union

Example

attributes weakness and evil to him/herself, and awaits transformation before
going out to live the Christ-like life. These illustrate the Union and Example
theories on the one hand and the Ransom, Victory, and Satisfaction theories on
the other.

James did not express a preference for one view of atonement over the
other. Nor did he espouse the value of once born over twice born, or vice versa.
He merely reported what was happening.[2]

Yet, there is a sense in which. James did not just describe. He was not
neutral in regard to the effects of the different types of religious experience.
While he did not evaluate type of experience or view of atonement he did make
judgments about results, he suggested that only those experiences which resulted in personality integration were of value (James 1902/1958). Irrespective of
the origin of religion, if it left the self divided, it was of little value. As James
said, not by "roots" but by "fruits" could religious experience be judged.

James understanding of the integration of the self merits further discussion. Without question, James was strongly concerned with mental or psychic
energy. He was suggesting in this case that good religious experiences resulted in
the individual being able to focus his/her energies toward single goals without
conflict or ambivalence. His model was a reflection of the concern in his day
with thermodynamics and the transfer of energy. It is interesting to note how
some of his ideas parallel those of Freud, even though the two did not consult.

James knew first hand through his own depressions the turmoil of the divided self. He valued experiences that reunited the parts of the personality and gave persons the feeling that they were integrated. He suggested that an individual knew when this had happened and that their behavior would reflect it.

James did not value the once born over the twice born person even though an examination of the preconditions suggests that the twice born person clearly feels disintegrated prior to conversion. In fact, there is the implication that James felt the twice born person to be more realistic. He described the once born person as able to repress part of reality better than the twice born person. This resembles a hysteric or dissociative tendency at worst and compartmentalization at best. Even the once born person must someday face evil in him/herself and the world. Perhaps, they are able to reunite themselves at that time because of not being as divided to begin with. But, this is by no means a foregone conclusion. James was a functionalist to the end.

Thus, in summary, William James attitude toward the need of a saving God was one of pragmatic functionalism. His prime concern was with experiences which would integrate or reunite the divided self. His descriptions of the good -results of conversion clearly attest to this. In this regard, he cared-little what view of the atonement characterized the experience so long as the fruits, or results, of faith helped people live without feelings of fragmentation and conflict.

JAMES H. LEUBA

Leuba could be termed a radical reductionist in regard to his view of Soteriology. He proposed, in contrast to Hall, that the Christ event had no ultimate truth to it and its meaning was simply the cultural vehicle by which persons moved from fear to inner peace. He went one step further and suggested that religion was a means by which persons asked God to do for them what could better be done through science, especially psychological science. Like many other scientists before and since his time, Leuba glorified science as a way of solving human problems and depreciated religion—calling it a cultural artifact that should be outgrown by mature individuals.

The term "radical" is appropriately applied to Leuba. Like Hall, he was a very religious person early in his life, but unlike Hall, he became singularly preoccupied with explaining away the content of faith. Whereas it is debatable whether James believed there was a God, there is no question about Leuba. He did not. He felt it important to show how God was a figment of projection, as Feuerback and others had suggested. Leuba saw himself as giving scientific evidence and rationale for what previous theorists had proposed.

This proclivity to psychologically explain rather than neutrally describe religious behavior is clearly seen in his distinction between "positive" and "negative" religion. These distinctions, interestingly enough, are not unlike James dichotomy of once and twice born persons. Leuba (1933) says both types are grounded in fear. Negative religion attempts to appease and persuade evil spirits while positive religion expresses appreciation for the good will and assistance of benevolent deities. Most often, negative appears earlier and even in the absence of positive religion. There is some question whether positive religion would ever appear—yet appear it does. Leuba's conviction is that in both cases the root emotion is fear of annihilation and an urge to survive. Leuba explains away, he does not simply describe.

Leuba even reduces to psychophysiology the essence of religion as detailed by James and others (i.e. the mystical experience). He suggests that it is grounded in lapses of consciousness, memory, and suggestibility. There is no scientific evidence for the *reality of the unseen.*

In regard to Soteriology, Leuba rejected the final validity of all interpretations at the same time that he clearly understood why the myth of Jesus as Saviour came into being. Like many of his contemporaries, he rejected religion as magic and affirmed science. He suggested science was the mode of' thought appropriate for the modern world and was convinced that progress included the rejection of religion. The title of his book *God or Man* (1934) clearly attested to this point of view that was in no small measure based on his survey of American scientists wherein an inverse relationship between belief in a God and eminence in the field was revealed.

Thus, Leuba was a radical reductionist in regard to the need of persons for a saving God. Faith is understandable but the need for it better satisfied through scientific endeavor.

O. HOBART MOWRER

Mowrer could be termed an ethical trans-valuationist in regard to his view of Soteriology. The person of Jesus has played a central role in his thinking. He has felt it was essential to reassert the importance of his ethical teaching.

The distinction between the life and the death of Jesus has not heretofore been clarified in this essay. This is important from Mowrer's point of view because he suggests the Christian church has almost exclusively perceived His saving power only in terms of His death and resurrection. This has been a gross historical error that needs correcting, according to Mowrer (1961). He concludes that the early church came too much under the sway of Paul who re-construed the Christ event almost entirely in terms of the last week of Jesus' life. It is Mowrer's opinion that this was a distortion of Jesus' own intention and that/ in fact, Paul created a new religion. True Christianity is that which is based on following the ethical teachings of Jesus. Obeying the Beatitudes is more to the essence of Christianity than is faith in a Saviour who forgives sins and restores persons to a right relationship with God.

It is widely known that much of Mowrer's thinking stemmed from his own depressive crisis that hospitalized him at the very time he was to be installed as president of the American Psychological Association. According to his report of his hospitalization, visiting ministers who urged him to repent of sins caught his attention far more than anything else being said to him by the hospital staff—including the hospital chaplain who was preaching a God who loved persons enough to die for them. Mowrer began to examine himself and purposed to confess his sins when next he went home on a visit. This he did. He became convinced that by confession and reconciliation he would get well.

Thus, Mowrer's understanding of the atonement is closely related to his views of mental illness. In contrast to psychoanalytic theory which suggested that release of the repressed brought health, Mowrer (1961) concluded that strengthening the super ego would lead to health. A too weak, rather than an overly strong, conscience causes psychopathology, according to him. He attributed his own depression to unacknowledged guilt. He saw most abnormality as resulting from self -deception.

Many of these ideas can be seen in Mowrer's (1961) two factor learning theory. In this model, the ego not only learns to solve problems but the super-ego learns how to deceive. Punishment by parents, not only shapes problem solving, it also results in children knowing around whom and where to misbehave. Some of the evidence about the results of punishment seems to support Mowrer.

Punishment by itself seems to result in the suppression of behavior at a given time and place but it does not, over the long run, reduce the number of times a behavior is exhibited. The individual simply becomes more crafty and cautious. Bad behavior is done in secret where parents cannot see or punish it.

Mental health for Mowrer is living wholeheartedly by standards, values, and ideals. It is listening to one's conscience and correcting one's errors. It is being just, kind, loving, and considerate of others. Anything that one does in violation of these ends is to be confessed and corrected. Thus, the deceitful learning patterns which led to inner conflict are confronted and obliterated.

Following Jesus's teaching about the good life is the way to mental health, Jesus called for high ideals. Those who would be integrated within His will follow His admonitions. Mowrer illustrates the example theory of atonement with his emphasis on the teachings of Jesus. He is an ethical trans-valuationist.

ALBERT R. ELLIS

Albert Ellis's position on Soteriology could be labeled that of a negative cynic. In contrast to Leuba, belief in God is not even understandable much less efficacious, according to Ellis (n.d.). Being ruthlessly rational and logical has been his ideal. He does not feel that it is ever necessary to posit a saving God—even as a point along the developmental way. It is more understandable when persons grow up thinking clearly (or rationally) and never assert belief in the divine. The need for God is always a distortion. It is never the norm. More importantly, Ellis opines that belief in the divine and dependence upon him is antithetical to good mental health. He does not see religious belief merely as a harmless crutch. It is a destructive force. It not only has no value—it has negative value.[3]

As a psychotherapist, Ellis (n.d.) perceives all his goals in working with people as the opposite of those inherent in the religious point of view. In addition to assisting persons in becoming minimally hostile and anxious, he attempts to help them become maximally self concerned, self directed, self accepting, tolerant, flexible, committed, and scientific in their thinking. Further, he is concerned to help them become more willing to accept uncertainty, to be courageous and to take more risks. According to Ellis, belief in the deity does not help persons reach these goals. In fact, it inhibits their efforts.

Religion encourages God interest, not self interest, according to Ellis (n.d.). For the religionist, the prime concern is whether God loves him or her. Masochistic self sacrifice directed toward pleasing God is a part of all religion. Human efforts are, thus, directed toward finding peace and freedom from guilt—by appeasing the deity. Religiosity equals masochism, according to Ellis. And this is the antithesis of mental health—all those goals toward which psychotherapy is directed. In fact, masochism and religiosity could both be conceived as forms of mental illness. Religion is the unhealthiest mental state imaginable, according to Ellis.

Belief in a God who saves not only diverts persons attention away from self acceptance, self concern, and self direction, it also leads to a fantasy of certitude which is the essence of the neurotic demand that everything must be fully predictable in order for persons to survive. This is a childish dream that should be outgrown, not perpetuated. The religious person is not open to change. She or he is prejudiced and inflexible. She or he is not open to change nor is she/he willing to subject his/her thoughts to scientific validation. The whole system borders on being obsessive-compulsive fanaticism. It is the antithesis of health.

These beliefs led Ellis to encourage psychotherapists to be intolerant of their patient's religion. Religion is to be opposed and obliterated. It is not one of those aspects of the patient's life that is to be understood and incorporated as part of the individual gestalt. Whenever a patient expresses religious faith in God, the psychotherapist should immediately combat it and root it out because such attitudes are the opposite of all that good mental health stands for. Ellis (n.d.) suggests that the goal of any psychotherapist should be to help the patient live without illness and, thus, to live without religion.[4]

Therefore, it is clear that Ellis, of all the theorists who have been discussed, is by far the most cynical in regard to persons' need for a saving God. He perceives the value of religion to be nil. His views of Soteriology fit none of the alternatives suggested. He would say that he agreed with no one of the possibilities and that the real meaning of the atonement was psychopathology. As he concluded, "If there was a god, it would be necessary to un-invent him" (Ellis, n.d.).

GORDON ALLPORT

Gordon Allport is the last of the psychologists to be considered. He could be termed an optimistic self-actualist. In contrast to Ellis, he was optimistic about the role that religion could play in life. His primary concern was with the development of mature personality within the individual and he conceived a vital role for faith in that process.

Allport (1951) defined mature personality as having three components. First, he suggested that the individual should have a number of interests that dominate over *viscerogenic* desires. These interests should be directed toward values or ideals—objects of greater worth than the individual him/herself. Second, a mature person should have the ability to be objective; meaning to stand apart from her or himself and to get some perspective on life. This includes being able to laugh at oneself and to see oneself through others' eyes. Finally, a person who is mature has a "unifying philosophy of life" (Allport, 1951, p. 59). Allport said that this philosophy does not *necessarily* have to be religious (emphasis mine). But he would agree that religion preeminently serves that function in the scheme of things. Its prime purpose is to resolve that fragmentation, aimlessness, and loss of meaning which characterize those personalities which have not yet matured.

It can readily be seen that Allport's understanding of mental health differs in some important ways from that of Ellis. He emphasized the importance of values and ideals above the self much more than does Ellis. When Ellis talks about allegiance to science he is thinking about what will pragmatically work for self—interest more than any ideal above the common life. While both authors write extensively about the "self" one gets the distinct feeling that Allport's mature person with commitment to high ideals and a unifying philosophy might be considered pathological by Ellis.

It may be that the difference between the two thinkers is understandable in terms of their roles. Ellis is a psychotherapist concerned with healing the disturbed while Allport was a social philosopher more concerned with the growth and development of fully functioning adults. On the one hand Ellis sees religion as a crutch from which disturbed persons need to extricate themselves while Allport saw religion as a means by which the average person could possibly enhance his/her inner potential.

In regard to Allport, his seminal distinction between the intrinsic and the extrinsic religious sentiment should be noted. There is no doubt that he valued one over the other, and that he, in fact, considered the extrinsically oriented religious person to be immature. He might even have gone so far as to agree with Ellis in saying that mental health would come only through the extrication of extrinsic religion. Needless to say, Allport placed supreme value on the development of an inner integrity and high religion could function in behalf of that development. Intrinsic religion, wherein persons loved God for God's own sake and not their self advancement or to please others, could be the essence of mature selfhood. Herein, persons would have a central purpose to their existence and that purpose would be to live in behalf of a high value with emphasis on the good of all humankind.

The question next arises as to what place the idea of a saving God had in the thought of Allport. Specifically it seems to have played only a small role in his thinking. In fact there is some indication that he explicitly rejected the classical views of the atonement. He spoke of himself as replacing the doctrines of his childhood with "some sort of Humanitarian religion" during college (Allport, 1968, p. 382).

This involved, for him, an active role in social action. Yet, interestingly enough, he later reacted to an "essentially Unitarian position" which he had adopted because it exalted his intelligence too much (Allport, 1968, p. 382). Like William James he spoke of the need to accept life with some humility and mysticism. He appears to have had a very meaningful private faith. Although he did not acknowledge it, it is known that he was an active member of the Episcopal church.

Nevertheless, the figure of Jesus was not of prime interest to him. The index to his book *The Individual and His Religion* (1951) does not include references to "Jesus," to "Christ," or to the "Atonement." At best it could be said that he accorded to Christ the place of one who exemplified all the qualities of a mature person—high ideals, self-objectification, and a unifying philosophy of life. Jesus's life was centered in himself and his behavior reflected full personality integration.

No doubt, Allport was optimistic about human beings. He defined sin as ignorance. There was no need for God to die to save mankind except by the example of Jesus we are shown how to live. Soteriology to Allport was the Example theory. By following Jesus persons could actualize their "selves"— which was the most important task of life. Allport, thus, was an optimistic self-actualizer.

CONCLUSION

What has the idea of a saving God meant to twentieth century psychologists? A variety of things, if these six theorists be any indication. The differences are not predictable nor are they progressive. By no means has there been a move toward scientism across these decades. Nor, on the other hand, has there been any systematic rapprochement between orthodox doctrine and psychological theory. If one considers the several labels applied to the psychologists discussed herein several groupings are in order.

First, all theorists reflect a prime concern for the function of religion rather than its objective validity. No one of the theorists was unbiased. Even Leuba was preoccupied with what religion could do for the individual's life. He just felt science could do it better. Second, two of the theorists, Leuba and Ellis, unequivocally assess religion to have negative value. The other four thinkers felt that belief in God could have positive effect in enhancing adjustment. Third, Mowrer and Ellis began with a basic model of psychopathology while Hall and Allport were concerned with normal personality development. However, Mowrer aligned himself with Hall and Allport in asserting the value of religion. Only Ellis, of these four, felt religion to be destructive.

Fourth, several of the psychologists distinguished between good and bad religion. The positive value they attributed to religion was confined to that type of religion that was productive of good fruits (James), altruism (Hall), confession (Mowrer), and maturity (Allport).

Fifth, it is apparent in considering such personages as these that psychologists in general tends toward the more liberal rather than the more conservative (or orthodox) views of Soteriology. Thus, they are, in the final analysis, optimistic about the ability of humankind to both achieve individual maturity and to create a just social order. Views of sin which perceive human beings to be unalterably sinful and needing redemption of a metaphysical sort are missing here.

Finally, scientism and the Freudian hypothesis about religion appear only to partially characterize these theorists. While all seem concerned with the impact of religion on culture, they are evenly divided as to whether religion perpetuates or combats injustice. They are by no means unified in their assessment of the social value of belief in a saving God.

One might wonder how typical these psychologists are of the several options available to psychologists in the last quarter of the twentieth century. The question could be asked, "Just what are the implicit or explicit Soteriologies currently in use in the contemporary psychological community?" This essay could provide the background for addressing such questions as these.

ENDNOTES

1. There is some evidence that Freud was oblivious to the developments in Liberal religious thought in his day. A Swiss pastor, Oskar Pfister, debated him on this issue. A recount of this dialogue can be read in Malony, H. N. and North, G. E. The future of an illusion and the illusion of the future—the Freud-Pfister dialogue. *Journal of the History of the Behavioral Sciences*, 1979.

2. James's personal beliefs are unclear. In the *Varieties of Religious Experience* there is a chapter on the "Reality of the Unseen" which reflects a faith in "something out there" which cannot be denied. Yet, he seems to take a basically neutral position overall. It does not matter whether there is a God or not. What matters is that some people believe there is and that belief has effect on lives.

3. Although, it could be noted that Ellis did soften on this position toward the end of his life.

4. This contrast may be more semantic than real. In all fairness it should be remembered that Ellis includes commitment to something outside the self in his definition of mental health.

REFERENCES

Allport, G. W. (1951). *The individual and his religion.* New York: Maontllan.

Allport, G. W. (1968). *The person in psychology: Selected essays.* Boston: Beacon Press.

Ellis, A. (n.d.) *The Case against Religion.* (Tape recording). New York: Institute for Rational Living.

Hall, G. S. (1917). *Jesus and Christ in the light of psychology* (Vol. 1 & 2). New York: D. Appleton and Company.

Hordern, W. E. (1968). *A layman's guide to protestant theology.* New York: Maonillan.

James, W. (1958). *The varieties of religious experience.* New York: New American Library of World Literature. (Original work published in 1902)

Leuba, J. H. (1933). *God or man? A study of the value of God to man.* New York: Henry Holt and Co.

Malony, H. N. & North, G. E. (1979). The future of an illusion—the illusion of the future and historic dialogue on the value of religion between Oskar Pfister and Sigmund Freud. *Journal of the History of the Behavioral Sciences, 15(2),* 177-186.

Mowrer, 0. H. (1961). *The crisis in psychiatry and religion.* New York: D. Van Nostrand.

Sellers, J. E. (1966). *Theological ethics.* New York: Macmillan.

FIVE

The Relevance of "Religious Diagnosis" for Counseling

This essay considers whether religious diagnosis is a relevant task for counselors to undertake in addition to their evaluations of personality, intelligence, and social history. The issue of the importance of religion in the current situation is debated and the conclusion reached that for a significant part of the population religion is still a vital component of life. Therefore religious diagnosis is considered to be relevant. Past attempts to undertake such diagnoses are described and the development of the Religious Status Interview is detailed. Other issues discussed are the uses of religious diagnosis in counseling, the relationship of religious diagnoses to DSM III-R Axes, the positive functions of religion in life, and an understanding of religious maturity. The intent of this essay is to provide a rationale for counselors to undertake religious diagnoses in their work with clients.

RELIGION: OF "MINOR" OR "MAJOR" IMPORTANCE IN LIFE?

In determining the relevance of making religious diagnoses in counseling, an initial question must be answered, namely, "How important is religion to the mental health of the average person?" The rationale for addressing such a question is this. If religion is an important dimension of human experience, then counselors should not neglect to evaluate its status. If, however, religion plays an insignificant role in the emotional adjustment of the average person, then counseling time might be better spent in other ways than in making a religious diagnosis. After all, counseling time is limited and counselors are always making judgments about what aspects of life to emphasize and what aspects to ignore.

There is some warrant for contending religion is a pervasive fact of human life. Sociology has long stated that every human society has three basic institutions—family, state, and religion. Often reported surveys of American culture would seem to support this presumption. They have concluded that 90% of Americans say they believe in God, over 50% belong to some religious group, and about 30% participate in weekly religious activity. A recent study by sociologist Barry Kosmin supports these statistics (O'Guinn, 1991). Only 7.5% of the population reported they had no religion, while 80% claimed to be Christian. Assuming that self-identification and attendance were synonymous with importance, it would seem logical to assume that religion would have import for the life adjustment of most persons and that some form of religious diagnosis should be included in the standard battery of tests administered by counselors (Malony, 1985). Along with social histories and family dynamics, religion might be assumed to be one of the more crucial factors influencing emotional disturbance and mental health.

In even stronger support for this presumption, I reaffirmed, in an earlier essay (Malony, 1983), the model of the social psychologist Theodore Sarbin that adjustment to the "transcendent" was an essential ingredient of social identity. Sarbin (1970) asserted that every individual had to adjust to transcendental reality in addition to accommodating to the physical, situational, interpersonal, and idealistic environments of life. Transcendental reality was understood to mean that province of life usually ascribed to religion. It included the supernatural, trans-empirical reality in terms of which persons found ultimate meaning to their existence. I agreed with Sarbin concerning the absolute necessity that persons come to terms with this transcendent dimension at the same time that they adjusted themselves to their bodies, their cultures, their associates, and their values.

I went one step beyond Sarbin, however, in suggesting that this transcendent reality was the most important of the five life-environments. Social identity, from this point of view, was not determined by adding-up adjustments across all of the environments but was a function of multiplying the sum of the other four by the individual's adjustment to the transcendent. If my contention about the primacy of adjustment to transcendent reality is correct, religion is not only one of the important life dimension that should be assessed by counselors, it would probably be the *most* important. If this is true, then making a religious diagnosis becomes a necessity, not an option.

However, my views about the importance of religion in contemporary life are not universally shared. There is a widespread contention that religion has become fairly irrelevant to daily life. I am convinced that many counselors have shared this view in the past, else why has there been only rare attempts to assess religious status along with evaluations of personality, social history, family background, intelligence, cognitive functioning, etc.

The management theorist Peter Drucker speaks for many such theorists in his reported statement, "Religion lives off the excess of society." By this

Drucker meant that religion, like hobbies and recreations, had become what most people do in their spare time. Religion is no longer central to their lives, indeed, if it ever was. Society's main thrust, according to this analysis, has become irreligious, or secular. Religion is passe; no longer central to society's life. According to this view, some persons continue to be religious, most do not. Religion is a private affair that is becoming less and less viable for the great majority of the public, quite apart from their identification of themselves as "Christian" and quite apart from their cultural accommodation to church attendance in their spare time.

Lesslie Newbign (1986) sums up this point of view in a penetrating account of cultural developments since the Enlightenment. He notes how ludicrous it is for church in societies which have become secularized and almost irreligious to continue to send missionaries into cultures which have become self-consciously religious and where the church is growing at a fast rate. Newbign (1986) sees this transition from the sacred to the secular as resulting from the influence of modern science and, especially, the work of Isaac Newton. He states, "The effect of the work of the new scientists, and above all the brilliant vision of Newton, was to replace this (divine purpose) explanatory framework with another. The real world disclosed by the work of science was one governed not by purpose but by natural laws of cause and effect" (p. 24).

The way in which these scientific changes came to affect individual existence and the importance of religion for daily life is critical to note. The central conviction of the scientists that reason, rather than faith, was the essential rule by which their research was to be undertaken became the basis for everyday interaction with the world. Reason meant those "analytical and mathematical powers by which human beings could attain (at least in principle) to a complete understanding of, and thus a full mastery of nature." (Newbign, 1986, p.25). The rational individual has become the norm.

"Rational individuals" were presumed to have the potential as well as the right to exercise their reason in search for reality. Out of this presumption came the ideals of the human right to life, liberty, and the pursuit of happiness, according to Newbign. Since teleology, or final purpose, had been obliterated from human understanding by the advent of the age of reason, happiness was no longer defined by life after death or, even, pleasing God here and now. Happiness became defined in this worldly terms by all rational individuals by themselves alone. According to Newbign, medieval people did not expect to find full happiness on this earth but rational persons did. He concluded: "The methods of modern science provide no grounds for belief that there is something beyond death. Hence the whole freight of human happiness has to be carried in a few short and uncertain years that are allowed us before death ends it all. The quest for happiness becomes that much more hectic, more fraught with anxiety than it was to the people of the Middle Ages" (Newbign, 1986, p.27).

This analysis of the cultural situation in the western world challenges the view that religion still has much import for the average individual. In contrast to the view that all individuals have to deal with transcendent reality and/or that their adjustment to this dimension of life colors the rest of their existence this analysis implies that religion is, indeed, as Drucker suggested, is an "excess" elective, not a requirement, of life. Religion is, thus, thought to be a private option rather than a public mandate.

In an innovative follow-up study of students in the Sierra Project, Day (1991) reported conclusions that support this view that there is a lack of religious concerns in many young adults. The Sierra Project was a living/learning project initiated by the University of California to raise the level of moral development in college students. In interviews some years later, Day (1991) was surprised to note the lack of religious influence and involvement among these students who, by the time of the interviews, were almost 30 years old. According to Day, the inference that there is still a "religious factor" to which counselors need to attend may be more a "guild" issue of professionals who define themselves as students of religion than a social reality. There may be no religious influence to measure among most adults. Those who want to study religion may be talking to themselves.

In spite of Day's conclusion that the day of religion may have passed, the fact remains that a significant percentage of the American public still consider themselves to be religious and they continue to participate in organized religious groups. One has to admit that there is an element of cultural conformity to these statistics in that participation is twice as high in the south than in the west. Certainly the data on Americana religion is duplicated nowhere in the western world. Religious participation in Britain and Europe is very slight.

It also has to be acknowledged, however, that there are innovative ways to express religious interest as can be seen in the appeal of the new religions and New Age movements. Nevertheless, the messages communicated by leaders in these religious experiences do not fall on completely deaf ears. Some people are still being influenced by trans-empirical, transcendent ideas and it would appear prudent to assess whether and how religion is impacting their lives, be they ever so few.

In a survey of California psychologists, a majority of those surveyed indicated that their clients presented spiritual problems to them in counseling (Shafranske & Malony, 1985) . These results were later replicated in a national sample (Shafranske & Malony, 1990). It would seem as if religious issues are still arising in counseling even if the larger society seems to be becoming more secular. While we may admit that counselees are a societal sub-group and/or that religion has become a private, sub-cultural affair, it would seem a strategic move to determine its importance among specific individuals in the face of clear mandates in the helping professions to consider cross-cultural influences in emotional disturbances. The rest of this essay is based on this judgment that religion is, indeed, at least a minor, if not a major, influence in some, if not all, persons' lives.

ATTEMPTS TO DIAGNOSE RELIGION

Chief among early attempts to undertake religious diagnoses among counselees were the efforts of psychiatrist Edgar Draper and his colleagues at the University of Mississippi Medical School (Draper, Meyer, Parzen, & Samuelson, 1965). They concluded that they could classify patients into valid psychiatric categories on the basis of patients' responses to the simple prompt, "Tell me about your religion." They only asked this one question and from the answer inferred the importance of religion for psychopathology. They made no judgment about the maturity of patient's faith. This illustrates the basic differ-ence between "diagnosis" and "research." Draper and his colleagues func-tioned in a medical school where the emphasis was more on treatment than on research. In diagnosis, treatment is the prime concern. In research, understand-ing is the prime goal. While it is true that the conclusions reached in research can be applied, in diagnosis the results are primarily directed to remediation. Thus, the critical aspect of diagnosis is that all assessments are brought togeth-er in a combined report designed to help counselors do a better job of helping persons. Typically, research investigations are undertaken for their own sake— the advancement of knowledge rather than the betterment of one individual. While the literature is replete with research studies of religion (e.g., Batson & Ventis, 1982; Spilka, Hood, & Gorsuch, 1985), the examples of diagnostic approaches have been fewer (Draper et al., 1965; Malony, 1988; Pruyser, 1965). Although many of us who have worked in mental hospitals know how seductive diagnosing can be and how rare are those occasions when counseling is truly based on diagnosis, we also know that this is not how it should be. Diagnosing cannot be an end in itself. Where the meaning of diagnosis is taken seriously information about persons is always used in their treatment.

USES OF RELIGIOUS DIAGNOSIS

There are a variety of ways that counselors can use the information they obtain in making religious diagnoses (Malony, 1991). The first option is to *disregard* the data. This may sound contradictory to the idea that all information obtained in the diagnostic process is to be used or not gathered in the first place. However, disregarding counselees' religion may be appropriate if they simply reported themselves to be religious out of cultural conformity when it turns out they are not. Further, if counselees1 religion is very weak and unformed, the counselor may choose to disregard it and work, instead, with stronger determinants of behavior. After all, time is a critical variable in treatment and no counselor is able to attend to every aspect of his or her counselees' lives. Religion is only one of the life-dimensions being evaluated, and there may be other more viable areas that need to be considered.

An even more radical option for counselors is to *annihilate* the religion of their counselees on the basis of their diagnostic conclusions. Without doubt, most counselors would argue against those types of religion where clients reported God telling them to commit violent acts or where they claimed to be Jesus Christ or the devil.

Sometimes the situation is less clear, however. Here is where *a standard of good religion* must be brought into consideration. Many counselors might shy away from trying to annihilate another person's faith either because they didn't know enough about a given religion or they feared that they might be imposing their interpretations or values into the situation. I recall a psychiatrist who sought my counsel as to whether a hospitalized nun who wanted to pray every hour for the sins of the world was being pathologically religious. She felt personally responsible. The psychiatrist asked whether this was normal behavior for nuns. I was able to help him to assess her religious behavior as pathological by concluding that she did not come from a cloistered convent nor was the order to which she belonged one that emphasized solitary prayer. The psychiatrist lacked a standard by which to judge her behavior and was hesitant to confront it.

Illustrative of this reluctance are the findings in the aforementioned study of the relationships between spiritual/religious orientations and the practice of psychotherapy (Shafranske & Malony, 1990). While over half of the psychologists in this survey felt it was appropriate to know the religious background of their clients and to use religious language, metaphors, and concepts in counseling, they, nevertheless, disapproved of praying or using the Bible or other scripture. While most of the psychologists felt they could handle religious issues, they readily admitted their knowledge had its limits.

In an effort to provide counselors with a diagnostic tool that had built-in criteria for judging the validity of clients' religion, we sought the counsel of theologians. Taking our cues from Paul Pruyser's (1976) challenge to psychologists to take the content of faith seriously, we designed an 8 category, 33 question interview that a group of theological scholars judged to be a comprehensive survey of the basic dimensions of optimal religious functioning (Malony, 1988). This Religious Status Interview is thought to be a scale which counselors, with proper training, can use to make diagnostic judgments without feeling they lack knowledge or are imposing their idiosyncrasies onto their clients. It should be noted, however, that this interview is designed to be used exclusively with Christian clients and is not applicable to persons who ascribe to other religions. There is a need for psychologists and theologians from other traditions to work together to produce reliable and valid measures for diagnosing religious status from their points of view.

Thus the next option available to counselors is to *correct* the religion of their clients. Like annihilation, correction should be undertaken on the basis of informed criteria rather than on biased judgments. For example, consider the case of Laura, a character in the novel *Men and Angels* (Gordon, 1986) who became overly religious in reaction to a disapproving and rejecting mother. She assumed a quiet, self-depreciating, masochistic role in which she imagined God had chosen her for some profoundly important role. She eventually committed self-sacrificing suicide, convinced that God was calling her to spill her blood in order to save her employer.

Had the Religious Status Interview (Malony, 1988), noted above, been used by Laura's counselor, her religion would have been identified as needing correction. The RSI includes a dimension "Experiencing Fellowship" in which one of the questions is "What does being part of the family of God mean to you?" Persons who claim a self-righteous exclusive relationship with God and a judgmental attitude toward others are rated as less mature in their Christian faith. Another question included in a dimension called "Knowing God's Leadership and Direction is, "How does your faith relate to your various roles in your family, occupation, and community?" Here having a sense of positive role-identity that is related to religion is rated as more mature. Both of these judgments are based on criteria for optimal religious functioning determined by Christian theologians. Laura would have been judged as correct in relating her vocation to God's will for her life, but as incorrect in assuming that she was destined to sacrifice herself in that endeavor. She was not purer than her employer nor did God intend that she sacrifice her life in a "Joan-of-Arc" fashion.

Counselors can use such a scale as the Religious Status Interview (RSIN) and/or the Religious Status *Inventory* (RSIv), that has also been developed, to correct the religion of their counselees, confident that their counsel represents valid professional judgments.[1] This is the same confidence that counselors express when they administer standardized measures of intelligence, brain damage, and personality. Counselors need such criterion-based measures so that they can assist clients to better conform to the norms of their religious traditions. Counselors can assume that such conformity will lead to higher personal satisfaction, less internal conflict, greater social approval, and more effective adjustment.

The last possible use of religious diagnoses by counselors is to *encourage* clients to apply their faiths to their lives. Where religion appears to be effective and valid, as judged by such measures as the RSI, counselors can offer support and reassurance. Clients can be reminded of the way the faith they have affirmed in the diagnostic interview should work in their lives. Clients can be encouraged to apply their faith to the problems for which they came to counseling. Of course, such encouragement should be based on the counselor's judgment that the individual's religion is already important and mature.

Religious Diagnosis and the DSM III-R

Since the 5-Axis method of diagnosis recommended in the American Psychiatric Association's *Diagnostic and statistical manual of mental disorders. 3rd edition, revised* (1987) has become the norm among mental health counselors, it would seem important to envision how religious diagnoses with such measures as the RSIn AND RSIv (Malony, 1988) can be interrelated with these concerns. The five axes of the DSM III-R are as follows:

Axis 1—the *symptom pattern* as it can be observed in the client's present functioning. Two examples might be: (a) an former atheist who suddenly becomes convinced that everything painted red symbolizes the blood of Christ and (b) a missionary child who becomes depressed six weeks after coming to the United States to attend college. A religious diagnosis would help determine whether religion was, or was not, an explicit part of the pathological symptoms that brought a given individual for counseling. On the surface, pathological religion does seem to be an aspect of the first case of the atheist but not an aspect of the second case of the missionary child. However, this last inference would need to be checked out via some measure such as the RSI in order to ascertain to what extent the youth interpreted his depression in terms of rejection by Christian parents and/or felt guilty as his own weakness and loneliness in the face of a new environment. Suffice it to say, making a religious diagnosis can have much import for Axis 1 decisions. The prime question to be answered is whether religion is or is not an overt or covert part of the observed symptoms. Religion's presence or absence among the symptoms is the issue.

Axis 2—the *underlying mental status* of the client prior to the outbreak of the symptoms. Two examples might be: (a) an older pastor with a long history of church ministry who suddenly becomes hyper-anxious about the quality of his sermons and cannot sleep, and (b) a mother who had reared her children apart from any organized religious involvement who becomes depressed after her daughter marries. Along with evaluations of the personality patterns and intellectual abilities that existed prior to either of these breakdowns, a religious diagnosis could be used to determine the maturity or immaturity of the pastor's and the mother's religious functioning before they became upset. Here the questions would be, is his or her religious faith a personality strength or weakness? Did his or her religion keep him or her from becoming more seriously disturbed or was it a vulnerable part of the personality adjustment? What was the status of religious functioning before he or she became sick?

Axis 3—the *physical state* of the person. Two examples might be: (a) a 55 year old arthritic man who suddenly becomes manic and withdraws all his money to invest in a high-risk scheme and (b) a slightly overweight young adult nurse who is trying to adjust to a divorce. The explicit question to be asked is, what are the confounding physical conditions that exist in these persons that might be affecting their emotional or mental state? Religious functioning would not seem to apply here. Yet, the interaction between physical maladies and faith could be extremely important. A religious diagnosis might conclude that although the 55 year old man suffered from a chronic physical condition, he had accepted it as part of the creative process in which physical deterioration was part of God's plan while in the case of the nurse, her overweight might be perceived as due to her overindulgence and her failure to take care of her body as God intended. In Axis 3, the interaction between faith and physical condition is the prime issue that might be considered in a religious diagnosis.

Axis 4—*stress during the past year* as rated on a five-point scale. Two examples might be: (a) an adolescent whose parents divorced and who had to change schools three months ago and (b) an elderly woman whose husband of 60 years had to be hospitalized for respiratory infection. Here the interaction between stress and faith could be explored through religious diagnosis. A religious history might be undertaken so that the way in which clients handled stress could be better understood. In one study utilizing the Religious Status Interview (Atkinson, 1986), elderly women who were more mature in their Christian faith tended to experience less distress (lower anxiety, depression, hostility) than did those who were less mature quite apart from the amount of stress they had experienced in their lives. This illustrates how Axis 4 considerations can include information from religious diagnoses.

Axis 5—*overall level of adjustment* in the past year. Two examples might be: (1) a college junior who had failed to be elected to a music honor society in the fall, who had difficulty sleeping during the winter, and who became suicidal after not being chosen for a senior jazz band in the spring, and (2) a business woman whose outstanding sales' record over the past twelve months resulted in a promotion to district manager over which she became extremely agitated. In the one case the level of past adjustment was very low while in the other case it was extremely high. Of critical import in Axis 5 would be the role religion played in these differing levels of adjustment. It might be found that the adolescent had simply accommodated himself to the religious patterns of his parents and had never applied his faith to any real-life problems while the business woman might have previously utilized her faith in a number of life-crises. Here religious diagnosis might give insight into the "trait" as opposed to the "state" of religion in the lives of clients. The subtle, and not so subtle, manner in which religious faith affected adjustment is the prime issue here.

As can be seen in the above discussion, religious diagnosis can play a critical role in decisions made on all five of the Axes of the DSM III-R. These include symptoms (Axis 1), mental status (Axis 2), reactions to physical condition (Axis 3), handling of stress (Axis 4), and religious trait effects on overall adjustment (Axis 5).

THE FUNCTION OF RELIGION IN LIFE

Much has been written about what religion does for people. Milton Yinger (1970) exemplifies this literature in his conclusion that religion is the way people handle life's basic enigmas, tragedies, and mysteries. In a previous comment on this definition, I suggested that, "Enigmas are the incongruities and injustices that result from breakdowns in the give and take of the social contract. Tragedies are unexpected disruptions, losses, injuries, and deaths that occur prematurely in life. Mysteries are the ultimate imponderables about purpose, meaning, and destiny that plague the human consciousness" (Malony, 1991, p.4). I would like to expand Yinger's definition and my elaboration into a taxonomy of ways in which religion can contribute positively to human adjustment. I see this as an extension to my previous essay on "The case *for* religion: A counter to Albert Ellis" (1985). In that essay, I argued that mature religion did much good for people in contrast to the bad things that religion did to people, as Ellis had contended.

The taxonomy of the functions of religion in life clearly applus to the tenets of the Christian tradition. They are separated into Defensive, Coping, and Transforming groups (see Table 1).

TABLE 5-1

Functions of Religion in Life

Positive DEFENSIVE Functions of Religion

- comforts persons in the face of disaster
- promises ultimate recompense to persons in the presence of injustice
- promises forgiveness and restoration into community when persons do wrong
- stimulates courage which leads to attempts to try again in the face of failure and disappointment
- offers persons a sense of joy and fulfillment in life
- gives persons a fellowship to which to belong
- security for persons in the midst of uncertainty
- assures persons there will be relief from drudgery and pain
- assists persons in accepting harsh realities

Positive COPING Functions of Religion

- encourages hope in the face of failure and tragedy.
- helps persons adjust to the demands of life.
- defines a reality in which persons feel treasured and needed.
- offers salvation through which persons can align themselves with a divine plan.
- provides a framework for understanding life as having purpose and meaning.

Positive TRANSFORMING Functions of Religion

- provides persons with a perspective by which to judge right from wrong; good from bad.
- calls persons to live by ideals above the level of selfish desire.
- furnishes persons a transforming perspective by which to make judgments and with which to identify.

The list in Table 1 is a first attempt to arrange the functions of religion along a continuum from a defensive to a coping to a transforming dimension. I conceive all of these functions as positive. I do not agree with James (1904) that the ethical "fruits" of religion are any more intrinsically valuable than religion's "roots," which promise compensation for the tragedies and enigmas of life. While we might all agree with the biblical writer of the book of James that faith should be followed by work (James 2:14-26), the prime way in which religion functions for most counselees, at least initially, is in a defensive, compensatory manner. In the midst of stress, religion provides security and that is as it should be.

Initially, diagnosis will find, almost always, religion serving a self-centered need. This is good. It is the very least that religion can do. Counselors should applaud, not discount, this religious function because they are interested, first and foremost, in helping persons readjust to life. While there may always be a need to probe this defensive function of religion in order to see that persons do not deny reality or withdraw from life, there is also the need to honor rather than disapprove of this basic positive role for religion. We scholars might prefer that persons go beyond defensive and coping to transforming faith but we need to remind ourselves of the caution expressed by James Dittes (1971) that such preferences may be an elitist scholarly bias that is unrealistic for most persons.

DEFINITIONS OF RELIGIOUS MATURITY

There have been numerous definitions of religious maturity (Allport, 1954; Elkins, Hedstrom, Hughes, Leaf, & Saunders, 1988; Propst, 1988). However, no one of these takes seriously that religion can be mature when it functions to enhance everyday adjustment nor are they specifically construed within the Christian tradition. In regard to everyday religious functioning, it is important for counselors who utilize religious diagnosis to remember that maturity, like health, can be defined in three ways: negatively, normally, and idealistically. Persons can be healthy if they are no longer sick (a negative definition), if they are as well as other persons their age (a normal definition), or if they are weller than well (an idealistic definition). Similarly, persons can be religiously mature if their religion is functioning for them as well as it is functioning for others in their culture (a normal definition of maturity).

Counselors should honor these negative and normal levels of religious functioning and not judge religious functioning idealistically by applying a standard in this area they would hesitate to apply in family relations, intelligence, or personality traits. In the terms I have been using in this essay, counselors should not discredit "Mini" and "Midi" criteria of religious functioning in their application of religious diagnoses.

The definition of maturity we have used in the development and use of the Religious Status Interview and Inventory (Malony, 1988) take these comments about levels of maturity into account. It also assumes that most persons are religious in terms of the major traditions provided by their culture (Sunden, 1974) and is, therefore, grounded in the affirmations of the Christian tradition.

"Mature Christians are those who have identity, integrity, and inspiration. They have 'identity' in that their self-understanding is as children of God, created by Him and destined by Him to live according to a divine plan. They have 'integrity' in that their daily lives are lived in the awareness that they have been saved by God's grace from the guilt of sin and that they can freely respond to God's will in the present. They have 'inspiration' in that they live with the sense that God is available to sustain, comfort, encourage, and direct their lives on a daily basis. These dimensions of maturity relate to belief in God the Father, God the Son, and God the Holy Spirit. They pertain to the Christian doctrines of creation, redemption, and sanctification. They provide the foundation for practical daily living" (Malony, 1985, p.28). It is my conviction that such a definition as this can serve the minimal, the moderate, and the maximal (mini, midi, maxi) understandings for counselors to make judgments about what they find in religious diagnoses.

As noted earlier, at given times in peoples' lives religion can function in defensive, in coping, and in transformative ways. While counselors might hope for transformative functioning, they should honor defensive and coping religious functioning when it is appropriate. After all, the goals of counseling can themselves be conceived in this manner. Most of the time, counselors are concerned to restore persons to normal adjustment. Only rarely do counselors have the privilege of assisting persons in living up to their potential.

CONCLUSION

This essay has considered the relevance of making religious diagnoses in counseling. After a discussion of importance of religion for contemporary life, it was suggested that religion still played a crucial role in the lives of a significant part of the population. Although there seems to be increasing secularization in the western world, religion plays more than a minor role in life according to counselor surveys. Under the rubric of "mini, midi, maxi" several issues pertaining to making religious diagnoses were discussed: the difference between diagnosis and research; the uses of religious diagnosis in counseling; the relationship of religious diagnosis to DSM III-R Axes; the positive functions of religion in life; and, definitions of religious maturity. It was proposed that the development of the Religious Status Interview and Inventory (Malony, 1988) met the need for a scale with valid theological criteria, normal maturity assumptions, and questions appropriate for making religious diagnoses among Christian persons.[1]

ENDNOTES

1. Those interested in obtaining copies of the Religious Status Interview and Inventory can contact Professor Malony at hnewtonm@yahoo, or call 541-302-2863, or write him at 2836 Kincaid St, Eugene, Oregon 97405. He will provide a packet that includes development, research, scoring of the instruments as well as copies for counselor use.

REFERENCES

Allport, G.W. (1954). *The individual and his religion.* New York: Macmillan.

Batson, C.D., & Ventis, W.L. (1982). *The religious experience; A social-psychological perspective.* New York: Oxford University Press.

Day, J.M. (1991, August). *Moral development, belief and unbelief? Young adult accounts of religion in the process of moral growth.* Paper presented at the 5th European Congress on Psychology of Religion, Leuven, Belgium.

Elkins, D.N., Hedstrom, J., Hughes, L.L., Leaf, A., & Saunders, C. (1988). Toward a humanistic-phenomenological spirituality: Definition, description, and measurement. *Journal of Humanistic Psychology* F 2.8(4) , 5-18.

Dittes, J.E. (1971). Typing the typologies: Some parallels in the career of church-sect and extrinsic-intrinsic. *Journal for the Scientific Study of Religion.* 10, 375-383.

Draper, E., Meyer, G.E., Parzen,, Z., & Samuelson, G. (1965). On the diagnostic value of religious ideation. *Archives of General Psychiatry.* 11(September), 202-207.

Gordon, M. (1986) . *Men and angels.* Hammondsworth, Middlesex, England: Penguin Books.

W, James, W. (1904). *The varieties of religious experience.* New York: Longmans Green.

Malony, H.N(Ed.). (1983). *Wholeness and holiness; Readings in the psychology/theology of mental health.* Grand Rapids MI: Baker Book House.

Malony, H.N. (1985). *The case for religion; A counter to Albert Ellis.* Unpublished manuscript, Graduate School of Psychology, Fuller Theological Seminary, Pasadena, California.

Malony, H.N. (1985). Assessing religious maturity. In M. Stern (Ed.), *Psychotherapy and the religiously committed patient* (pp.25-33). New York: Haworth Press.

Malony, H.N. (1988). The clinical assessment of optimal religious functioning. *Review of Religious Research.* 30 (1), 3-15.

Malony, H.N. (1991). The place of religious diagnosis in evaluations of mental health. In F.W. Schumaker (Ed.), *Religion and mental health.* New York: Oxford University Press.

Malony, H.N. (1991). The use of religious assessment in counseling. In L.B. Brown (Ed.), *Religion, personality and mental health* (pp. 41-69). New York: Springer-Verlag.

Malony, H. N. (1992). How counselors can help people become more spiritual through religious assessment. In H. Grzymala-Moszcaynska (Ed.), *Religion, mental health and mental pathology.* Amsterdam: Rodolpi, in press.

Newbign, L. (1986). *Foolishness to the Greeks; The gospel and western culture.* Grand Rapids, Ml: William B. Eerdmans.

O'Guinn, G. (1991). 8 of 10 Americans claim to be Christian. *The United Methodist Reporter.* April 12, 3.

Propst, L.R. (1988). *Psychotherapy in a religious framework; Spirituality in the emotional healing process.* New York: Human Sciences Press.

Pruyser, P.W. (1976) *The minister as diagnostician.* Philadelphia: Westminster Press.

Shafranske, E.P., & Malony, H.N. (1985, February). *Religion, spirituality, and psychotherapy; A study of California psychologists.* Paper presented at the meeting of the California Psychological Association, San Francisco.

Shafranske, E.P., & Malony, H.N. (1990). Clinical psychologists' religious and spiritual orientations and their practice of psychotherapy. *Psychotherapy.* 17(1), 111-120.

Spilka, B., Hood, R.W., & Gorsuch, R.L. (1985). *The psychology of religion; An empirical approach.* Englewood Cliffs, NJ: Prentice-Hall.

Yinger, M. (1970). *The scientific study of religion.* New York: Macmillan.

SIX

Brainwashing and Religion: The Influence Process Revisited

Throughout human history people have tried to influence one another (cf Brown, 1963). I can just hear my wife's response to such a statement as that. She would say, "Any fool knows that. Is that what you psychologists do all day: Come up with statements that sound profound but are nothing more than common sense?" In part, I agree. Psychology is, indeed, little more than organized common sense. We psychologists have skills in understanding, predicting, and changing human behavior that are just a shade above tea-leaf reading. Our only claim to fame is that these skills lead us to conclusions that are significantly better than chance alone.

So when I begin with the statement that "throughout human history people have tried to influence one another," I acknowledge that I have spoken a truism that is already well-known. I think it important to remind ourselves, however, that attempts to change people's opinions and/or their identities did not begin with the Communists in China and will not end with the Cult Awareness Network's attempts to control the proselytizing activities of new religions. Attempts to change people are as current as the advertisement of Anthony Robbins in a *LA Weekly* (August 18-24, 1995) newspaper ad where he billed himself as a "master of persuasion" who could teach attendees at his seminars how to influence anyone, anytime and as recent as the theme of Singer & Lalich's newest book entitled *Cults in our midst: The hidden menace in our everyday lives.*

SOCIAL INFLUENCE IS INEVITABLE

As a matter of fact, there would be no human beings without influence from the outside. Human beings come into being through a process of interaction with those who are trying to influence them. Persons do not emerge; they become. Persons do not pop into life full blown like bathing beauties or clowns jumping out of cakes. Persons grow and develop; they come to be. Like mirrors, they reflect all the experiences of life in which others tried, intentionally or unintentionally, to shape, to mold, to change them. The bard spoke for all of us in stating, "I am a part of all that I have met." Socialization is the term we use for how families and schools shape the cultural adaptation of the young. "Self-actualization" is the term we use to describe how people seek out those experiences to shape themselves into becoming the persons they intend to be.

Freud and his followers have convinced us that the mind is, indeed, what John Locke said it was, "a blank tablet on which experience writes." In spite of Kant's contentions, there are probably next to no innate ideas. But Freud further has reminded us is that the vitalists were right in asserting that the pencil that does the writing on the mind's blank tablet is a basic inborn urge to survive, to relate, to become, to exist, to live. The human being is not a passive parasite that takes its entire sustenance from the environment, but an active, participant in the interaction. Were there no basic, in-born motivation to become somebody, there would be no interaction in the first place.

It is this interaction between Person and Environment that is the province of psychology. Person times Environment equals behavior. Over time, $P \times Es = Identity = Personhood$. Note that the mathematical function which ties person and environment together is multiplicative rather than additive. It is the interaction between the two, not simply the combination, that makes for personhood. Both the individual and the environment are active forces in the process. How people come to be the persons that they are is what psychology is all about. Psychologists take whole courses in "Learning" -- psychology's term for this process of personality formation. Applied psychologists, such as counselors, give their lives to helping people "Unlearn" and "Relearn." Of course we never know enough about persons' "Leaning Histories" to be totally successful in our understanding, much less in our efforts to help. But the record of counseling suggests that people can and do change. Old dogs can learn new tricks.

And the whole process combines intentional, or planned, as well as incidental, or accidental, associations of people and experiences. Further, behavior at any given moment can be provoked by conscious, pre-conscious, or unconscious motivations. But, it is crucial to remember that there is no behavior anytime, anywhere that is completely undetermined, that has no history in past P X E interactions. Nature and nurture are intertwined from the very beginning. Behavior can seem novel, but it is never completely so, as many psychological analyses of St. Paul's conversion have demonstrated (Johnson and Malony, 1982). There are no such things as out-of-the-blue acts.

CONTROL OF BEHAVIOR

Overt behavior and, most particularly, the mental life which lies behind it, is indeed, "controlled," even "mind controlled." It is determined and it is influenced. However, my conviction is that this control is as often internal as it is external, unless one chooses, as the Cult Awareness Network seems compelled to apply yet another distorted Barthian analysis of participation in new, as well as old, religions.

It will be remembered that Barth's doctrine of God was very strong. He contended that the need for God never determined when God would come into a human life (Barth & Brunner, 1935). God, according to Barth, does not play a waiting game off stage delaying his entrance until humans call Him to join them on the stage of life. Nor is God dependent on evangelists to awaken a need for Him so that people will acknowledge His presence when He comes. God acts alone; on His own good time. God determines his own entrances onto the stage of life, according to Barth. God makes his own "point of contact" with human beings. He does not depend on human awareness of sin, sorrow, or sadness to provoke peoples' need for a Savior -- contrary to the position Emil Brunner so forcefully supported. In Christ, God takes the initiative and breaks into life on His own terms. Those who perceive new religions as dangerous cults whose leaders are brainwashing professionals, pervert Barth's analysis by insisting that these groups force their way into innocent converts' lives and completely change persons against their wills, quite apart from any personal motivation or desire. They contend that new devotees were not in the market for a religion just as Korean war prisoners did not want to be exposed to Communist theory. They further contend that, in spite of this absence of motivation, both Korean war prisoners as well as those who join new religions were, and are, overwhelmed by the brainwashing power of authoritarian manipulators who coercively influence helpless people to change to a totally new outlook on life. From this point of view, people become zombies or robots who slavishly do the will of their masters (Hunter, 1960; Singer & Ofshe, 1992). As a psychologist, I strongly doubt that this is true. Unmotivated behavior is rare, if not nonexistent. People do not read the ads for cars in the newspaper unless they are in the market to buy a car. People do not join health clubs unless they have a desire to exercise. People do not accept Christ who do not sense their need for a Savior. People do not join a new religion who are satisfied with their old faith (Tippett, 1977). Behavior, even religious behavior, is controlled from within; it is motivated. The mind that controls behavior belongs to us, not to some force outside of us.

In my opinion, Emil Brunner and Paul Tillich were right. The point of contact we have with God is through our anxieties, our needs, our wants, our desires. As James Sellers concluded in his book *The outsider and the Word of God* (1961) the relationship of the gospel to life is always indirect. It is filtered through the stress and strain of life. Tillich stated this truth poignantly "Life asks the questions to which faith is the answer" (Tillich, 1952).

On the other hand, powerful persuaders can, indeed. induce "overt conformity." However, these "compliance professionals," to use Cialdini's (1984) label, are far less successful at inducing "covert conviction" and heart-felt agreement. For example, the US Department of Defense reported that out of a total of 7,190 prisoners in the Korean War, only 21 choose to remain with the Communists. Yet, 2397 were guilty of some form of collaboration with the enemy (Brown, 1963, p.255). Of these 21, eleven eventually returned to the United States. Only 10 became residents of China (Wolff, 1960). Now it should be admitted that by the end of the war only 4449 servicemen were offered repatriation because 2641 of them had died in prison. All the prisoners were subjected to some form of coercive persuasion or efforts at thought reform but less than 1% were convinced enough of the truth of Communism to remain in a Communist society when the war was over. Nevertheless, over 50% complied or collaborated to some degree while they were in prison. Ninety- nine percent of those who collaborated returned home when they were freed. Many conformers; few real believers. And even the behavior of the few who remained has been explained by their own life experience prior to the war rather than the overwhelming influence of their captors (Paisley, 1955 quoted in Anthony, 1995, p. 18). As I stated before, if brainwashing existed in the Korean War, it was singularly unsuccessful. Interestingly, 51% or 88,000 of the Korean prisoners held by the United Nations forces at the end of the war refused repatriation back into Communist hands (Schein and Bauer, 1962, p. 95 cited in Anthony, 1995, p.

This is, by all odds, far greater evidence for the mastery of brainwashing on the part of the United States than of China or North Korea. And, in fact, the Communists argued as such in their complaint before the United Nations (Anthony, 1995, p. 20). Somewhat similar figures are true of the new religions, although none of them have used imprisonment to insure belief. New religions have had a very difficult time with recruitment. Their recruitment success has been far below the law of averages which is the maxim behind retail sales. Very few are converted and even fewer converts remain (Malony, 1988). For example, although they have gotten a great deal of public press, there have been probably never more than 15,000 Moonies and it is estimated that there are less than 10,000 of them today in the United States. While all of us have heard horror stories about strong pressure not to leave these groups, I have heard many more stories of those who left of their own accord without any harassment. Most persons leave new religions within two years. It should be noted, for example, that Larry Wallersheim, the young man who sued Scientology for making him mentally ill, always lived in his own apartment during the eleven years he was in the group. Although it is true that he was strongly encouraged not to leave after he had been promoted to a responsible position in the church, he, nevertheless, departed of his own accord. During a long period after he left the church, he went about his life without any overt expression of concern about his time as a member of Scientology. Only after two years did he decide to sue the church for damages. All of this is to state that the myths about the power of brainwashing and coercive persuasion have been greatly exaggerated.

Persuasion

Turning next to the issues of persuasion, it goes without saying that human needs can be awakened by outside influences. All good evangelists know that the first thing that has to be done is to make people conscious of their need for God. One evangelistic technique has been to cultivate a conviction of sin. What is the first question the Kennedy plan of Evangelism recommends be asked when contact with a non-believer is made? The answer: "Where would you spend eternity if you died tonight?" The Scientologists knew this when they invited Larry Wallersheim to take an intelligence test. Since all scores on their tests indicate that potential converts are functioning at less than their full potential, it follows naturally that Scientologists should ask, "Would you like to hear about a way to increase your intelligence and improve your life?" Does that not sound strangely like the message of humanistic psychology that we are using only 10% of our brains and should become active in self- actualization groups? Is this not the message from those who encourage us to engage a direc- tor who can help develop our spiritual gifts?

Yes, all persons may have a need for God, as Augustine proclaimed in his famous prayer, but not all people know it. Awakening a need requires influence and persuasion. We may differ as to whether the provoking of such needs by non-Christian groups is appropriate, but I encourage you to acknowledge three things:

(1) behavior does not develop or change in the absence of motivation,

(2) behavior does not occur without influence, and

(3) the processes involved in the interaction between motives and influ- ences are the same whether they are occur at a Billy Graham Crusade or at a Moonie retreat; in a store selling Serta mattresses or at a used car dealership; in student decisions to go to Dartmouth or join the Americorps; when a cus- tomer is buying a MacIntosh computer or deciding to repeat Hari Krishna mantras on a public street. All of these include social Manipulation.

IS ALL INFLUENCE EVIL MANIPULATION?

Not everyone agrees with my benign assessment of the similarity of influence processes across situations. Some time ago, Farber, Harlow, and West (1956) proposed a 3D model which they felt characterized the unique procedures used in brainwashing. They wrote of "debility" or putting persons in an impoverished, incarcerated situation; "dependency" or disempowering persons so that they had to plead for the satisfaction of their most basic needs; and "dread" or inducing fear of reprisal if a person did not conform. Singer (1995) expanded this to a 5D model by adding "deception" and "desensitization" to the list. A better description of what was attempted among restrained and locked-up persons in Korean prisons or what occurs today in deprogrammers' cabins would be hard to find. That such is drastically different from normal influence processes in daily life must be affirmed. This is the reason that the diagnosis of Post-traumatic Stress Disorder (PTSD) should not be used to describe the travail of those who claim that they have been harmed by participation in religious groups. The kinds of events that provoke the anxious flash- backs in PTSD must be, according to the *Diagnostic and statistical manual of mental disorders, 4th Revision, DSM-IV* (1994), the kind of events that are outside the range of normal human experience. Examples given are rape, earthquakes, wars, and airplane crashes. Surely joining a religious group in a nation where over sixty percent of the population are members of some religious group cannot be considered abnormal. The *DSM-IV* suggests that for events to provoke PTSD they would have to be markedly distressful to almost anyone and they usually evoke fear, terror, and helplessness. These experiences are qualitatively different from willing involvement in new, old, or any religion. Religious participation is almost always experienced as pleasureful and satisfying at the time (Malony, 1990). As one well-trained lawyer who was a Moonie said to me, "At no time in my life have I felt as much joy and happiness as those first two months in the Unification Church." In no way did he feel forced against his will. The experience was positive not negative. His memories of that time were good and he had no symptoms of dread or anxiety. I judge his experience to be typical.

However, Margaret Singer has used this 3D model as the basis for her Systematic Manipulation of Social and Psychological Influence (SMSPI) theory, which she believes involve the insidious and dangerous techniques which underlie all social interaction—both in and out of prison. Robert Cialdini, psychologist at Arizona State University, seems to agree with Singer in his book *Influence: The new psychology of modern persuasion* (1984). His book has been called a "landmark publication" by those psychologists who want us to become aware of the widespread ominous tricks being used to influence us to do things that violate our best interests. While he does not use the term, Cialdini believes that there are forces out in the world that can, and will, brainwash and coercively persuade us. We are helpless in the face of these "compliance professionals," according to Cialdini. One wonders how humans could ever become anything other than zombie robots if they took seriously this judgment that all influence is evil and manipulative. Cialdini illustrates vividly Singer's view that human beings are weak organisms who constantly stand in great danger of being exploited by powerful forces over which they have little control. Cialdini's paradigm for illustrating the ways he thinks unsuspecting persons are controlled is detailed in the following incident:

> I was walking down the street when I was approached by an eleven- or twelve-year-old boy. He introduced himself and said that he was selling tickets to the annual Boy Scout circus to be held on the upcoming Saturday night. He asked if I wished to buy any at five dollars apiece. Since one of the last places I wanted to spend Saturday evening was with the Boy Scouts, I declined. "Well," he said, "if you don't want to buy any tickets, how about buying some of our big chocolate bars? They're only a dollar each." I bought a couple and, right away, realized that something noteworthy had happened. I knew that to be the case because: (a) I do not like chocolate bars; (b) I do like dollars; (c) I was standing there with two of his chocolate bars; and d) he was walking away with two of my dollars. (1984, p. 47)

What Cialdini does with this story, as well as with a numerous other anecdotes and research reports, is to picture human beings as at the mercy of malevolent persuaders, like Boy Scouts selling chocolate bars, who know human weakness well enough to trap and ensnare people into unwanted, even evil, decisions. Among these weaknesses are:

• Reciprocal Concession—the tendency of persons to please salesmen by giving into a smaller request after they have rejected a larger offer. Cialdini's purchase of the chocolate bars is an example.

• Pretty Face—the tendency of persons to give into demands made by those who are physically attractive. The "seduction" of Larry Wallersheim into the Scientology office by a pretty woman is an example.

• Consistency—the tendency of persons to respond to logic. Giving in to the realtor's pitch that "You want to buy a house, this is a good house, why waste your time looking further?" is an example.

• Low Ball—the tendency of persons to jump at a bargain and become psychologicly committed to the sale—only to learn that the price was not what they it thought it was when the final figures are presented. The car salesperson's statement after the bargain had been reached, "I'm sorry that, after checking your offer, my boss said we'd be giving the car away at that price; You wouldn't mind paying $500 more for this great car, would you?" is an example.

• Social Proof—the tendency of human beings to follow the crowd. Being influenced to think something is funny by canned laughter when watching a sit-com video is an example.

• Hero Worship—a variation of Social Proof; the tendency of human beings to follow the recommendations of celebrities. LA Dodger former manager Tommy Lasorda's suggestion that people should buy a cellular phone from a certain company is an example.

• Imitation—another variation of Social Proof; the tendency of human beings to follow the crowd. High school students' slavish adherence to the latest fashion in campy dress codes is an example.

• Promise—the tendency of human beings to believe outlandish guarantees. The promise that elixirs will cure everything from warts to appendicitis is an example. Cialdini asserts that these tendencies are "fixed action patterns" rooted deep within human nature. They work like electrical responses to temperature change on air-conditioner thermometers. When the gauge senses that the temperature has reached a certain degree, the power clicks on and the motor starts. He calls it the "Click-Whirr" pattern. Human beings are so vulnerable that these "Click-Whirr" weaknesses function as automatically as instincts. He concludes that these tendencies are inborn biases to respond that are known and used manipulatively by compliance professionals for their selfish ends. The world is full of evil, powerful, insincere, self- centered persuaders who are just waiting to trick us into following them down dangerous roads, according to Caildini. Even Boy Scouts selling candy bars are included among these dangerous influences.

Cialdini may well have captured a set of human behavioral inclinations. Reading books on advertising, sales, and evangelism should convince us that these principles have been well-known for many years. What he has observed is not new. These principles have been studied by providers of human goods and services across a range as wide as Maytag washing machines, on the one hand, to Young Life Fellowship groups, on the other. But these processes are not brainwashing, regardless of what Cialdini or Singer contend. They are different from the conditions and processes seen in Chinese war prisons and deprogrammers cabins.

As a Christian, I certainly hope that many evangelists will read Cialdini's book if they are unacquainted with the human behavioral tendencies which he so well describes. I sometime despair of those church persons who claim they know for sure that strange religious groups are using deceptive and coercive techniques but who passively and smugly wait for potential converts to come to their 11:00 Sunday morning worship services. Seemingly they would never think of establishing a store front office open at all hours or meeting buses and inviting lonely travelers to supper as Scientology and the Moonies have done in every major city in the nation. They think it is somehow more Christian to simply sit and wait. A store which followed this plan and never had a sale would go out of business—and it would have no one to blame but itself.

All of this is to say that, in my mind, all Cialdini has done in describing the actions of his "compliance professionals," is to describe some of the learning principles known to psychologists, evangelists, advertisers, and salespersons for many years. These influence techniques are not the unique province of cult leaders who want to manipulate people for their own ends. They belong to anyone with the good sense to use them. The problem lies with those in society who want to be left alone and who indulge in the self-deceptive privatism that they have been, or can be, the sole masters of their fate.

More importantly, Cialdini has revealed himself to be an individualistic idealist and a positivistic rationalist—neither of which positions, I believe, provide a tenable foundation for living in a post-modern environment. As an individualistic idealist Cialdini asserts an innocent, but very passive, view of the human being. He seems to believe that people can become human and live their lives without any significant interaction with the social world. His view of personhood is as naive as that of Carl Rogers who implied that any and all interaction with others involved a sacrifice of the self. One wonders how Cialdini can ascribe such pervasive "fixed reaction patterns" to the human being at the same time that he claims that people know what is good and what is bad for them. He has a negative view of human nature and an vacuous understanding of self-actualization. Needless to say, he also presumes that becoming a self implies no need for religion.

This leads to my second analysis of Cialdini. I depicted him as a positivistic rationalist. Like many 19th and 20th century natural and social scientists, Cialdini is probably quite confused as to why any metaphysical, much less religious, ideas have survived to the present day. He seems unaware of the basic human need to find answers to the problems of meaning, to the anxieties of finitude, and to the tragedies and enigmas of life. He looks as if he is oblivious to the "black holes" of existence, as the Christian sociologist Peter Berger so vividly labeled them (1969). Further, he appears to lack an understanding of his own cultural biases which have inappropriately caused him to defend the status quo and pathologize the new or different. Finally, it seems to me that he has made the "is" of his own outlook, the "ought" for the rest of society and does not realize that every theory has its apriori assumptions or that he may simply be expressing an opinion rather than stating a fact. Needless to say, such an opinion comes close to violating the basic right to freedom of religion guaranteed in the first amendment to the constitution and reaffirmed in the past year by the Restoration of Religious Freedom Act.

Michael Langone is another psychologist who disagrees with me. He is the director of the American Family Foundation which is affiliated with the Cult Awareness Network. Langone is better informed about normal social influence than Cialdini seems to be. Instead of implying that all social influence is bad, he proposed a model that distinguished between "mundane" and "destructive" influence behaviors. His model was included in the report of the Task Force on Deceptive and Indirect Methods of Control which was presented in 1987 to the Board of Social and Ethical Responsibility for Psychology (BSERP) of the American Psychological Association (Singer, Goldstein, Langone, Miller, Temerlin, & West, 1987). Although this report, in which Langone's model appeared, was soundly rejected as policy by BSERP because it was unscientific and deficient, the model does provide a continuum which recognizes the differences among various forms of social influence. My disagreement is not with the steps that he lists, but with where to draw the line between forced and self- chosen compliance; mundane and destructive social influence. Langone's model follows:

TABLE 6-1

Langone Model of Influence Behaviors

MODE OF INFLUENCE	METHOD OF INFLUENCE	TECHNIQUE
I. Choice Respecting (emphasis on message)	A. Educative/Therapeutic	1. reflection 2. clarification 3. discussion 4. information giving 5. directed questioning 6. creative expression 7. commenting on problem or alternatives 8. suggesting ideas or solutions
	B. Advisory/Therapeutic	1. recommending solutions 2. rational argument: 3. message oriented 4. hypnosis (some forms) 5. rational argument: 6. emotional appeals 7. compliance tactics: consistency, reciprocation, social proof
II. Compliance Gaining (emphasis on response)	C. Persuasive/Manipulative	1. gross deceptions 2. hypnosis (some forms) 3. isolation from social support 4. selective reward/ punishment 5. denigration of self and critical thinking 6. dissociative states to suppress doubt
	D. Controlling/Destructive	1. alternation of harshness/ threats and leniency/ love 2. control-oriented guilt induction 3. active promotion of dependency 4. physical restraint 5. pressured public confessions

Overall, I find this model to be a fairly accurate list of influence techniques. However, I do not agree that the line separating mundane and destructive techniques can be drawn as clearly as Langone does. While I would venture, along with Langone, that the more coercive and force dependent the method, the more likely one might obtain compliance without real agreement, I do not agree with the implication that the best decisions are those made without emotional involvement. Nor do I agree with the use that Langone and others have made of this model. They have erroneously asserted, in my opinion, that there are groups in society called "cults" that can be identified by their use of persuasive/manipulative and controlling/destructive methods and other groups which do not use these approaches. Do not misinterpret my disagreement with Langone. I definitely feel that a line can be drawn between mundane and destructive social influence. But I would draw it almost at the end of his model where physical confinement and threat are involved. In my opinion, where such methods are used, legal action should be taken to protect peoples' right to free choice of association and belief. Our society has laws against abuse and violence—family as well as public. Nor do I mean to imply that I think there are no evil leaders in new or old religions who at times have resorted to such methods for their own aggrandizement. There is evil in the world; sin has not been abolished. When people are forced to act against their will and are abused, I think it appropriate for personal damage suits to be filed.

For example, during the 1950s and 1960s, the C.I.A. conducted mind-control experiments at McGill University in Montreal. D. Ewen Cameron, M.D., an imminent psychiatrist, directed research which attempted to wash the mind completely clean of previous mental habits through conditioning procedures (Anthony, 1995, p. 28-30). He "placed subjects in a drug-induced sleep state, around the clock for anywhere from 15-65 days. They also were administered electroshock treatments two to three times a day during this period. Cameron continued this regimen until the subject had lost all of her memories of previous events, and had very little sense of personal identity" (Anthony, 1995, p. 29). This kind of brutal misuse of research authority would probably not be allowed today. and should certainly result in claims of damages. The C.I.A. continued these efforts to demonstrate that brainwashing was possible for over twenty-five years. But, the program "was never able to change people's political attitudes against their natural inclinations, nor to implant a new sense of self loyal to different political masters" (Anthony, 1995, p. 33). These kinds of investigations illustrate how far down Langone's list of methods one would have to go to get anywhere near to the classic idea of washing the brain.

However, I think the best examples of such coercive attempts at thought reform today cannot be found in the so-called cults but in the action of deprogrammers, now called "exit counselors." Their characteristic methods have

included kidnapping people against their will, taking them to isolated mountain cabins, and then exposing them to prolonged argumentative and harassing
attempts to change their minds about their beliefs. Often this abuse lasts for
days and includes food rationing and interrupted sleep. Personally, I am convinced that such deprogramming is the nearest thing we have to Communist
efforts at brainwashing. I am also convinced that, although they have recently
denied it, such deprogramming has been supported by the very groups that are
most active in anti-cult activity and that modified efforts of this sort still go on
in such places as the WellSpring Retreat Center in Ohio.

CAN FREE WILL BE OVERCOME?

As long as we affirm free will, persons should be supported in the choices they
make, even when we consider that those choice are bad for them. However, we
should resist the temptation to imply that because their decisions seem ill-
advised to us, their free will has been overcome. As Robbins and Anthony
(1994) correctly concluded:

> Models which embody what has been called "hard determinism"
> definitely affirm that victims actually lose their capacity for
> voluntary social action under the impact of mental conditioning
> regimens variously called brainwashing, menticide, the
> "Dependency, Dread, Debility ("3-D") syndrome, etc... The
> problem with these models, which are potentially legally powerful
> because they do indeed affirm a stringent socially reduced
> incapacity, is that research has shown them to be stigmatizing
> myths rather than credible scientific accounts. Insofar as science
> has been able to determine, there are no specialized techniques of
> social influence which are capable of overwhelming free will.
> (emphasis added, p. 129).

What Robbins and Anthony are asserting is that free will is not overcome
in religious conversion. No matter how disconcerting such a decision may be
to family and friends, it is still the person's own decision for which the person
must take legal, moral, and psychological responsibility. Except under dire conditions of life threat, there is no such thing as the overcoming of the will—and
even then, compliance is probably more the case than agreement. Certainly,
there will always be groups that are out of favor with general culture, but there
is no scientific warrant for saying that they exert a qualitatively distinct kind of
social influence that overcomes free will. One father of a young man who died
in the Branch Davidian raid was interviewed on national television. He said
that he had journeyed from Detroit to talk to his son. Asked why he did not

forcibly remove his son from the compound, he replied, "I became convinced that this was a rational, yet passionate, decision my son had made. Someone tried to change my religious convictions when I was young. I did not want to commit the same mistake with him.. I'm convinced my son knew what he was doing." At a recent meeting of American and European clinical psychologists of religion, I heard of a young woman who had joined a hippie-type, new-age group to which her parents were strenuously objecting. Before this radical change in her upper-middle class demeanor, this college student had been a loner who had few friends and no romantic relationships. After she joined the group, her dress became campy and she was constantly meeting and talking with her new found friends late into the night. To say that she had been brainwashed into a radically new way of life would be to miss the point of her long-standing semi- depression over her social isolation and insecurity which, while not fully explaining her behavior, certainly goes a long way in helping us understand it. Her family would be misguided if they accorded all the power to the new group and missed her free decision to change her affiliations.

In another situation, I firmly agree with the judge's ruling in the Stephen Fishman case in San Francisco (Jensen, 1990). The judge ruled that social/behavioral scientists who were willing to testify that they could prove that hard determinism had caused Fishman's behavior were out of order. He said that these psychologists and sociologists were expressing their personal opinions rather than stating the majority opinions of their disciplines when they said that Mr. Fishman, who was accused of defrauding the government of over a million dollars, was under the robotic influence of Scientology which he joined some years after he had begun his fradulent behavior. Those of us, who lent our expertise to the government in this case, expressed what we felt was the general opinion of our disciplines, namely, that Mr. Fishman's decision to be a part of Scientology as well as his decision to defraud the government were unrelated. His behavior was not due to some type of mind control or brainwashing in which he hypnotically followed Scientology's control of his brain. Mr. Fishman is now in federal prison.

OPERANT IS A BETTER MODEL THAN CLASSICAL CONDITIONING

Frankly, as a psychologist, I believe my colleagues in the social sciences who have accused religious groups of mind control, thought reform, and brainwashing have been using the wrong type of learning theory on which to base their conclusions. They seem to imply that joining a religion is controlled by automatic association processes of the click-whirr variety. These automatons are similar to the classical conditioning processes of Pavlov's dogs who could not help salivating to bells once they were associated with food. Surely decisions to adopt a religious world view are more self-conscious and explicitly motivated than that. Surely radical changes in life style and beliefs do not occur in "robots" who are as mindless as zombies. It would seem better to use the operant conditioning models of B.F. Skinner, who although he thought religious behavior was superstitious, still afforded psychological learning theory a model in which the person "operated" or acted upon the environment. I prefer to think that decisions made in old, as well as new religions, are of this kind. Religious persons are not robots; they are converts who confess their need and are attracted to an answer that is offered to them.

In this regard, I am more inclined to agree with sociologists John Lofland and Rodney Stark (1965) who suggested a step-wise sequential model of youths' decisions to join the Moonies. They called this a "problem solving" theory of "conversion to a deviant perspective," i.e. a new religion. I suspect it could also be called a problem solving model of conversion to a traditional perspective or old religion, also. They suggested that the first step in the conversion process was a state of tension, strain, frustration or deprivation. This is the inner need to which I have been referring. This state of tension leads to a problem-solving perspective which provokes potential converts, in the second step, to explore solutions in their environment for reducing the stress they were experiencing. This approach is based on the human tendency to want to reduce tension in life and maintain a sense of safety and security. One might call this a state of "religious seekership for spiritual homeostasis or peace." Modern "Seeker" churches owe their stance to this model, although they may not know it since the Lofland and Stark article was published in a scholarly journal in the mid 1960s.

These "predisposing tendencies," to use Lofland and Stark's terms for the first two steps, make potential converts susceptible to the "situational contingencies" which follow. Persons in the third step find themselves in religious environments where conversion can occur. How potential converts come to be in these environments is noteworthy. Whether by intention or coincidence, in every case the experience involves interpersonal contact. Research indicates that most persons who join or change churches do so because friends take them. Even in such deviant conversions as to the Moonies and to Scientology, a friendly interpersonal contact initiates the experience. Moonies met the buses in San Fransico and invited lonely-looking passengers to supper after which they began to "love bomb" them with affection. An attractive young woman invited Larry Wallersheim into the Scientology office. Conversions only occur after interpersonal contact is made and nourished. We might call interpersonal contact, or friendship, a prologue to step 3—being in a conversion environment.

THE FOURTH STEP IS ONE OF CUTTING OFF PAST RELATIONSHIPS.

This, of course, is the step that has most disturbed the families out of which converts have come. However, those who have protested this separation of converts from former friends and family would do well to remember the separatist words of Jesus in Matthew 10:34-39 that he came to set sons and daughters against their parents and "Whoever loves father and mother more than me is not worthy of me." They should also recall the teachings of the late Fuller professor, Allan Tippett, who wrote extensively about "bridge burning" of former fetishes and religious associations in his description of conversions on the mission field (1977).

Further, it has been noted that Jewish young people were particularly susceptible to conversion to new religious movements (Richardson, 1986). However, in many cases, the alienation that resulted was from cultural, but not religious, Jewish families in which youth were bereft of any serious faith experience. Although not a universal fact, this lack of a vital religious background has been typical among non-Jewish converts as well. As the Finnish psychologist of religion, Nils Holm, observed (1991, 1995, p.226), some religious training in families is so mild that it would be miraculous if youth did not reject it. He termed this type of cultural, but not committed, religious atmosphere as "unconfident transmission" of faith. Unfortunately, some families need to acknowledge that they have no one to blame but themselves.

In my opinion, negative reaction to these explicit admonitions to cut off contact with one's past is understandable, but is essentially inappropriate. We counsel juvenile delinquents to not continue their friendships with those who got them into trouble. So, it is legitimate for new or old religions to counsel converts to spend their time with those who agree with them if they are to maintain their new convictions and grow in their faiths.

Aggrieved families would do better to take the advice of Melton and Moore in their helpful book entitled *The cult experience: Responding to the new religious pluralism* (1982) to not discount their youths' conversions but be open to listening to them explain why they made the decision they made. By criticizing or attempting to deprogram their children, they make enemies of them and increase the alienation. By being open and understanding, they, at least, make it possible that family unity can be maintained.

In our family, we took this position when my son decided to worship at Lake Avenue Congregational Church. He responded so well to our attitude that he allowed our United Methodist minister to rebaptize him by immersion in the Lake Avenue baptismal pool. We never let our love and acceptance of him change even though we strongly wished he had remained in our church. Further, families might do well to recall what Charles Stewart concluded in his helpful book *Adolescent Religion* (1967). Adolescents respond to the religion of their parents in one of three ways, according to Stewart. They continue to espouse their parents religion, they deviate from it, or they leave it entire ly. My three sons illustrate all three: one son has remained in main-line Christianity by becoming a part of the United Church of Christ; one son has deviated from it by becoming a part of the Southern Baptist church; and one son is active in the Church of Religious Science.

Now, I grant you that our concern has not been as great as if one or more of our sons had joined a new religious movement such as the Moonies but the principle is just the same. Adolescence is a time when youth shift from dependence to independence. Questioning the religion of their childhood is normal. In fact, it should come as no surprise to us that one of the first ways that students assert their independence as college students when they leave home is to quit going to church. Religion is often a hang-over from childhood conformity (Malony, 1995). Hand-me-down religion is hum-drum and aseptic, as William James observed in his classic Varieties of religious experience(1902). It might be helpful to take the position that, although the religion to which a son or daughter has joined is different from that of the family, some religion is better than no religion. After all, in almost every case these groups espouse high ethical standards. New religions are religions, they are not the Mafia or street gangs. As the psychiatrist Mansell Pattison observed, in most cases, "There are usually strong interdictions against drug use and the active promotion of healthful life styles. They generate strong ethic norms, built on explicit religious ideologies" (1983, p. 124).

The last step in the Lofland and Stark model is a "series of intense interactions within the new group." These interactions are both interpersonal and informational. New converts acquire the lingo of the new group in situations with others with whom they have become best friends. Note how the content of the religion is always contextualized within a social situation.

BELIEFS ARE ALWAYS SOLIDIFIED WITHIN RELATIONSHIPS.

Pattison notes how these interactions provide for their members what the nuclear family used to provide its members but which it can no longer do in modern urban, instrumental society. He suggests that while the family served both continuity and identity in rural and small town cultures, it cannot adapt rapidly enough to the changing, transitory nature of modern urban life to provide the personal meaning and depth of relationships which are needed for achieving personhood (1983, p. 116-117). He suggests, instead, that modern life is best built on non-familial "social networks" to overcome "existential dislocation." New religions, or cults, often meet this need. As problematic as it may seem, the role of the family may need to change. While we may all have some nostalgia for the past, the day in which the family is central to personal identity may have passed. This Lofland and Stark model has been labeled the "seduction" syndrome", "manipulation by the management", and "coercive persuasion" by critics. However the steps in this model of conversion probably add up to just good common sense. I venture that the Lofland and Stark model is the basis for any good evangelism—wherever it occurs, in new religions or old. While it is a "program," as critics have suggested, it is no different from the methods of social influence which permeate our society and it is, by no means, overly coercive or criminal. If we mandate that members of new or old religions be "de-programmed" we will have to extend that mandate to much of the rest of our culture.

All of what I have been saying is an attempt to ground our discussion of brainwashing and religion within the context of normal social influence and traditional learning theory. Further, I have insisted that in almost no case is the free will or the motivation of the person overwhelmed by some outside force. While behavior is determined, most often it is determined by the person, not some outside force.

REFERENCES

Anthony, D. (1995). Brainwashing and totalitarian influence: An exploration of admissibility criteria for testimony in brainwashing trials. Doctoral dissertation, The Graduate Theological Union, Berkeley, California.

Barth, K. & Brunner, E. (1935). *Natur und Gnade (Nature and Grace)*. Zurich: Zwingli Verlagl.

Berger, P. (1969). *A rumor of angels*. Garden City, NY: Doubleday.

Brown, J.A.C. (1963). *Techniques of persuasion: From propaganda to brainwashing*. Baltimore, MD: Penguin Books.

Cialdini, R.B. (1984). *Influence: The new psychology of modern persuasion*. New York: Quill.

Farber, I.E., Harlow, H.F, & West, L.J. (1956). Brainwashing, conditioning, and DDD: Debility, dependence, and dread. *Sociometry, 20*, pp. 271-285.

Holm, N.G. (1991, 1995). Tradition, upbringing, experience: A research program for the psychology of religion. In H.N. Malony (Ed.) *Psychology of religion: Personalities, problems possibilities*. Grand Rapids, MI: Baker Book House. Republished by Integration Press, Fuller Theological Seminary, Pasadena, CA., pp. 223-230.

Hunter, E. (1960). *Brainwashing: From Pavlov to powers*. New York: The Bookmaster.

James,W.(1902). *The varieties of religious experience: A study in human nature.* Cambridge, MA: Harvard University Press, 1985. (Original edition 1902)

Jebsen, J.(1990). Judges Ruling: United States v. Stephen Fishman (No. CR-88-0616 DLJ). 743 Federal Supplement. 713 (N.D. Cal. 1990), 713-723.

Johnson, C.B. & Malony, H.N. (1982). *Christian conversion: Biblical and psychological perspectives.* Grand Rapids, MI: Zondervan.

Lofland, J. & Stark, R. (1965). Becoming a world-saver: A theory of conversion to a deviant perspective. *American Sociological Review, 30,* 862-874.

Malony, H.N. (1988). The psychology of proselytism. In M.E. Marty and F.E. Greenspahn (Eds). *Pushing the faith: Proselytism and civility in a pluralistic world.* (pp. 125-142). New York: Crossword.

Malony, H.N. (1990). Expert testimony on residual effects of participating in new religious movements. Paper presented at the annual meeting of the Religious Research Association, Virginia Beach, VA.

Malony, H.N. (1995). Religion, science and the humanities in the undergraduate curriculum. In S. Gill (ed.) *Religion in the classroom: Essays by the Good professors.* In Press.

Melton, J.G. & Moore, R.L. (1982). *The cult experience: Responding to the new religious pluralism.* New York: The Pilgrim Press.

Pasley, V. (1955). Twenty-one stayed: The story of the American GI's who chose Communist China -- Who they were and why they stayed. New York:

Pattison, E.M. (1983). Religion and compliance. In Max Rosenbaum, Ed. *Compliant behavior: Beyond obedience to authority.* New York: Human Sciences Press, pp. 107-136.

Richardson, J.T. (1986). Jewish participation in new religions. Paper presented at the annual meeting of the Society for the Scientific Study of Religion, Washington, D.C.

Robbins, A. (1995). How to influence anyone, anytime. *L.A. Weekly,* August 18-24, p.3.

Schein, E. and Bauer, E. (1962). Statement: To set straight the Korean POW episode. *Harvard Business Review,* V(40), 94-95.

Sellers, J. (1961). *The outsider and the word of God: A study in Christian communication.* New York: Abingdon.

Singer, M.T. and Ofshe, R. (1992). Thought reform programs and the production of psychiatric casualities. *Psychiatric Annals, 20*(4), 188-193.

Singer, M.T., Goldstein, H., Langone, M.D., Miller, J.S., Temerlin, M.K., & West, L.J. (1987). Report of the Task Force on Deceptive and Indirect Techniques of Persuasion and Control. Unpublished manuscript. American Psychological Association.

Singer, M.T. & Lalich, J. (1995). *Cults in our Midst: Thehidden menace in our everyday lives.* San Fransico: Jossey Bass.

Stewart,C. (1967)*Adolescent Religion :A Developmental study of the religion of youth.* New York: Abingdon.

Tillich, P. (1952). *The courage to be.* New Haven, CT: Yale University Press.

Tippett, A. (1977). Conversion as a dynamic process in Christian mission. *Missiology, 5,* 203-221.

Wolff, H. (1960). Every man has a breaking point— the conduct of prisoners of war. *Military Medicine, 125* (February).

SEVEN

John Wesley, John Calvin, and Martin Luther: An Unholy Triumvirate of Import for Psychology

Do you promise to tell the truth, the whole truth, and nothing but the truth?," This question is asked by the bailiff as witnesses take the stand in every court in this nation. This query might well be posed to a 20th century scholar bold enough to claim he was delineating the importance of an 18th century divine for modern psychology. The accuracy of such an enterprise is enhanced, however, by two truths: One, the 18th divine under consideration, John Wesley, put many, if not most, of his opinions down on paper. In fact, it is has been said that Wesley never had a thought that he didn't write down. Since this was a pre-typewriter age, one wonders when it was that he wrote what he wrote. I feel sure it was not in that setting where he spent so much of his time—atop a horse on the highways across the British Isles. Nevertheless, though dead, yet Wesley lives through the words that he wrote and our opinions about his thoughts can usually be referenced. The second truth about Wesley is that the content of his writings reveal him to be essentially ecumenical, rather than sectarian, in his approach. It must be remembered that the Wesleyan movement was part of the Enlightenment, not the Reformation. Wesley lived two hundred years after Luther and Calvin. He appreciated them both but his was a renewal movement within the Church of England—essentially an English language derivation of Roman Catholicism. There is a plaque on the pulpit of the Anglican church of South Leigh, just outside Oxford, which attests to Wesley's background and orientation. It reads, "John Wesley, the founder of Methodist movement preached his first sermon here, but he remained a faithful priest of the church until his death." Although Wesley came to have significant differences with both Calvin and Luther, as well as Anglicanism and Catholicism, he was not essentially sectarian. Today, Wesley may be pictured as at the opposite end of most of these movements but it was not always so. He recommended his pastors read widely in the Christian classics and he reprinted with strong recommendation *A treatise on the religious affections* authored by the New England Calvinist Jonathan Edwards. And, it should not be forgotten that Wesley experienced his heart strangely warmed while listening to Luther's commentary on the book of Romans within the setting of a Moravian prayer meeting.

All of this is to say, that as I try to tell the truth, the whole truth and nothing but the truth about the impact of Wesley's relations with Calvin and Luther on psychology, it should be kept in mind that his voluminous writings reveal that, although he took strong stands about a some of their ideas, he was essentially an ecumenical Christian who appreciated their contributions.

This is not the first effort I have made to explore the import of John Wesley for psychology. In a forthcoming issue of *The Journal of Psychology and Christianity* which explores the thinking of a number of classical figures, I have written the article on Wesley. I do indeed consider Wesley to have been the most psychologically astute religious figure of his age. His own life experience is fraught with psychological introspections and reflections. Although a ordained cleric, his faith ebbed and flowed and, even at its best, he was never able to establish an intimate relationship with a member of the opposite sex. A more perceptive combination of personal experience with the mandates of the gospel would be hard to find.

In yet another publication, I have written about Wesley's compassion for the poor and his sensitivity to the impact of the social environment on behavior. He established free health clinics in London and Bristol and complained bitterly about physicians who provided service when they were paid. I think he deserves to be called an "18th century *health* psychologist." He could also have been called a *social* psychologist. Everywhere he preached he showed a sensitivity to injustice. He preached against low pages paid to potters at Stoke-on-Trent and he chastised the good citizens of Penzance for their involvement in smuggling after provoking shipwrecks by moving the lighthouses. No Bible-thumping, narrowly focused evangelist was Wesley. He knew well the impact of the environment on behavior.

Further, in yet another article, I noted that while others persisted in opposition to the new science of Sir Issac Newton, Wesley quickly overcame his concern that persons would look to the "the book of Nature" instead of "the book of the Bible" for their salvation. He came to view the former as testimony to God's action in creation and the latter as God's action in redemption. Both were important: there was no inherent contradiction between them. He eventually published a five volume treatise on the science of his day entitled *A survey of the wisdom of God in the Creation: A compendium of natural philosophy* (1777, 1809). More importantly, he revealed his openness to the way that scientific discoveries could enrich human life by his fascination with electricity. Electricity was, according to Wesley, "God's elixir of life" put on earth to correct many of the maladies caused by the fall (Wesley, 1760). He put a hand-operated electrical stimulation machine in each of his free clinics and recommended "being electrified" as the cure for many illnesses in his book entitled *Primitive physick: Or an easy and natural method of curing most diseases* (1751)—a home health-care manual which went through thirty six printings in Britain and America.

This is my first attempt, however, to deal directly with the ways that Wesley's interactions with the thought of Calvin and Luther impact one of the basic foci of contemporary psychology, namely, behavior change in human beings. I define the discipline of psychology broadly as "the attempt to understand, to predict, and to control human behavior." Through reformulations of Calvin's teachings on predestination and Luther's conceptions about grace, Wesley's approach to Christian perfection provides a means for viewing behavior that is in close accord with the hopeful, yet realistic, conceptions of contemporary psychology. Although his formulations about human expectation referred to religious, or idealistic, behaviors, the ideas can be generalized to all behavior change wherever it occurs.

As a prologue to the discussion, let me remind you that both Calvin and Luther were 16th century leaders in the Protestant Reformation who had been dead almost two hundred years by the time that Wesley began to critique them. His interaction was with their writings, not with them personally. A major problem to which Calvin, Luther, as well as Wesley, addressed themselves was the fact that not everyone accepted the good news of the gospel. Furthermore, among those who did, a great many people returned to their old ways of behaving. These observable facts required secondary or corollary theologizing as addenda to the basic truth all three of them affirmed that "God was in Christ reconciling the world unto Himself." Calvin explained the facts of non-acceptance and lack of persistence as due to God's "double predestination" of some people to damnation and other people to salvation. Luther dealt with these behaviors through asserting that nothing really changed in conversion. People remained sinners until they died but God accepted them as righteous anyway. After Jesus death on the cross, judgment became God's grace – a changed way of looking at human beings. God considered humans as righteous for Christ's sake. This is what is meant by God's grace.

Wesley's counter to these theological rationalizations for the lack of universal conversions and for the failure of Christians to remain faithful was to deny Calvin's contention that God could condemn anyone to damnation and to reinterpret Luther's understanding of God's grace as an active agent within the hearts of believers, not just a new set of spectacles God put on in viewing human beings. Wesley's doctrines of "salvation" and "perfection" asserted that acceptance of the Gospel was possible up to the moment of death and it was possible for ALL persons to grow in grace to the point where they were totally committed to love of God and neighbor five minutes before they died. This is the gist of Wesley's theologizing that I will present. I will now turn to a fuller explication of how these ideas developed in Wesley's thinking. I hope to demonstrate the way in which his reflections on these issues are profoundly relevant to the ways psychology understands the potentials of human at the end of the 20th century.

WESLEY AND LUTHER

Justification, making things right with God, was, for Luther, dependent solely on faith. To no degree was it a result of something humans did to prove themselves to God, as in the purchasing of indulgences to guarantee salvation. Justification was something God did for us in Christ. It was a free gift to us. Our only task was to accept justification through faith. It must be remembered that Luther was reacting to the Roman church's sale of pardons from punishment that were offered as a means of saving one's loved ones from hell. Luther felt that this was tantamount to buying God's favor. He reaffirmed the Pauline/Augustinian sola fide (faith alone) doctrine as a basis for justification. Essentially Luther was reasserting a doctrine that placed the initiative of grace entirely within God's graciousness. God imputed righteousness to human beings by looking at them through the spectacles of Jesus Christ. It was as if God chose to put on a new set of eye glasses—all on His own initiative. In no way did God, according to Luther, base his perception on human righteousness or accomplishments.

As we shall see, Wesley agreed with this emphasis on God's unsolicited love for us in *justification*, but felt it led to a disregard of human effort in *regeneration*. Of course Wesley knew about Luther, but his first hand knowledge of Lutheranism came through his contact with the Moravians (Wainright, 1995, p. 109). Their *quietistic* doctrine of passive waiting took Luther's "faith alone" ideas to the extreme. In addition to insisting that God did not require good works for salvation, they bordered on claiming that neither sins of omission or commission mattered in the least to God before, or after, conversion.

Wesley termed this *Antinomianism* and accused Luther of a gross misunderstanding of salvation. Wesley claimed that behavior did matter and that while we never proved ourselves to God, God expected us to "grow in grace."[1] In a conversation with his brother and close confidants in May 1744, Wesley defined Antinomianism as the doctrine which makes void the law through faith. The main tenets of Antinomianism were:

1. *That Christ abolished the moral law;*
2. *That, therefore, Christians are not obliged to observe it.*
3. *That one branch of Christian liberty is liberty from obeying*

the commandments of God.

*4. That it is bondage to do a thing because it is commanded, or
forebear it because it is forbidden.*

*5. That a believer is not obliged to obey the ordinances of God,
or to do good works.*

*6. That a Preacher ought not to exhort good works; not unbe-
lievers because it is hurtful; not believers because it is needless"*
(Wesley, 1872, Vol. Viii, p. 278).

With Wesley's activistic preoccupation, it is not surprising that he was
appalled when he read that Luther called the New Testament book of James
"an Epistle of Straw."[1] For Wesley, faith without works was indeed "dead."
Like many theologians before him, Wesley contended that the image of God in
which humans were created (Genesis 1:27) was lost in the fall but restored in
justification by faith. Subsequently, God, through His grace freely given,
empowered persons to become fully what they were intended to be. This was
Wesley's doctrine of *perfection* that placed great confidence in humans being
able to actualize their God-given potential through God's grace working in and
through them. Compared to Luther's understanding that God's grace was simply a new way that God looked at people (*imputed righteousness*), Wesley
understood God's grace to be a substantive seed placed in the human heart that
needed nurturance to grow up into *real righteousness.*

Wesley was so convinced that perfection in love of God and love of
neighbor was possible that he claimed it could happen before death. In fact,
there is an apocryphal story that suggests the difference between Luther and
Wesley was one of "five minutes before and five minutes after death." Because
Luther felt that even after conversion converts lived off of the imputed righteousness of Christ and remained sinners until they died, only five minutes after
death would God give persons new, "really righteous," bodies, In contrast,
Wesley felt that all good Christians should set for themselves the goal of becoming "really righteous" (perfect) five minutes before death.

This has led Lutherans from that day to this to accuse Wesleyans of
Pelagianism and works righteousness—accusations which Wesley denied contending that from the beginning to the end of the Christian life it was God's
grace that undergirded whatever change occurred. Nevertheless, he insisted
that this movement toward perfection never occurred apart from human permission and cooperation.

WESLEY AND CALVIN

This comment about human effort and free-will leads naturally into Wesley's interaction with Calvin. As George (1988, p. 231) stated, "Wesley owed more to Calvin than he (Wesley) was willing to admit." This is true. Calvin predated Wesley in his affirmation of growth toward Christian perfection. In his sermon on Job 42:1-5 Calvin stated "Repentance "is never perfect at the start, but after God planes us, he also needs to polish us." And in his commentary on Phillipians 1:9 he concluded "Growth in faith must be accompanied by a growing measure of sanctification. "The true stages in the growth of Christians are when they make progress in knowledge and understanding, and afterwards in love"(Wainright, 1995, p.146). Wesley would agree with every word. The problem between the two arose, however, over when it was possible to attain perfection. Wesley held on to the view it was possible in this life while Calvin contended otherwise

Although writing two hundred years before Wesley, Calvin stated in the *Institutes* IV.1.20 (Wainright, p.144) that "Confident belief in the attainability of perfection is a devilish device." Yet, he contended in the same sentence that "we are nevertheless not to labour feebly or coldly in urging perfection or in striving towards it."

In his cautions about the difficulties in attaining perfection, Calvin has been thought by some to be even more psychologically sensitive than Wesley to the human proclivity toward self-interest. These words of Calvin show an awareness of the difficulties that Wesley often ignored: "Even though we have experienced the victory by the grace of God, and sin has not reigned within us, yet it still dwells within us always, and there are stains and spots on our life...Even though each day we see a million faults within us, yet we must always seek to get beyond (Sermon on Deuteronomy 5:21, Wainright, 1995, p. 145). Calvin's contention that Christians should make the effort even though they knew they could never fully attain perfection was the essence of his doctrine called "The Perseverance of the Saints."

Wesley's concern, on the other hand, was the problems caused by the pretentious claims of some of his followers that they had already attained perfection. While he resisted equating their charismatic gifts with either spontaneous or gradual perfection, he still held on to the possibility of attaining perfection before death (Wesley, 1850, 1777, p. 166ff).. Yet, the best illustrations he gave of perfection, for example Jane Cooper (Wesley, 1850, 1777, p. 96ff), were persons who were dying with only a short time to live. Wesley urged those who "professed perfection" to use great caution in their claims (Wesley, 1872, 1958, vol. VII, p. 22). Yet he never fully discounted "enthusiasm" (the religious expression of emotions) as did Jonathan Edwards (1746, 1959). In fact, in his preface to his own republication of Edward's *Treatise concerning the religious affections*, Wesley (1872, 1958, Vol. XIV, p. 269), Wesley countered Edward's tendency to discount emotion as having any value in comparison to reason. He could have profited, nevertheless from appropriating some of Calvin's wisdom in his Perseverance of the Saints doctrine while retaining his positive view of human capabilities. As Calvin stated in his comments on Ephesians 5:27, "We are never truly wholehearted in our response to Jesus Christ; the Holy Spirit is never able to occupy the whole of us. We are required to make constant progress and so long as there is daily progress, there cannot be perfection." (Wainright, 1988, p.144). Wesley was keenly aware of the distinction between human frailty and sin, but he did not seem to be as aware as was Calvin of the temptations that continued to plague even the most diligent Christians.

Wesley's major difficulty with Calvin, however, was over Calvin's view of predestination. It should not be forgotten that Calvin started out training for the priesthood but switched to law. As contrasted with Luther who began legal training but changed to become a workaday priest, Calvin's legal education led him to became a systematic theologian who thought in catechetical terms. According to Calvin, the reluctance of people to accept the gospel was antithetical to belief in an all powerful God. He reasoned that if God is, indeed, omnipotent and if God acted to save the world in Christ Jesus, then it must be that God pre-destined some persons to be saved and others to be damned apart from anything that hey did. The only explanation Calvin could give as to why everyone did not receive this gift of God whole heartedly was that God predestined some people to damnation just as He had predestined others to salvation. This is called *Double Predestination.*

When Wesley realized that this was what Calvin meant, his reaction was strongly negative. His traveling over 40,000 miles throughout England, Wales, Ireland, and Scotland was based on a conviction that the good news of salvation was available to anyone who would receive it. To think that in his audience there were folk who were already condemned to hell was a deep affront to Wesley's basic convictions. His words to his preachers on several occasions between 1744-1789 (Wesley, 1850, vol. VIII, p. 336) are evidence of his disdain for *Calvinism*, which Wesley identified with predestination:

> *Q (question). 74. What is the direct antidote to Methodism, the doctrine of heart-holiness?*
>
> *A (answer). Calvinism: All the devices of Satan, for these fifty years have done less toward stopping the work of God, than that single doctrine. It strikes at the root of salvation from sin, previous to glory, putting the matter on quite another issue.*
>
> *Q.75. But wherein lies the charms of this doctrine? What makes men swallow it so greedily?*
>
> *A.(1) It seems to magnify Christ; although in reality it supposes him to have died in vain. For the absolutely elect must have been saved without him; and the non-elect cannot be saved by him.*

Wesley even wrote a hymn ridiculing Calvin's predestination doctrine:
Thou has compell'd the Lost to die
Hast reprobated from thy Face
Hast Others sav'd, but them past by;'
Or mock'd with only Damning Grace.
How long, thou Jealous God, how long
Shall impious Worms thy Word disprove,
Thy Justice stain, thy Mercy wrong,
Deny thy Faithfulness and Love.
Still shall the Hellish Doctrine stand?
And Thee for its dire Author claim?
No—let it sink at thy Command
Down to the Pit from whence it came
(George, 1988, P. 231-2)

These are extremely strong words. Suffice it to say that for Wesley the freedom of the will and the collaboration of human acceptance with the grace of God in both justification and sanctification was a conviction that was at the core of his theology. A doctrine of God that ignored such human action or that intentionally condemned some people to eternal damnation was, to Wesley, anathema.

WESLEY AND PSYCHOLOGY

What is the legacy of John Wesley for modern psychology? More specifically, what is the legacy of Wesley for modern psychology that can be gleaned from his interaction with Martin Luther and John Calvin. Simply put, it is this: Wesley advocated a view that took seriously the ontological validity of human behavior, on the one hand, and that advocated the possibility of change for better or worse, on the other. While Wesley's arguments for these convictions pertained primarily to religious behavior, the underlying presumptions about human capacity are consonant with the basic assumptions of modern psychology (Myers, 1993). No modern psychologist would doubt for an instance the strategic importance of behavior for human destiny – regardless of whether that destiny be in this world or the next. And, while all applied psychologists would agree with William James (1902, 1958), as well as all other theorists from that day to this, about the difficulty of habit change, they would, nevertheless, retain Wesley's basic optimistic outlook on the possibility of behavior change.

The recent debate over Judith Rich Harris's book *The nurture assumption* (1998) is noteworthy in this regard. In her presentation before last summer's meeting of the American Psychological Association, she reiterated her contention that parents have almost no importance in determining behavior of their children. Basic temperament shaped by peers are the controlling factors. Her views have been met with disagreement by ormer APA president, Frank Farley (1998), among others. Farley commented that Harris ignored much data from developmental psychology in suggesting that home environments are unimportant. This dialogue is but a revival, in a novel form, of the old *nature/nurture* debate. But it important to note that neither Harris nor her critics emphasized the *nature* side of the equation, as Calvin or Luther might have done.

Behavior changes—that Harris, Farley, and all modern psychologists would contend. The only issue is how and when, not whether. Wesley would applaud this conclusion. In fact, Wesley would hold out for complete transformation of that behavior into the image of God. In 1734, four years before his own heart-warming experience, Wesley defined religion as "a renewal of our minds in the image of God, a recovery of the divine likeness, a still-increasing conformity of heart and life to the pattern of our most holy Redeemer" (Wainright, 1995, P. 156). In agreement with Harris about peer relationships, he advocated intense small group interaction. After each of his revivals, groups were formed where persons came together each week and shared the state of their souls. He wrote in his Journal for April 4, 1739 about the establishment of the very first of these "class meetings, as they came to be called: (three women and four young men) "agreed to meet weekly to confess their faults to one another, and toi pray for one another that they may be healed" (Wesley, 1872, Vol. 1, P.185-186). The Wesleyan class meeting became the genius of the movement. Today's 12 Step groups, that are helping people change their lives, are the indirect result of Wesley's insight that people need other people to make change possible. Modern psychology could ask for no better friend.

Of even greater interest, however, has been the call of the current president of the American Psychological Association, Martin Seligman, for a "positive psychology"—one that emphasizes the contribution psychology can make to the acquisition of positive character traits such as virtues and strengths.. Seliigman notes correctly that much of psychology has been directed toward the alleviation of suffering and the alteration of maladaptive behavior. At best, psychology has been focused on the functional value of adjustment to culture. He recently stated, "By working in the medical model and looking solely for the salves to heal the wounds, we have misplaced much of our science and much of our training" (1998, p. 2) Now is the time, according to Seligman, to see what psychology can contribute to acquisition of values and the achievement of human potential. He has called for the setting up of a number of centers across the nation to advance the tenets of this positive understanding of the role of psychology. He calls the effort the "building of buffered strengths" and suggested that the one word which should typify psychology in the future would be hope. (1998, p. 2).

Such a revision of psychology's prime foci would be to adopt a *normative* understanding of its role. Third force, or humanistic, psychology, has been calling for this kind of change for years. Normative mental health, for example, emphasizes the ideal—what humans could become, if they would. This normative approach can be contrasted with *negative* and *normal* mental health. Negative mental health is defined in terms of "no longer being sick," and normal mental health is defined in terms of "adjustment to the environment" (cf Malony, 1983, pp. 15-27). Negative and normal concerns have dominated psychology long enough, according to APA's president.

John Wesley would be pleased with this change in psychology's role from curing people or helping them function to assisting them in achieving their potential—becoming what they could become. Becoming what God intended persons to be would be a synonym for perfection in Wesley's eyes. In fact, his view of this new psychology might be similar to his view of the electrical machine. He might see them both as *secondary divine revelations* put here by God to help redeem humans from the results of the fall. Just as the electrical machine, a manipulanda created by human technology, harnessed electricity and could be used to restore God-intended health to people, so psychology, a set of functional understandings of how people behave likewise created by the human mind, could be conceived as a way of enhancing persons' God-intended possibilities and lead them on into perfection. In fact, Cobb (1995) goes so far as to suggest that today's application of Wesley's moral understanding could be better understood in terms of psychological development rather than moral achievement. If this be true, Wesley would feel right at home in the halls of contemporary psychology. "Hope" would, indeed, be the name of the game.

CONCLUSION

This essay has considered the ways in which the 18th century divine, John Wesley, interacted with the two cardinal figures of the 16th century Reformation, Martin Luther and John Calvin. It was the thesis of this presentation that Wesley's corrective to Luther and Calvin had crucial relevance for the central conviction of modern psychology that behavioral change is possible. Although their theorizing was focused on religious conversion and Christian living, the basic assumptions about human nature underlying Luther's, Calvin's, and Wesley's convictions are pertinent for modern psychology's assertions about human potentiality. Wesley challenged what he felt was Luther's *Antinomianism*—the idea that behavior did not matter. Wesley also challenged what he felt was Calvin's *Double Predestination*—the idea that God had already made up His mind as to who was saved or damned; yet a further implication that behavior had no ultimate value. He affirmed the possibility that behavior had ultimate meaning and that humans could not only stop doing evil but they could start doing good. He even asserted that they could become perfect—the final goal of goodness. With the current interest on using the discipline to enhance strength and virtue, Wesley's ideas would be right at home in most contemporary psychology texts and classrooms. When we add to these seminal ideas Wesley's insight about the importance of interpersonal support, I think we could label Wesley an 18th century personality as well as social psychologist.

ENDNOTES

1. In his Journal for Monday, June 15, 1741 (Wesley, 1872, vol 1, p. 315-16), Wesley stated: "I set out for London, and read on the way, that celebrated book, Martin Luther's "Comments on the Epistle to the Galatians." I was utterly ashamed. How I have esteemed this book, only because I heard it so commended by others; or, at best, because I had read some excellent sentences occasionally quoted from it! But what shall I say, now I judge for myself? Now I see with my own eyes? Why, not only that the author makes nothing out, clears up not one considerable difficulty; that he is quite shallow in his remarks on many passages and muddy and confused almost on all; but that he is deeply tinctured with Mysticism throughout, and hence often dangerously wrong. To instance only in one or two points: - He does he (almost in the words of Tauler) decry reason, right or wrong, as an irreconcilable enemy of the Gospel of Christ! Whereas, what is reason (the faculty so called) but the power of apprehending, judging, and discoursing? Which power is to be no more condemned in the gross, than seeing, hearing, or feeling. Again, how blasphemously does he speak of good works and the Law of God; constantly coupling the Law with sin, death, hell, or the devil; and teaching, that Christ delivers us from the Law of God, than that he delivers us from holiness or from heaven. Here (I apprehend) is the real spring of the grand error of the Moravians. They follow Luther, for better for worse. Hence their "No works; no law; no commandments." But who are thou that "speakest evil of the Law, and judgest the Law?"

REFERENCES

Cannon, W.R. (1946). *The theology of John Wesley*. New York: Abiingdon-Cokesbury Press.

Cobb., J.B. (1995). *Grace and responsibility: Wesleyan theology for today*. Nashville, Abingdon.

Edwards, J. (1746, 1959). A treatise concerning religiouis affections. Edited by J.E. Smith. In *The works of Jonathan Edwards, Vol. 2*. New Haven, CN: Yale University Press.

Farley, F. (1988). We've known for centuries that parents count. *L.A. Parent Magazine*, November, p. 66.

George, T. (1988). *Theology of the Reformers*. Nashville, TN: Broadman.

Harris, J.R. (1998). *The nurture assumption: Why children turn out the way they do*. New York: The Free Press.

James, W. (1902, 1958). *The varieties of religious experience: A study in human nature.* New York: Mentor.

Malony, H.N., ed. (1983). *Wholeness and holiness: Readings in the psychology/theology of mental health.* Grand Rapids, MI: Baker Book House.

Malony, H. N. (1995). John Wesley and the eighteenth century therapeutic uses of electricity. *Perspectives on Science and Christian Faith,-47*, 244-254.

Malony, H.N. (1996). John Wesley's Primitive Physick: An 18th century health psychology. *Journal of Health Psychology, 1*, 147-159.

Malony, H. N. (1998). John Wesley and psychology. *Journal of Psychology and Christianity.*, in press.

Seligman, M.E.P. (1998). Why therapy works. *The Monitor of the American Psychological Association, 29*(12), p.2

Singleton, J. (1998a). At the roots of Methodism: Marriage revealed in Wesley's own humanity. Nashville: TN: United Methodist News Service (Internet http://www.umc.org/unms/98/nov/670t.htm).

Singleton, J. (1998b). At the roots of Methodism: Wesley intensely interested in social issues. United Methodist News Service #734. Nashville, TN: United Methodist Church.

Sleek, S. (1998). Blame your peers, not your parents, author says. *American Psychological Association Monitor,* October, p. 9.

Wainright, G. (1995). *Methodists in dialogue.* Nashville, TN: Kingswood Books.

Wesley, J. (1751). *Primitive Physick: Or, an easy and natural method of curing most diseases,* London: J. Palmar

Wesley, J. (1760). *The desideratum: Or, electricity made plan and useful by a lover of mankind and of common sense.* London: Bailiere, Tindall, & Cox.

Wesley, J. (1777, 1809). *A survey of the wisdom of God in the creation; Or, a compendium of natural philosophy.* Originally published in 1763 in 3 volumes, it was expanded in 1777 to 5 volumes. The 1809 edition was a republication of the 5 volume edition.

Wesley, J. (1850, 1777). *A plain account of Christian Perfection as believed and taught by the Rev. John Wesley from the year 1725, to the year 1777.* New York: Lane and Scott.

Wesley, J. (1872). *The works of John Wesley, 14 volumes.* Grand Rapids, MI: Zondervan.

Wesley, J. (1872). Predestination calmly considered. In *The works of John Wesley, volume X,* (pp. 204-259). Grand Rapids, MI: Zondervan.

Wesley, J. (1872). A dialogue between an Antinomian and his friend. In *The works of John Wesley, volume X* (pp. 266-276). Grand Rapids, MI: Zondervan.

Wesley, J. (1872). A second dialogue between an Antinomian and his friend. In *The works of John Wesley, volume X* (pp. 276-284). Grand Rapids, MI: Zondervan.

EIGHT

Religion
and Psychotherapy:
A Futuristic View

I recently co-authored, with Ed Shafranske, a chapter entitled "Religious issues in psychotherapy: A critical assessment" which will appear in a forthcoming American Psychological Association book on psychology and religion (1996). In that chapter we contended that the need to attend to religion in psychotherapy would persist for the following reasons:

1. the professional ideal to be inclusive (i.e. to not ignore ethnic, gender, and cultural dimensions in efforts to understand and help people). This ideal must include religion;

2. the fact that religious involvement is a cultural fact among many, if not most, of those who come to counselors for help. Religion is normal, not abnormal or atypical;

3. the relevance of religious issues for a fuller understanding of the 5 Axes of The Diagnostic and Statistical Manual of Mental Disorders; Fourth Revision *(1995). Religion can function as a strength, as well as a weakness, in symptom formation, mental status, and adjustment to physical and situational stress;*

4. the essential importance of religion in the sense-making and meaning-finding tasks of life. Religion deals with questions which science cannot answer. Fate, tragedy, morals, and meaning are the province of religion; and

5. the increasing inclusion of religion in the redesign of professional training. Many medical schools and a number of psychology graduate programs are offering prescribed training in dealing with religious issues. Being able to deal with religion in psychotherapy is a need widely acknowledged in professional surveys (cf. Shafranske & Malony, 1990).

Although I still affirm these basic considerations, I would like to take a different tact in this essay. Herein I contend that, while religion will continue to have importance, the approach toward religion that psychotherapists take in the future will have to change or the cultural trend toward trivializing religion (cf. Carter, 1994) will undermine religion's significance in the years to come.

OLD DEBATES ABOUT RELIGION THAT WILL DISAPPEAR

Initially, psychotherapists in the 21st century will have to recognize that there are some 20th century controversies that should be declared null and void if the centrality of religion is to be retained. These include debates over: whether science will finally obliterate religion, whether there is a valid difference between religion and spirituality, and whether there exists such entities as good and bad religion. As important as these may still be to some late 20th century apologists, such issues as these will become meaningless in the 21st century.

Consider, first, the debate over whether religion will disappear some time in the next century. Contrary to Freud's prediction that religion was an illusion that had no future (Freud, 1927, 1964), religion has, indeed, survived. Religion in the late 20th century is alive and well. I predict it will continue to thrive well into the 21st century.

Although Oskar Pfister (1928) may have been overly grandiose in proclaiming, in his review of Freud's *The future of an illusion*, that religion was the only illusion that had a future, there is no sign that religion is about to disappear. The almost two hundred year old prediction of August Comte that the advancement of science would result in the demise of Christianity has not proven true. His science-based "religion of positivism" has failed to take hold among the general public.

Peter Berger noted the basic reason for the individual and social fact of religion's persistence in his book *A rumor of angels; Modern society and the rediscovery of the supernatural* (1969). According to Berger, the experience of being human inevitably includes "black holes," the meaning of which surpasses all that science has to offer. Religion will continue to address questions of ethics, of fate, of tragedy, of mystery, and of purpose (Yinger, 1970). Apologists may continue to bemoan the fact that science does not have all the answers. But in the years to come, such statements as the following by Margaret Singer will be relegated to the side lines more and more. In a bold proclamation of her scientistic sentiments she stated:

> *I became particularly interested in the new cults as they spring up because it was an era in which many liberal political advances had been achieved: scientific reasoning had come to the forefront of our thinking and rationalism had become widely accepted. Yet, I saw many young adults turning to extremely authoritarian groups. ...dropping the world of science, liberalism and rationalism and entering a world of magic and primitive thinking.*
> (Singer, 1978, p.14).

Apparently Singer did not realize that her critique was not limited to "new cults," but applied, in a general sense, to all religion—old as well as new. Such thoughts as these will appear quaint and dated in the 21st century. Religion is here to stay. It is an indisputable individual and social fact that must be taken into consideration by psychotherapists if they would do adequate work in the future.

The second issue that will become passé is distinction between spirituality and religion, which has been ardently promoted by humanistic psychologists in their disdain for social institutions (Moore,1992; Watts, 1996). The difference between religion and spirituality is moot, at best, and socially naive at worst. It confuses motivation with behavior, impulse with action.

Unfortunately, the hyper-individual-privatism that has continued to fuel such a distinction has permeated much individual psychotherapy and many major traditional religious organizations. Although, some may continue to emphasize a preference for individual spiritual growth over institutional religious involvement, such a preference will become increasingly judged as esoteric and unimportant from a psychotherapeutic point of view. As provocative as psychodynamic theorists (cf. Fowler, 1981) may continue to find personal spirituality, the fact remains that private spiritual perceptions are usually adaptations of major religious traditions (Melton, 1982).

Furthermore, where such personal religiosity has any significance for the psychotherapeutic process it will, most often, involve a relationship to participation in some social group. Where personal spirituality does not express itself in group involvement, it will probably not be a vital enough part of life to spend time on it in psychotherapy (Malony, 1995). Although some may continue to contend that there is an innate spiritual urge in all human existence (Halligan, 1995), it is only in its social, corporate expression that religion has any chance of having an impact on life—either good or bad. Accusations made against Irana Huffington's involvement with the Hindu based Movement for Spiritual and Inner Awareness in the late US Senate race in California clearly illustrates this fact. Here, the public judged her participation in this group to be "cultic" and socially irresponsible in terms of the influence she might have on her husband, should he be elected. The public paid little or no attention to her private spirituality or her individual beliefs. Only her organizational involvement mattered. In this, and in most other situations such as psychotherapy, it is proper to judge people by their organizational involvement because religion resembles vocational interests: unless those interests are well above average, and involve participation with others, they will predict nothing (Malony, 1995).

There may be a valid difference between private and public experience, but what else is new? To be truly spiritual is to be religious and to be religious is the way persons become spiritual in any serious use of the term. While not synonymous, the terms are sequentially related in a manner that leads to the conclusion that making a radical distinction between the two may be wasted energy, as far as psychotherapy is concerned.

Deciding to ignore the artificial difference between religion and spiritual may result in a renewed emphasis among psychotherapists on the value of social networks for motivation and for health (Cohen, 1988). Although Alcoholics Anonymous encourages persons to depend on God "however they may define Him (or Her)," there is no doubt in my mind, or AA's for that matter, that social involvement with like-minded believers has greater influence on behavior than private experience. In the future, as in the past, involvement in some social group will probably be the key to religion's impact on the psychotherapeutic process.

Thus, the *DSM-IV's* (1995) distinction between of "spiritual" and "religious" in its V-codes may have limited overall value although this distinction does identify the one significant exception to the general rule that only religiousness has import for psychotherapy (Lukoff, D., Lu, F., & Turner, R., 1992). This is the case in which persons experience unexpected trans-empirical, alternative realities which they cannot explain and which are not necessarily related to organized religion. Typically, these have been the types of experiences reported to San Francisco's Spiritual Emergency Network and the Alister Hardy Religious Experience unit at Westminster College, Oxford, England.

These mystical-like experiences have usually been disturbing and anxiety provoking, according to Spiritual Emergency Network accounts, while those reported to the Oxford group have been pleasant and enticing. However, the impulse to share and to better understand them has been the same in both cases. Both groups reassure persons that the experiences are within conventional experience and they help them incorporate the events into daily life. These experiences are accepted as part of the higher mental potentialities naturally available to human beings (cf Greenwood, 1995). They are not pathologized nor are they theologized. They are simply accepted. These experiences could legitimately be called "spiritual" instead of "religious" in the sense that most often they are not contextualized within the framework of traditional religious explanations.

Similar events experienced among traditional religionists are explained within the theological schemas of those social constructions of reality (Luckman & Berger, 1966). Sunden's (1966) role theory, as interpreted by Holm (1995), and Proudfoot and Shaver's (1975) attribution theory, as interpreted by Spilka and McIntosh (1995), are examples of how these experiences can be contextualized in more traditional manners.

The third 20th century battle that may not be worth much more of psychotherapists' time or energy in the future is the effort to distinguish between

"good" and "bad" religion (Sloat, 1986; Arterburn & Felton, 1991). Ever since
the finding of (Tellegen, Gerrard, Gerrard, & Butcher, 1969) that snake han-
dlers in the Carolinas were as mentally healthy as Methodists, such distinctions
have been on the decline. It must be remembered that, while certain forms of
religion may be preferred by the hyper-sophisticated, highly educated group
called "psychotherapists," in the end those judgments are personal preferences,
pure and simple, as the Tellegen, et. al. research demonstrated.

Although many have insisted that their judgments were based on
research based, expert opinions about constructive personality and social development, it is clear to others that, in many cases, the dominant concerns of these
analysts have been repudiation of religion in general or disdain for the beliefs
of specific groups with which they disapprove (Singer & Lalich, 1995).

A hyper-rationalistic elitism has dictated many of these opinions. The old
"liberal-enlightened" versus "conservative-fundamentalist" distinctions have
been belabored ad nauseum (cf. Altemeyer & Hunsberger, 1992). Participants
in such groups as the Christian Coalition have been pathologized by some who
conveniently forget that communist stereotypes were ascribed to liberals when
they became socially active in the 1950s. Moreover, these critics have disguised
their discomfort with cultural plurality by marginalizing new or different religious groups as if they utilized deviant influence processes (Cialdini, 1984) .

Such debates as these have no future, as far as psychotherapy is concerned. Religious judgments in the next century will become entirely pragmatic. Psychotherapists should assert anew their inability to address the validity
questions about which religions are better or truer than others.
Psychotherapists should be solely invested in whether individuals' religions
work for them or not—an approach first recommended by William James
(1902, 1958). Psychiatrists have routinely been better at making such pragmatic judgments about social realities than psychologists. I well remember the way
in which questions about religion were asked in case conferences at Topeka
State Hospital where I was a pre-doctoral intern in clinical psychology in the
1960s. Without hesitation, the social worker would describe a patient as, for
example, "a Baptist housewife." Without any prejudgment of that or any other
religion, the psychiatrist would ask, "Is she involved in a women's group at her
church where she could receive social support when we discharge her?"

I would venture that most, if not all, of us at the case conference, had
long since abandoned whatever "Baptist" background we might have had. Our
graduate training had taken us far beyond much conservative religion. It was
beneath our sophistication. But we were concerned with pragmatism; if a
Baptist women's group worked to help our patient, we would use it without
hesitation or scrutiny.

A recent report of the experience of a member of the Church Universal

and Triumphant in Boise. Idaho illustrates how this pragmatic approach to religion should even be extended to less traditional, more modern religious movements. Members of her Catholic background family joined with an estranged
husband to kidnap this church member and try to deprogram her away from
this somewhat unique group of persons who listens to their leader's "dictations" of messages she receives from the great religious leaders of the distant
past while in a trance. In the trial where she was accusing her kidnappers of
violating her civil rights, it was revealed that she was a person of good mental
health, a responsible mother of teen age-children, a full-time secretary, and a
member of this different religious group for over a decade. Although the judge
reflected the public's distrust of such a group by allowing the defendants to
claim that they kidnapped her because of the greater evil of her membership in
such a strange group, it was demonstrated conclusively that the group had not
damaged her emotionally and, had, in fact, contributed significantly to her
mental health. Surveys of the mental health of new religious movements
(Richardson, 1995) have found her situation to not be the exception. Religion
in the future should be judged on its effects, not its beliefs.

PSYCHOTHERAPY AND MANAGED CARE

This last discussion of the difference between good and bad religion leads easily into some comments on the changing nature of the psychotherapeutic task.
Worthington (1995) proposed a helpful model to illustrate the way that psychotherapy has become a process which society will only underwrite to increase
social functioning but which society will no longer support for the purpose of
personal growth and development that has no overt social results. This change
has immense importance for the future of the religion/psychotherapy relationship because religion has typically been aligned with personal, rather than
social, effectiveness.

Worthington's model compares the changes in influence of three major
forces on psychotherapy between 1975 and 1995. These forces are The Client,
the Counselor, and Society. These forces can be envisioned as three points of a
triangle with lines of influence pointing to a circle in the middle labeled "psychotherapy."

In 1975 the lines connecting the psychotherapy circle to the Client and
the Counselor were decidedly shorter and the line from Society was long. This
diagram indicated that in 1975 the decision for type and length of psychotherapy was heavily influenced by the recommendations of the Counselor and the
desires of the Client. Although Society had begun to note the heavy cost of
much psychotherapy, it had little to say about the type and extent of the
process. Society approved, and insurance companies supported, growth-orient-

ed, personal-development approaches.

These years were the hey-days of long-term therapy based on the presumption that deep personality change was necessary and worthy of societal support. The voice of society, expressed through insurance companies, was fairly helpless to control the process. Society knew very little about how to challenge the power of the mental health professions whose goals for treatment were dominated by a focus on individual mental health.

By 1995, however, the situation had drastically changed. "Managed Care" had made its entrance into the Client, Counselor, Society matrix (Goodman, Brown & Deitz, 1992). It would be unwise for psychotherapists to ascribe the growing influence of managed care solely to cost containment, although controlling expenditures has definitely been one prime concern. However, underneath this apparent decreased emphasis on individual health lies a change in societal values.

It is definitely true that managed care, i.e. health insurance of whatever variety, will no longer support long-term therapy and will require demonstrated effect of whatever help is supported. It is also true that there will be a reduction of payment-for-service based on level of training. Doctoral level professionals will likely be paid no more than those with only masters level training. Yet beyond the simple issue of cost a deeper philosophical issue is at stake.

The emphasis now is less on intense care for a few and short-term care for the many. Further, and more importantly, the focus has shifted from internal self-understanding to adequacy in social functioning. This has been due to a dramatic change in social conscience. The good of society as a whole has assumed more importance in health care than the fulfillment of the individual. Thus, according to Worthington (1995), the triangular diagram places the psychotherapy circle much closer to the Society pole and much farther away from both the Counselor and Client points of influence. Society's concerns have become social functioning rather than personal growth and development. Society will no longer support counselor's prescriptions for individual self-fulfillment unless such therapy results in a return to functioning. Reassuming a minimally contributing social role at home, at work, or at play has become munch more important than individual growth or personal mental health.

"Performance" rather than "health" has become the goal of psychotherapy. Role performance has become the basis on which treatment will be evaluated and supported. In terms of social philosophy, this change reflects a definite trend toward social Marxism and away from laze faire individualism. Once the roles of society are understood (be they parent or worker), treatment will be directed toward social cohesion rather than individual fulfillment.

Such is the environment in which the psychotherapists will have to function in the future. If they intend for religion to have any meaning in such circumstances, religion will have to takes its place alongside all other aspects of life that either enhance or detract from social functioning. The absolute truth of a given religion will be of no consequence. As noted in the Topeka State Hospital example, religion will be judged by its power to strengthen or weaken a person's social functioning not by self-reports of the meaning it gives to persons' self-esteem, which, in turn, has its effect on social identity and role performance.

The day of personal development counseling is over save in Los Angeles, Chicago, and New York where the culture of psychoanalysis is still alive and well. It should be noted, incidentally, that at least one, if not more, of the psychoanalytic societies located in these cities has intentionally declined to be a part of managed care. Their practitioners have remained fee-for-service and they are not listing themselves among any groups of professionals who can be assigned cases by health maintenance organizations (HMOs).

I predict that the cultural influence of psychoanalysis will speedily decline and psychoanalysts will become marginal professionals who are only available to the rich. Any efforts to conceive of religion's importance to the psychotherapeutic task that aligns itself with such long-term therapy as psychoanalysis will be side-lined in the future.

THE FUTURE OF RELIGION IN MANAGED CARE

Since I, for one, think that it has been clearly demonstrated that religion is too important a part of life (cf Malony and Shafranske, 1996) to be relegated to only an issue dealt with in long-term, growth-oriented psychotherapy, it is crucial to delineate the ways which religion can play a vital role in the world of managed care. I will group my comments under the dual categories of "diagnosis" and of "treatment."

In a previous publication, I suggested how a religious diagnosis could be related to the five axes of the *DSM-IV* (Malony, 1993). At the time that this essay was written, I was under the spell of the old model. Following the longstanding approach proposed by William James (1904), I conceived of the issues as primarily directed toward answering the question "How does this individual's religion contribute to or detract from their deep-level, personality integration?"

For example, under Axis 1 (symptoms) the question might be, "Is religion an overt part of the symptom picture or not?" and under Axis 2 (mental status) the question might be, "Was religion a strength or weakness in the premorbid personality structure?"

In a re-conceptualization of religion in the managed-care environment, the questions to be asked of each Axis will be significantly different. This newer set of questions can be seen in the following outline. In each case, the primary goal of adequate social functioning, rather than personality integration, will guide the way that the role of religion is evaluated.

Axis 1: Presenting Symptom—"Was the breakdown in social functioning which brought this person into psychotherapy due to religion?

Axis 2: Underlying Mental Status—"Was this person's religious practice before the breakdown of social functioning an underlying strength in preventing, or a weakness in provoking, the crisis in social functioning?"

Axis 3: Physical Complications—"Assuming a physically-challenged condition, did religion play a positive, negative, or neutral role in helping the person maintain social functioning under such physically handicapping frustrations as might exist?"

Axis 4: Situational Crises—"Assuming environmental stress, did religion play a positive, negative, or neutral role in helping the person maintain their social functioning in the face of social stress?"

Axis 5: Overall Level of Adjustment in the Past Year—"Has religion contributed to or detracted from this person's total social functioning across all areas of life in the immediate past?"

Although many may decry becoming indentured to the *DSM-IV* (cf.Watts, 1996), the psychotherapeutic parameters prescribed by managed care are destined to become more, not less, restrictive. For years we have described ideal training for psychologists as within a "scientist/practitioner" model that envisioned applied psychology as grounded in general psychology. Much psychotherapy has been undertaken apart from that model. Neither the giving of standardized tests or the routine use of assessment tools has characterized intensive, long-term psychotherapists. Psychotherapists have adopted, with a vengeance, the old adage that " clinician are their own best tools." Future managed care psychotherapists will have to rejoin the "human race" of scientist/professionals. This means they will have to contextualize their work within the limits of the *DSM-IVs* five axes and demonstrate in objective manners that their diagnoses have validity and are directly related to social dysfunction.

Adequate measures of religious status can become helpful adjuncts to the short-term therapy which managed care will support. While there are available assessment tools for most other aspects of personality, there are practically no standardized measures of religion. It is incumbent on each religious tradition to state the essence of its "functional theology," a term which applies to the ways its core beliefs relate to adequate social adjustment. The Religious Status Inventory (Malony, 1988) is just such a measure designed to assess functional theology from a Christian point of view. This is a reliable and valid means of determining individual religious status grounded in the core affirmations of the

Christian faith. It can be used by psychotherapists quite apart from their own religious beliefs. It makes no judgments about the truth or falseness of these beliefs but judges the way they function in daily life.

Increasingly social scientists from within other religious traditions will be providing psychotherapists the means to assess religious status from within the practice of their unique points of view. As noted earlier, if they are religious, most clients will express their spirituality within institutionalized traditions. Where this is not so, religion will likely have little impact on daily life or on psychotherapeutic outcome.

Turning finally to treatment in managed care. What future does religion have in the kind of short-term psychotherapy which is likely to become the norm? My conclusions about this issue may surprise those who have presumed that the inclusion of religious was meaningful only toward the end of intensive, long-term psychotherapeutic relationships (Watts,1996).

I, for one, think that Jung was right in his proverbial statement that he had never counseled anyone in the second half of life the answer to whose problems could not be found in the tenets of the world's great religious traditions. My only criticism of his contention would be that "tradition" should be broadly defined to include the plurality of religious options available to people today and the timing of these solutions should be extended downward to embrace those who are in the first, as well as the second, half of life.

This point of view may sound apologetic, and I confess that it is. Understanding religion as that which "ties together" the strands of existence, I am convinced that the theologian Paul Tillich (1952) was correct in asserting that social dysfunction (which he called "neurotic anxiety") was based in lack of faith (which he called "basic anxiety"). The goal of "personal empowerment" (Gibson, 1991), which has come to dominate the goals for long-term therapy, is equally appropriate for time-limited treatment. The only difference is that in managed-care psychotherapy, the role of the therapist may become less constrained and more directive than where the sessions are not limited by cost controls.

Rebecca Propst, in a conceptual rethinking of the servant role of women in our society (1982) and in a book-length report of her treatment of depressed women (1988), has masterfully demonstrated the way in which religion can become a central part of short-term treatment. Using Bandura's model of "self-efficacy," she provides a model for re-conceptualizing culturally defined gender specific roles within the way in which Jesus assumed his life task. She extended this approach in a major research study of the value of using religious ideas in the treatment of depressed women. She demonstrated conclusively that the use of religious convictions, even by psychotherapists who were themselves NOT religious, had a significantly greater effective on treatment outcome among women who were overtly religious.

Propst provides a clear example of how the type of treatment which includes religion can be utilized in empowering those who have become socially dysfunctional. I am convinced that such use of religious resources in the future will become standard psychotherapeutic procedure in the world of managed care.

CONCLUSION

Does the 21st century portend a negative or positive role for the inclusion of religion within the psychotherapeutic task? Hopefully, this essay has engendered hope for those who consider religion to be among the most valuable of culture's creations. I am among that group. While I recognize that all religious traditions are just that, i.e. human creations, I yet affirm their functional ability to provoke social adaptation.

Nevertheless, times are changing and whatever sense psychotherapists have had that religion is only appropriate in long-term, self-initiate, personal development relationships needs to be confronted with both the falseness of that perception and the reality that this kind of treatment will no longer be supported by society. There are ways and means to incorporate religion into managed care psychotherapy and, hopefully, this essay has left practitioners with some possibilities for application and re-conceptualization.

REFERENCES

American Psychiatric Association (1995). *The Diagnostic and Statistical Manual of Mental Disorders: Fourth Revision*. Washington, DC: American Psychiatric Association.

Altemeyer, B. and Hunsberger, B. (1992). Authoritarianism, religious fundamentalism, quest, and prejudice. *International Journal for the Psychology of Religion*, 2, 113-134.

Arterburn, S. & J. Felton (1991). *Toxic faith; Understanding and overcoming religious addition*. Nashville, TN: Thomas Nelson.

Bergen, P.L. (1969). *A rumor of angels: Modern society and the discovery of the supernatural natural*. Garden City, NY: Doubleday.

Carter, S.L. (1994). *Culture of disbelief; How American law and politics trivialize religious devotion*. New York: Bantam, Doubleday, Dell Publishing Group.

Cialdini, R.B.(1984). *Influence; How and why people agree to things*. NY: Quill.

Cohen, S. (1988). Psychosocial models of the role of social support in the etiology of physical disease. *Health Psychology*. 1, 269-297.

Fowler, J. (1981). *Stages of faith; The psychology of human development and the search for meaning*. San Fransico: Harper & Row.

Freud, S. (1927, 1964). *The future of an illusion*. Garden City, NY: Doubleday (originally published 1927).

Gibson, C. (1991). A concept analysis of empowerment. *Journal of Advanced Nursing*. 16. 354-361.

Goodman, M., Brown, J. & Deitz, P. (1992). *Managing managed care: A mental health practitioners survival guide*. Washington, DC: American Psychiatric Press.

Greenwood, S.F. (1995). Transpersonal theory and religious experience. In R.W. Hood, Jr. (ed.) *Handbook of religious experience* (pp.495-519). Birmingham, AL: Religious Education Press.

Halligan, F.R. (1995). Jungian theory and religious experience. In R.W. Hood (ed.) *Handbook of religious experience* (pp. 231-253). Birmingham, AL: Religious Education Press.

Holm, N.G. (1995). Role theory and religious experience. In R.W.Hood, Jr. (ed.) *Handbook of religious experience* (pp.397-420). Birmingham, AL: Religious Education Press.

James, W. (1902, 1958). *The varieties of religious experience*. New York: Mentor Books.

Luckman T. and Berger, P.L. (1966). *The social construction of reality: A treatise on the sociology of knowledge*. Garden City, NY: Doubleday.

Lukoff, D., Lu, F., & Turner, R. Toward a more culturally sensitive DSM-IV: Psychoreligious and Psychospiritual problems. *Journal of Nervous and Mental Disease. 180*. 673-682.

Malony, H.N. (1993). The uses of religious assessment in counseling. In L.B. Brown (ed.) *Religion, personality, and mental health* (p. 16-28). New York: Plenum.

Malony, H.N. (1993). The relevance of "Religious Diagnosis" for counseling. In E.L. Worthington, Ed. *Psychotherapy and religious values*. Grand Rapids, MI: Baker Book House.

Malony, H.N & Shafranske, E. (1996). Religious issues in psychotherapy: A critical assessment. In E. Shafranske (Ed.) *Religion and the clinical practice of psychology* (in press). Washington, DC: American Psychological Association.

Malony, H.N. (1995). Religion as "interest" rather than "instinct:" Or why religion has such little impact on behavior. Paper presented at the annual meeting of the Christian Association for Psychological Studies, Virginia Beach, Virginia.

Melton, J.G. (1982). *Religious bodies in the United States: A directory*. NY:Garland.

Pfister, O. (1928). Die illusion einer Zunkunft; Eine freundschaftliche Auseinandersetzung mit Prof. Sigm. Freud. *Imago, 14*, 149-184.

Propst, L.R. (1982). Servanthood redefined: Coping mechanisms for women within Protestant Christianity. *Journal of Pastoral Counseling, 26*. 14-18.

Propst, L.B. (1988). *Psychotherapy within a religious framework*. New York: Human Sciences Press.

Proudfoot, W. & P. Shaver (1975). Attribution theory and religious experience. Journal for 'the Scientific Study of Religion. 14.317-330.

Richardson, J.T. (1995). Clinical and personality assessment of participants in new religions. *International Journal for the Psychology of Religion.* 5. 145-170.

Shafranske, E. & Malony, H.N. (1990). Clinical psychologists religious and spiritual orientations and their practice of psychotherapy. *Psychotherapy,* 27, 72-78. (Reprinted in H. Newton Malony, Ed. *Psychology of religion; Personalities, problems, possibilities.* Pasadena, CA: Integration Press, 1996, 549-560).

Shafranske, E. (1996). *Religion and the clinical practice of psychology.* Washington, DC: American Psychological Association, in press.

Singer, M.T. (1978). Therapy with ex-cult members. *Journal of the National Association of Private Psychiatric,* 9(4). 14-18.

Singer, M.T. & Lalich, J. (1995). *Cults in our midst; The hidden menace in our everyday lives.* San Fransico: Jossey Bass.

Sloat, D.E. (1986). *The dangers of growing up in a Christian home.* Nashville, TN: Thomas Nelson.

Spilka, B. & D.N. McIntosh (1995). Attribution theory and religious experience. In R.W. Hood, Jr. (ed.) *Handbook of religious experience* (421-445). Birmingham, AL.: Religious Education Press.

Sunden, H. (1966). *Die Religion und die Rollen (Religion and Roles).* Berlin: Alfred Topelman.

Tellegan, A., Gerrard, N.L., Gerrard, L.E. & Butcher, J.N. (1969) Personality characteristics of members of a serpant-handling religioius cult. In J. N. Butcher (Ed.), *MMPI research developments and clinical applications.* New York: McGraw-Hill.

Tillich, P. (1952) . *The courage to be.* New Haven, CN: Yale University Press.

Watts, P. (1996). Are we becoming a soulless profession? *The California Psychologist.* XXIXO) 15-16.

Worthington, E.L. (1995). The new relationship between counseling and managed care. Paper presented at the annual meeting of the Christian Association for Psychological Studies, Virginia Beach, Virginia, April, 1995.

NINE

Why We Need the American Psychological Association

A s far as graduate training in the integration of psychology and theology in the preparation of clinical psychologists, I am a has-been. As the Australians might put it, I have "been there, done that." I am almost totally retired from 33 years of teaching in the Graduate School of Psychology at Fuller Seminary. The title I hold, Senior Professor, is more honorific than functional. The school still gives me an office and secretary but I have no vote in the faculty and teach only when I want to. My dean graciously puts up with my extensive eccentricities.

The Fuller program had been in existence only four years when I came. Although I was not on his committee, I attended the very first dissertation defense which had been undertaken on "the de-conditioning of snake phobia," if you can believe it. The much loved administrative assistant to the dean feared that one of the snakes that got lost might come out of the heating vent under her desk. Since that time in late 1969 we have graduated several hundred doctoral level clinical psychologists. I was present during our first attempt to obtain approval from the American Psychological Association and have been a part of the five renewals since that time. That process of renewal has never been easy.

Mine has been a career that has been deeply satisfying and fulfilling. I remain committed to the task of training "Psychologist Christians." You will note that by labeling what we do as training "Psychologist *Christians*" I make "Christian" the noun. Our primary vocation is to be a "Christian." "Psychologist" is simply the way we have chosen to actualize that vocation. In the language of occupational psychology, Christian is our career; Psychologist is our job. In two of my early publications I attempted to show how this can be done. The first volume was titled *Psychology and Faith: The Christian Experience of Eighteen Psychologists* (1978). The second was titled Is there a shrink in the Lord"s House? These publications were but the beginning of a persistent attempt to "put Christ in the heart of psychology" – as John Finch, the Tacoma, Washington whose influence led to the founding of the Graduate School of Psychology at Fuller Seminary often said.

I think it is important for us to seek the approval of the American Psychological Association for what we are doing. Why is this so? The answer is "because we are *psychologists.*"

- "Psychologist" is the job we fill among society's occupations;
- "Psychologist" is the role we play in life;
- "Psychologist" is the *license* that allows us to provide service to the public without supervision;
- "Psychologist" is the culture-specific vocation in which we engage;
- "Psychologist" is the title society gives to those professional skills we claim to have acquired.

We seek APA approval because American society has given to the American Psychological Association the role of defining the term and overseeing the training of those who represent themselves as embodying the title "psychologist." In his zeal to have us embody our Christian uniqueness John Finch would sometimes say during times of frustration "tell the APA to stuff it; we don't need them." He was wrong. We do need the APA if we intend to function as psychologists in this culture and at this time in history.

WHAT PSYCHOLOGISTS DO

So, let us be clear on who we are in APA terms. Psychologists are "experts in the study of human behavior." This is who we are. Expertise in human behavior is that body of knowledge we profess to have. Two words need to be unpacked in this definition of psychologists as experts in the study of human behavior. Those words are "study" and "human behavior."

- First, "Study" means to *Understand*: to Comprehend, Empathize with, See how it could be, Not be surprised by, Make sense of, Identify alongside, Intuit what is going on in human behavior
- "Study" also means to *Explain*: to Probe the causes of, Analyze the determinants of, Construe the sequence of events leading up to, Lay out a model that lies behind, identify the antecedents of human behavior.
- "Study" further means to *Predict*—to Recommend, to Treat, Advise, Forecast, Plan, Counsel, Change, Control human behavior.

And what is it that we Understand, Explain, and Control as Psychologists? *Human Behavior.* Humans BEHAVE. They think, they feel, they speak, and they act. Human Behavior includes what we can't see or hear (thoughts and feelings) as well as what we can (speech and actions).

So psychologists are those who are experts in the study of human behavior. They are experts in understanding, explaining, and predicting the thoughts, feelings, words and actions of human beings. This is what the APA expects those we train to be able to do, and rightly so, if the APA gives it stamp of approval to our work. And rightly so, if licensing boards of the states require that those admitted to its examinations graduate from APA approved programs.

ALL PSYCHOLOGY IS CULTURE SPECIFIC

Take this discussion one step further. Note that the APA has the word "American" as its first word. All psychology is "culture specific." All human beings think, feel, speak, and act but they do so in very unique, culture-specific ways. The APA does not presently approve any training programs outside the United States. Nor does it approve programs in any language other than English. This may soon change as our culture becomes less homogenous. One university in south Texas now requires all its graduate students to be bilingual in Spanish as well as English.

Nevertheless, there is still a general thing called "American culture" and the APA oversees those trained to function in that culture, nothing more, nothing less. Culture matters and its appropriate that the APA has *American* as its first word. While I belong to the International Council of Psychologists and am a fellow of APA's Division 52, International Psychology, I recognize that there are vast cultural differences among human beings in the nations of the world. All psychology is "culture specific." There are Indian, German, Chinese, Russian, Canadian and British Psychological Associations – and rightly so – to name only a few. All human beings think, feel, speak and act but they do so with a great variety of emphases and in amazingly different ways. "How" people behave varies with their culture.

Now, one of the "culture specific" aspects of American culture is that we are a religious people. The great majority of citizens in the United States report they believe in God and a significant number of them attend religious meetings on a regular basis. The late psychiatrist, David Larsen, called religion the "r factor" as he surveyed research results that indicated that there was a significant positive inter-relationship among studies of religious behavior and health.

Such empirical validation of religion in American culture has led the American Psychiatric Association to mandate that all approved psychiatric residency training should include seminars on religious/spiritual issues. The American Psychological Association may soon follow suit if APA's recent publications are any indication. Among these publications are *Religion and the Clinical Practice of Psychology* (Shafranske, 1996) and *The Handbook of*

Psychotherapy and Religious Diversity (Richards and Bergin, 2000). And it is noteworthy that The American Psychological Association has officially included religion among its list of diversities to which clinicians should routinely attend in their practices. Religion/Spirituality is there along with gender, age, culture, ethnicity, and sexual orientation. It goes without saying that the APA has approved programs who train "Christian psychologists" with the specific expectation that graduates will be the experts in the way that religion impacts treatment.

Society has every right to think of those who graduate from such program as Fuller's, Rosemead's, Regent's, Wheaton's, Western's, Pepperdine's, etc. to be specialists in religion. Just as society should expect those graduating from the University of Arizona to be specialists in behavioral conditioning and those graduating from the William Alanson White Institute to be specialists in psychoanalysis. I don't mean just specialists in the *Christian* religion, though that may happen, but I mean specialists in *religion in general*. In my opinion our graduate curricula should always include courses in the psychology of religion and in comparative religion.

Most clinicians are *pragmatists*—the do what works to help clients. In most cases clinicians have less than an hour per week with each of their clients. They are not primarily evangelists, as inviting a role as that may be. They should know how to work with the religion of the client, whatever that may be.

Several years ago we published in the *International Journal for the Psychology of Religion* an article by a psychologist from the University of Peshewar in Iran called "Third force psychotherapy." (Jahangir, 1995) She told of treating two depressed Muslim students while she was on sabbatical leave at the University of Glasgow in Scotland. The counseling service of the University asked for her help after trying all they knew to do to help the students. She brought them out of their depressions in a few sessions by including their Muslim faith in the treatment. She began by asking them if they believed Allah was present in the sessions. She used their affirmation of Allah's presence as the basis for helping them solve their depression. She called Allah the "third force."

I think APA should expect graduates of programs it approves that portend to relate psychology with religion should have have been able to help depressed visiting Muslim students at the University of Glasgow, Scotland without the counseling service having to find a Muslim counselor. APA approved program should graduate student who would know immediately that remembering the constant presence of "Allah" would help relieve their depressions had they been on the counseling staff. They, too, would have included "Allah" early on in their treatment even if they were not themselves Muslim.

APA's Meaning of Health

By using the religion of the client in the pragmatic process of finding what works, most modern psychologists affirm the APA's understanding of what "health" entails. The American Psychological Association defines *health* as *being able to function successfully in society.* This is quite different from earlier definitions where health would be understood to be "self understanding" or "restructuring of the personality." The technical term for health understood by the APA is *adequate social functioning.* Mothers are healthy if they are mothering, workers if they are working, friends if they have friends, students if they are studying, fathers if they are fathering.

Now, I would wager that many clinicians would say: "Counseling or psychotherapy is more than this; the goal of counseling is not to just good role performance in a given culture, i.e. "adequate social functioning." I acknowledge the discomfort. Of course it is a minimal definition of health, but it is what APA sees as the core of health in any culture. And "adequate social functioning" it is what most Health Maintenance Organizations (HMOs) and Preferred Provider Organizations (PPOs) will use in determining whether to reimburse clinicians for their treatment. They will ask, "is the person able to return to work, walk the streets, shop for groceries, make friends, feel happy without being suicidal, relate to wife or husband, achieve future goals, concentrate on studies, rear children who have positive self concepts, flourish in intimate relationships." HMOs and PPOs will no longer pay for "insight" unless it leads to behavioral change.

I affirm this emphasis on the goal of counseling being return to social functioning. In fact, such a goal may be a far more *Christian* understanding of our role than the old emphasis on extensive personality change that could possibly leave a person with new self understanding but little behavioral change. Most people cannot afford long term counseling anymore.

Most importantly, Christians are *Christian*—not Buddhist. The Christian faith emphasizes action in the world, here and now, rather than withdrawal from the world. Jesus admonished us to be active in this workaday world and to aspire to love one another in our daily lives. Even more important is our Christian conviction that we are to join God in helping to bring Christ's kingdom into the world by our actions for love and justice here and now.

So, a workable definition of what we clinical psychologists do in our daily work might be "Counseling—efforts by a person to help others adjust to or adapt the environment in which those persons choose to live." With this definition of counseling and the APA's understanding of health in mind I have often challenged my students to think of themselves as *Mechanics*—

Mechanics repair cars and help get them back on the road.

Mechanics will not be paid for conversations with the owners about where their cars have been or what plans they have for future travel.

Mechanics just help people get going again.

Functional mechanical help—that could be seen as the work-a-day world of the clinical psychologist.

USING RELIGION IN COUNSELING

Religion can be an integral part of the mechanical help that clinicians provide. In an article entitled "The prevalence of religious coping among persons with persistent mental illness" (Tepper, Rogers, Coleman, Malony, 2001) my colleagues and I found over 80% of 406 day-treatment psychiatric patients in Los Angeles used religious beliefs and/or practices to cope with daily difficulties or frustrations. While a variety of religious traditions were noted, there was a tendency for Judeo/Christian convictions and rituals to be those most often reported as effective in buttressing these persons against further deterioration.

Of course, not every person who comes for counseling is "religious" in the traditional, institutional, organizational sense of that word. In fact, it is becoming common for many to say they are "spiritual" but are not "religious." We need some definitions of these terms to assist us in the counseling we provide. It could be said that *Spiritual* refers to experience while *Religious* refers to expression. To be spiritual means to experience transcendent reality; To be religious means to give words and practice to that experience.

The ability to *experience* transcendent reality is like a sixth sense. Human beings are born with this added ability in addition to being able to see, to taste, to feel, to hear, and to smell, . They have the capacity, therefore, to be spiritual. It is a spiritual sense alongside the other five senses. Robert Emmons, of the University of California at Davis, has postulated that there is such a thing as "spiritual intelligence"(Emmons, 1998) Everyone has it as a capacity but the ability to exercise it may differ from person-to-person in a normal curve fashion.

I have become convinced that Emmons might be right after reading Swartz and Simon's recent book *The Afterlife Experiments: Breakthrough Scientific Evidence of Life after Death* (2002) where mediums, such as John Edwards who hosts the TV program *Crossing Over*, were accurate nearly 70% of the time in reporting details of deceased family members while those who claimed no such ability could never achieve higher than 20%accuracy. And these readings were done in controlled experiments with respectable designs. This is not to say that the ability to experience transcendent reality cannot be trained and increase (see Clark, Malony, Daane, & Tippett, 1973), but it is to say that the innate capacity may be distributed unequally. This is spirituality. It is an experience.

Whenever words or practices are put to this experience of transcendent reality, the spiritual experience becomes a *religion*. When two or more people agree on the name of the experience and on what one is to do to sustain or solidify the experience, there a religion exists. Whereas spirituality is experience; religion is expression. When persons experience the transcendent, they talk about and engage in active response to it. That is religious *expression*.

When people come to clinicians for help, they differ in the spiritual *experiences* they have had and the religious *expressions* in which they have engaged. Psychologists with special expertise in these matters should be especially interested in the spiritual/religious history of their clients. As those with skills in the study of human behavior, psychologists should be particularly concerned about whether they can rely on the strength of persons' spiritual/religious habits to be of significance in the therapeutic process. All counselors have to decide which parts of clients' lives to emphasize and which to ignore during the limits of treatment.

Counselors should be interested in helping clients return to successful living as soon as possible. Religious practices are one, but not the only resource, that is available. In our study of persistent mentally ill persons Rogers, Poey, Reger, Tepper, G. M., & Coleman (2002), we asked the following three questions.

1. Before you became upset, did you consider yourself to be a spiritual or religious person?

2. When you became upset, did religious/spiritual practices help you?

3. Which religious/practices did you find most helpful?

These could be asked of every client.

Note the way these questions are phrased. In the first question, persons are asked whether they are *SPIRITUAL/religious persons* but in the last two questions they are asked about *RELIGIOUS/spiritual practices*. This is intentional. In the first question we were interested in having them share with us whether they have had spiritual experiences and whether those have become spiritual expressions. However, in using religion in our treatment, we were less interested in spiritual *experience* and more interested in religious *practice*— what they did in actual behavior. We were not interested in what they believed but in how they acted on the basis of that belief. As clinicians who saw ourselves as pragmatic mechanics our basic interest was in what would still work; what they could still do that would help them return to good social functioning. Obviously, what were good questions for seriously mentally ill persons are good questions for those less emotionally disturbed.

When we asked the persistently mentally ill which practices they engaged

in, they reported six religious expressions:
- Prayer
- Attending religious services
- Private worship of God
- Meditation
- Reading Scriptures
- Meeting with a spiritual leader

By no means, will these be the answers one always gets in answer to the question of what religious/spiritual practices clients find most helpful. But, if they were spiritual/religious before they became upset and if they found religious practices to be helpful when they did become disturbed, and if they can identify which practices they found most helpful, therapists will have a head start in efforts to include religion in their clinical work.

Of course, it goes without saying, that religion doesn't always work and it is just as important to know which expressions clients did not find helpful. Not only did we find that some religious ideas did not work. In fact, some religious practices actually were reported to be destructive (Rogers, Malony, Coleman, Tepper, 2002)

RECOMMENDATIONS FOR CHRISTIAN PSYCHOLOGISTS

I conclude with three short personal comments about work as a Christian psychologist. First, just as it is appropriate to ask spiritual/religious questions of every client, it is also appropriate to say to each client, "At any time during our work together, if you have a question of me about why I emphasize one thing or another, feel free to ask it." This gives the clinician the chance to say, "We have found that spirituality and religion is often an important part of life and religion often provides some help to persons in their getting healthy again."

In this regard, I used to give clients a sheet of paper that told something of my approach to psychotherapy. I stated on this sheet that I emphasized the processes of Transactional Analysis and the values of the Christian faith. I listed a number of activities that I might include in therapy from time to time. In that list was "reading selected verses from the Holy Bible." During my first session, a new client said to me as he pointed to the statement about Bible reading, "I want you to know that I am not religious." "Fine, I said, it is good for me to know that; I will not impose religion on you against your will." Several weeks later he brought in the sheet again and pointed to the item about Bible reading, saying as he did "Is there something I should be reading in this book?" Be open to their questions.

My second observation is this—Have resources available: prayers, practices, scripture readings. Clinicians should be able to tell clients how to "work their religion"—i.e. how to express and practice their faith. Be ready to give suggestions. Test these options out and see if they work for the client. Now, I assume that the practices we will be most familiar with are *Christian*, but prepare yourself for other traditions you may face. Learn something about what non-Christian traditions do to express their faiths and be able to suggest options to their adherents should the occasion arise.

My last comment is this: Don't be afraid of dependency; Always be available. It is somewhat fanciful to think that the usual 50 minute, once weekly model of counseling should have any effect on the lives of those psychologists try to help. One prime concern of every clinician should be "How can the effect of the session be extended to all the other hours of the week when the client is not there?" If I had identified religious practice to be a healing force in a client's life, I would never hesitate to say to them, "You will be in my thoughts and prayers during the week we are apart; Call me if you need help in putting our work together into practice." This means that I think clients should be able to call their therapist day or night. My recommendation would be, "Don't play hard to get. Be available." The caution about clients becoming too dependent is a false issue. The therapist can control dependency as treatment progresses. When clients progress in treatment and become stronger in their own right, the counselor can encourage independence.

In conclusion, this essay on the value of the endorsement of the American Psychological Association for training in Christian clinical psychology has included reflections on the nature of health, the meaning of counseling, and the use of religion within the therapeutic process. Taken as a group , these thoughts are the musings of a semi-retired professor as he looks back on a career as an educator of Christian psychologists.

REFERENCES

Clark, W.H., Malony, H.N., Daane, D., and Tippett, A.R. (1973). *Religious experience: Its nature and function in the Human Psyche*. Springfield, IL: Charles C. Thomas, Publishers.

Emmons, R.A. (1998). Is spirituality an intelligence? Presentation at the annual meeting of the *American Psychological Association*, August, San Francisco.

Jahangir, S.F. (1995). Third Force therapy and its impact on treatment outcome. *International Journal of Psychology*, 5(2), 125–130.

Malony, H.N. (1978). *Psychology and faith: The Christian experience of eighteen psychologists*. Washington, D.C.: University Press of America.

Malony, H.N. (1986). *Is there a Shrink in the Lord's house: How psychologists can help the church*. Pasadena, CA: Integration Press.

Richards, P.S. and Bergin, A.E., Editors (2000). *Handbook of psychotherapy and religious diversity*. Washington, D.C.: American Psychological Association

Rogers, S. A., Poey, E. L., Reger, G. M., Tepper, L., & Coleman, E. M. (2002). Religious coping among those with persistent mental illness. *International Journal for the Psychology of Religion, 12*, 161–175.

Rogers, S. A., Malony, H. N., Coleman, E. M, & Tepper, L. (2002). Changes in attitudes toward religion among those with persistent mental illness. *Journal of Religion and Health, 41*, 167-178.

Shafranske, E.P., Editor (1996). *Religion and the clinical practice of psychology.* Washington, D.C.: American Psychological Association.

Swartz, G.E. and Simon, W.L. (2002). *The afterlife expepriments: Breakthrough scientific evidence of life after death.* New York: Atria Books

Tepper, L., Rogers, S. A., Coleman, E. M., & Malony, H. N. (2001). The prevalence of religious coping among persons with persistent mental illness. *Psychiatric Services, 52*, 660–665.

Toward
a Christian
Clinical
Psychology

SECTION TWO

The
Psychology
of Religion

TEN

Analog Measures of Religion: Experimental Psychology of Religion Revisited

Flakoll (1977) listed 20 methods which were used in the psychology of religion from 1900 to 1960. Only one of these was experimental. The rest were variations of self report methods; questionnaires, rankings, personal diaries, Q-sorts, and interviews, for example. During this period, experimental methods, defined as controlled and contrived laboratory approaches where the effect of differences in independent measures on dependent measures were assessed, were almost non-existent. In fact, Klausner (1964) reported that less than two percent of psychology of religion studies between 1950 and 1960 used laboratory experimental methods. Warren (1977) found only three such studies during the succeeding decade. Batson (1983) reported that a later survey of the 1970s and early 1980s revealed no greater use of the experimental method. Some twenty-five years earlier, Stolz (1937) spoke for many in the field in concluding that "laboratory type of experimentation in religion has not proved successful." (p.145)

While the success of experimental approaches may be debated, this type of methodology has not been in vogue, to say the least. Cline and Richards (1965) summarized the state of affairs which exists even to the present by writing, "significant empirical studies of the psychology of religion are a real rarity, and this has certainly not been a popular area of study for psychologists" (p.570). As Warren (1977) observed, "If it weren't for the Pearson product moment correlation coefficient, 90 percent of the studies in this field could not have utilized statistical analysis." (p.95-96)

Nevertheless, the creativity and profundity of a number of experimental studies in the psychology of religion years have added greatly to the field. My intent in this essay is to review a selected few of these studies as illustrations of how religion can be brought into the laboratory and subjected to experimental methodology. It is my contention that psychology of religion in the future will be greatly enriched by serious attempts to study religion through these methods. I have termed this type of research "analog" because in many, if not most, cases these studies have involved procedures which were similar to, but not exact replications of, religion in structure as well as function. The early work of Sir. Francis Galton illustrates this approach. In fact, he has been identified as the first to "conceive of a wholly DISINTERESTED experimental approach to religion." (Wulff, 1991, p. 8) In an effort to comprehend the experience of devotion to a divine being, Galton tried to induce in himself a similar feeling to a cartoon figure of Punch. He meditated on the figure and tried to allow his feelings to become adorational and worshipful. Wulff quotes Galton in stating, "I addressed it (the figure of Punch) with much quasi-reverence as possessing a mighty power to reward or punish behavior of men towards it, and found little difficulty in ignoring the impossibilities of what I professed. The experiment gradually succeeded; I began to feel, and long retained for the picture a large share of the feelings that a barbarian entertains for his idol, and learnt to appreciate the enormous potency they might have over him." (p.8)

Batson and Ventis (1982) defined this experimental, or analog, approach thusly: "An experiment might be described as a causal caricature. This caricature is an artificial, usually simplified, reconstruction of some natural phenomenon; it selectively emphasizes essential components. A caricature is not a mirror of reality; it is an intentional distortion. Yet it may reveal reality better than a mirror, because the essential components stand out." (p.314)

With this definition in mind the four studies that I will consider are: "From Jerusalem to Jericho": A study of situational and dispositional variables in helping behavior (Darley and Batson, 1973); "Physiological state deviation, prior religiosity, setting variation, and the report of religious experience" (Spradlin, 1981); "Health versus holiness: Self-esteem, self-sacrifice, and perception of Christ's ethics (Christ concept)" (Raney, 1984); and "Autonomic effects of visualizing a sinful act" (Forman and Malony, 1987).

"FROM JERUSALEM TO JERICHO"

A Study of Situational and Dispositional Variables in Helping Behavior Using the parable of the Good Samaritan, John Darley and Daniel Batson (1973) attempted to study the environmental and personality variables that might determine who acted as Good Samaritans in a contrived situation. Male students at Princeton Theological Seminary were sent to another campus building after completing paper-and-pencil scales to measure their religiosity. Each student had to pass by a confederate "victim" who was slumped over in the alley. The dependent measure was whether the students would stop to help him. The "victim" rated each student as he passed by. If the student did not stop, he was given a rating of "0." Ratings of "5" were at the opposite extreme and reflected stopping, refusing to leave, and insisting on taking the "victim" for help.

Those students who received higher ratings were inclined to be those who were told they did not have to hurry to the next building. There was no difference in the helping behavior of those students told to prepare a speech based on the Good Samaritan story and those assigned a less religious topic. The only measure of religiousness that correlated with helping was doctrinal orthodoxy.

Seemingly, being in a hurry or not was the chief determinant of helping behavior. Among those students who were told to hurry because they were late, only 10% stopped to help while 63% of those students not told to hurry stopped. Although being asked to make a speech on the Good Samaritan did result in 59% of the students stopping, 29% of those asked to make a secular speech also stopped. This difference was not significance.

This research was an ingenious attempt to replicate the Good Samaritan situation under controlled conditions. The results are astounding. What determined the behavior of the priest and Levite in the biblical story was observed to be the dominant factor here, i.e. being in a hurry to get somewhere. The importance of doctrinal orthodoxy to helping suggests that deep structure religiosity, i.e. adherence to doctrine, may be more influential than states of mind, i.e. whether one has been asked to think about a given biblical passage or not. This possibility is supported in the next study to be discussed also.

PHYSIOLOGICAL STATE DEVIATION, PRIOR RELIGIOSITY, SETTING VARIATION, AND THE REPORT OF RELIGIOUS EXPERIENCE

This research by Spradlin (1981) was a test of attribution theory defined as persons' explanations of why they do what they do. Based on a classic study by Schacter and Singer (1962) in which participants were given a disguised agent of arousal (adrenalin) and exposed to either a euphoric or angry confederate, a volunteer sample of women were exposed to paintings in the Norton Simon Museum of Art in Pasadena, California, USA. Half of the sample had no religious orientation while the other half had a religious background. One gallery in the museum featured early Christian Renaissance art while another gallery contained modern abstract sculpture and abstract paintings. Half of the participants with and without religious orientation were assigned to go through each of these galleries. Physiological arousal was manipulated by audio-taped suggestions to the participants to put themselves in either an excited or relaxed state. While they walked through the galleries, all subjects listened to a guided fantasy containing aspects of a mystical experience as noted by Pahnke and Richards (1966).

Thus, the independent variables were the settings (religious and nonreligious galleries), the personal religiosity of the participants (religious and nonreligious background), and the arousal instructions (aroused and relaxed). The dependent measures were four assessments of the religiousness of the experience of walking through the galleries while listening to the tape designed to induce a mystical experience. These assessments included the Religious Episodes Experience Measure Hood (1970), the Mysticism Scale (Hood, 1975), and self-report ratings of the religiousness of the taped message and the total experience.

The only variable that significantly predicted who would have a religious experience in the experiment was prior religiosity. Those women who had a religious background prior to participation in the study tended to report they had a religious experience quite apart from which gallery they went into or whether they were in an aroused or relaxed state. This result confirms the finding in the Darley and Batson (1973) research that those students who were more doctrinally orthodox, i.e. were committed to a religious tradition, were more likely to function as modern Good Samaritans. It further suggests that the trait of religiousness brought to the experience by the women with religious backgrounds was more determinative of their perceptions that the state of mind provoked by their environment.

Health Versus Holiness:
Self-Esteem, Self-Sacrifice, and Perception of Christ's Ethics

Raney's (1984) study examined the impact that instructions to follow Christ's example had on a type of behavior in which persons had the opportunity to be selfish or altruistic. Sixty college students, half of which reported low and the other half of which reported high self-esteem on the Coopersmith Self-Esteem Inventory, Adult Form C (Coopersmith, 1981), were engaged in a modification of the Prisoner's Dilemma game. Further, half of each sample measured intrinsic and half extrinsic in their religious orientation as determined by scores on the Gorsuch and Venable (1983) "Age Universal" I-E Scale.

Unbeknown to the participants, they were paired with a confederate in the playing of a rotating presentation of three imbalanced "games" in which participants could increasingly deny themselves by choosing to play the blue chip. The players were seated at opposite ends of a desk divided by a partition to make non-verbal communication impossible. The players were instructed to make a choice by holding up either a blue or red poker chip after which they received white poker chip payoffs.

The participants were unaware that the confederate was instructed to choose the red poker chip on the first trial and, thereafter, to choose the response which the other player had chosen on the previous trial. The participants received one of two cards instructing them to play the game as they would normally play it or to play it as they thought Jesus Christ would play were he in their situation. Both players were also told that the number of white poker chips they acquired by playing the game would be equal to the number of chances they would have in a drawing for $100. This provided an incentive for them to win as much as they could. Using the set to play the game normally or as Christ would play it, the 3 games was played for 20 trials each for a total of 60 trials. At the end of these 60 trials, the instructions given to the participants were switched. Those instructed to play the game normally were now instructed to play it as Christ would play and those instructed to play the game as Christ would play it were now instructed to play normally. Then the 3 games were played for another 20 trials each. The dependent variable was the number of white chips each player had at the end of each 60 trials. Of particular interest was the difference in white chips after playing the game normally or as Jesus Christ would play.

Irrespective of level of self-esteem or of order of presentation of the normal or Christ roles, participants were much more self-denying in the Jesus role. However, participants were much more self-denying in the Jesus role when it followed the normal role than when it preceded it. Further, they were significantly more self-denying in the normal role when it followed the Jesus role. In regard to self-esteem, high self-esteem participants were significantly more self-denying when the Jesus role was presented second but no difference was found in low self-esteem subjects regardless of whether the normal or the Christ role came first. In addition, the high self-esteem participants were significantly more self denying than the low self-esteem participants when the Jesus role came second but there was no difference based on self-esteem when the Jesus role came first.

These results suggest that the mental set with which persons approach a task significantly influences their behavior. These data also suggest that self-esteem interacts with mental set to effect the degree to which persons are able to switch from self-indulgence to self-denial. It seems as if higher self-esteem provides a basis for non-defensive self-denial, i.e. behaving more like Christ would behave. Since the participants in this study were all from a Christian liberal arts college, it was not possible to assess whether prior religiosity was a significant determinant. Therefore this research cannot be compared with the two previously discussed studies.

AUTONOMIC EFFECTS OF VISUALIZING A SINFUL ACT

In this Forman and Malony (1986) study 60 seminary students were measured on changes in heart rate, breathing rate, and skin conductance when they were imagining themselves to be committing sinful acts as compared to resting states. Participants for whom the religious importance of acting righteously was high or low were exposed to these conditions in an A-B-A-B sequence. The A conditions were resting states, while the B conditions were sinful visualizations of stealing or ignoring cries for help. One was a sin of commission and the other was a sin of omission. The assumption was that if the guilt theory of O. Hobart Mowrer (1968) was correct, then those who were more concerned about behaving ethically would find the experience of imagining themselves sinning anxiety provoking and evidence this emotion through physiological indices of stress. Furthermore, it was assumed that this concern for righteousness would be based, in part, on the teaching of Jesus that thinking about sin was tantamount to sinning (Matthew 5:27-28). Contrary to prediction, there were no significant differences in physiological arousal between sinful and neutral visualizations nor did those for whom righteousness was more important evidence greater measures of physiological stress than those for whom righteousness was less important. Because of an artifact in the experimental methodology it was not felt that the hypothesis was truly tested. At the time of this study the ethics regarding deception in research were being reconsidered. It was felt that concern for the welfare of participants made it necessary to forewarn them that the experience they were about to engage in might prove stressful and might involve them in thinking they were engaging in unethical acts.

Although this communication made the participants fully aware of the dangers in the experiment, it resulted in an adaptation effect. The measures of heart rate, breathing rate, and skin conductance tended to be highest on the first condition (a neutral resting state) and subside over the following three conditions (the first sin visualization, the second resting state, and the second sin visualization). It was thought that the participants became anxious initially and then found that the experiment was not as stressful as they thought it was going to be. Thus, they became more relaxed over time regardless of whether they were imaging they were sinning or not.

The methodology in this study is suggestive of ways to provide analogues to real-life situations in which persons experience guilt when their behavior contradicts with their values.

CONCLUSIONS

This essay has illustrated several experimental approaches to the psychological study of religion. While I may not be as pessimistic as Dittes (1969) or Batson (1977) are in their statements that laboratory research is the only way that scientific theory can be developed, I do agree with these writers that such research is sorely needed because "the chief problem (in psychology of religion) appears to be in the realm of theory and in the theoretical relevance of the data" (Dittes, 1969, p.603). On the other hand, I am not as optimistic as Yeatts and Asher (1979) who stated that experimentation in the psychology of religion was not only possible but feasible in almost every case. I am more inclined to agree with Batson (1977) that we may have to settle for quasi experimental designs since the ethics of manipulating various types of religion is highly questionable. The study of Pahnke and Richards (1966) in which LSD was used to assess the drug's effect on mysticism may be an example. There was always the possibility that the ingestion of LSD would evoke a bad trip which might have been irreversible. The ethical and legal ramifications of such methods would be highly questionable today. Nevertheless, the examples I have given in this essay illustrate how heuristic the conclusions can be where laboratory controls and religious analogues are employed. Hopefully the day will come when correlational and experimental studies will appear with equal occurrence in the literature rather than with the 90% to 10% respective frequency of such methods in the past. Contrary to what Batson (1977, p. 415) stated, I believe an experimental psychology of religion is likely to be developed.

REFERENCES

Batson, C. D. (1977). Experimentation in psychology of religion: An impossible dream. *Journal for the Scientific Study of Religion.* 16, 412-418.

Batson, C. D. (1979). Experimentation in psychology of religion: Living with or in a dream? *Journal for the Scientific Study of Religion,* 18, 90-93.

Batson, C. D., & Ventis, W. L. (1982). *The religious experience: A social-psychological perspective.* New York: Oxford University Press.

Cline, V. B., & Richards, Jr., J. M. (1965). A factor-analytic study of religious belief and behavior. *Journal of Personality and Social Psychology,* 1, 569-578.

Coopersmith, S. (1981). *Self-esteem inventories booklet.* Lafayette, California: Self Esteem Institute.

Darley, J. M., & Batson, C. D. (1973). "From Jerusalem to Jericho"; A study of situational and dispositional variables in helping behavior. *Journal of Personality and Social Psychology,* 27(1), 100-108.

Deconchy, J. P. (1978). L'experimentation en psychologie de la religion: Pourquoi ne pas rever. *Archives de Science Sociales des Religions.* 46, 176-192.

Dittes, J. E. (1969). Psychology of religion. In G. Lindzey & E. Aronson (Eds.), *The handbook of social psychology,* (Vol.5), (pp. 602–659). Reading, Massachusetts: Addison-Wesley.

Flakoll, D. A. (1977). A history of method in the psychology of religion (1900-1960). In H. N. Malony (Ed.), *Current perspectives in the psychology of religion,* (pp. 77-92). Grand Rapids, Michigan: William B. Eerdmans Publishing Company.

Forman, R. H., & Malony, H. N. (1986). Autonomic effects of visualizing a sinful act. *Journal of Psychology and Christianity*, 5(1), 11-21.

Gorsuch, R. L., & Venable, G. D. (1983). An "Age Universal" I-E scale. *Journal for the Scientific Study of Religion*, 22(2), 181-187.

Hood, R. W., Jr. (1970). Religious orientation and the report of religious experience. *Journal for the Scientific Study of Religion*, 4(4), 285-291.

Hood, R. W., Jr. (1975). The construction and preliminary validation of a measure of reported mystical experience. *Journal for the Scientific Study of Religion*, 14, 29-41.

Klausner, S. (1964). Methods of data collection in studies of religion. *Journal for the Scientific Study of Religion*, 3(2), 193-203.

Mowrer, 0. H. (1968). New evidence concerning the nature of psychopathology. In M. J. Feldman (Ed.), *Studies in psychotherapy and behavior change*. New York: University of Buffalo Press.

Pahnke, W. N., & Richards, W. A. (1966). Implications of LSD on experimental mysticism. *Journal of Religion and Health*, 5, 175-208.

Raney, R. W. (1984). Health vs. holiness: self-esteem, self-sacrifice, and perception of Christ's ethics (Christ-concept). (Doctoral dissertation, Fuller Theological Seminary, 1984). *Dissertation Abstracts International*.

Schachter, S., & Singer, J. E. (1962). Cognitive, social, and physiological determinants of emotional state. *Psychological Review*, 69(5), 379-399.

Spradlin, W. H. (1981). Physiological state deviation, prior religiosity, setting variation, and the report of religious experience. (Doctoral dissertation, Fuller Theological Seminary, 1981). *Dissertation Abstracts International*.

Stolz, K. R. (1937). *The psychology of religious living*. Nashville, Tennessee: Abingdon-Cokesbury Press.

Warren, N. C. (1977). Empirical studies in the psychology of religion: An assessment of the period 1960-1970. In H. N. Malony (Ed.), *Current perspectives in the psychology of religion*, (pp. 93-100). Grand Rapids, Michigan: William B. Eerdmans Publishing Company.

Wulff, D. M. (1991). *Psychology of religion: Classic and contemporary views*. New York: John Wiley & Sons.

Yeatts, J. R. & Asher, W. (1979). Can we afford not to do true experiments in psychology of religion? A reply to Batson. *Journal for the Scientific Study of Religion*, 18, 86-89.

ELEVEN

The Clark School
of Religious Psychology,
1889–1929

(Contributions of G. Stanley Hall and his students,
James H. Leuba and Edwin S. Starbuck)

The Clark School of Religious Psychology was so called because it was centered at Clark University in Worcester, Massachusetts between the years of 1889 and 1929. These years mark, on the one hand, the establishment of the University under the presidency of G. Stanley Hall and, on the other hand, the publications of books on the psychology of religion by E. S. Conklin, G. Betts, and E. T. Clark.

Conklin, Betts, and Clark were the last among a group of psychologists trained at Clark who dominated the field of the psychology of religion in America for forty years. For example a selected sample of fifteen issues of the American Journal of Religious Psychology and Education in the years 1904, 1905, 1912, 1913, and 1914 reveals that fully twenty-eight of the fifty-nine articles were written by psychologists associated with Clark University! This was no mean accomplishment for a young institution.

The distinction was early in coming. Pratt, writing in 1908, was bold enough to say that the psychological study of religion was "hardly more than a dozen years old" (cf. Clark's founding in 1889) and that "the Clark School had contributed almost half the work of any value that has yet been done in this country" (p. 20) on this subject. There was no other center wherein a group of scholars mutually supported each other in the psychological study of religious phenomena. As such it was the American school (Selbie, 1924).

In regard to the influence of the Clark School, Beit-Hallahmi (1974) suggests that the rise and fall of religion as a popular topic of study in American psychology occurred between 1880 and 1930. It is noteworthy that the demise of the movement is dated one year after the last publications of the Clark scholars (cf. Clark, Betts, Conklin, 1929) and that the beginning of the movement precedes by only two years the first publication of the most focal figure in the field, G. Stanley Hall. This last was Hall's article on "The moral and religious training of children" (1882).

THEMES OF THE CLARK SCHOOL

The three aforementioned authors (Conklin, Betts and Clark) illustrate three of the important themes in the movement. Their books, all published in 1929, typify interests in making the psychology of religion a legitimate branch of general psychology, the study of developmental phenomena (conversion) through empirical means, and the investigation of the beliefs of imminent leaders. Conklin's *The psychology of religious adjustment* continued the tradition of seeing religion as one among the many human experiences to be studied with psychological methods. Clark's *The psychology of religious awakening* was almost a replication of Starbuck's 1899 studies of conversion. Betts1 *The beliefs of 500 ministers* was similar to Leuba's 1921 report on the beliefs of scientists. Hiltner (1947) has called these three "imitators of the pioneers", and indeed they were. It is to their credit that their writings so faithfully continued themes which, while not exhaustive of the group's concerns, were, nevertheless, central to the thrust of the Clark School

In an attempt to explicate several of these central concerns of the Clark School of Religious Psychology, a considerat ion of three persons is in order. They are G. Stanley Hall, the founding president of Clark University from 1889 to]920 and two of his students, James H. Leuba (professor at Bryn Mawr) and Edwin D. Starbuck (professor at Stanford). The unique interests and continuing contributions of each will be noted. Let it be said that while 1930 was the date after which religion became one of those "taboo topics" for American psychology, there were those who continued the Clark traditions. Further, in these times of renewed interest in the psychology of religion, there are those who depend heavily on the persuasions of Hall, Leuba and Starbuck.

G. STANLEY HALL

G. Stanley Hall did not distinguish himself through his writings even though his article in the Princeton Review of 1882 proved to be of seminal importance. In this article he proposed ideas which were to be later elaborated in his chapter on "The adolescent psychology of conversion" in the second volume of his monumental work on *Adolescence* (1911) and in his two volume work on *Jesus, the Christ in the light of psychology* which appeared in 1917. The themes were: first, the importance of the years of childhood, especially the years from

12 to 16; second, the epigenetic evolutionary theory that ontogeny recapitulates phylogeny postnatally in the life of the individual; and third, that adolescent conversion is natural and that the figure of Jesus Christ is the focal means through which adolescents find the meaning for their lives.

Although Hall speaks of his life as being full of "fads and crazes", these three concerns remained constant. They are grounded in the three prime values of his life: pedagogy, psychology, and religion. Psychology represents his firm commitment to the scientific study of mind. He began a trend in 1883 through an article on "The contents of children's minds" It is interesting to note that a 1903 bibliography of Hall's writing by the librarian at Clark University, L. N. Wilson, included 196 items only 13 of which pertained to religious themes. Many of these were addresses to Sunday School teachers and administrators. This evidences his persistent concern for the practical application of his ideas. This grew so much that by 1915 over 194 questionnaires had been developed by Hall and his students for the study of children's attitudes toward, anger, death, religious experience, dreams and dolls (to mention only a few).

Further, he felt that there was ample evidence for applying evolutionary epigenesis to individual development. Others had applied it to human biology (the fetus seems to go through all the biological stages of development characteristic of lower forms of life) and to culture (the history of the race has followed a parallel course of development from primitive to modern civilization). Hall's contribution was to propose that the individual, in the course of growing from infancy to adulthood, progresses through the stages which culture has gone through from ancient to contemporary times. Thus, infancy represented primitive time, childhood represented ancient time, late childhood represented the middle ages, adolescence represented the Renaissance, and adulthood represented modern times.

Hall's most lasting contribution to society at large was the impetus he gave to the child study movement. This included not only the scientific study of children but also a concern for appropriate educational procedures. He had made a rapid tour of schools in Germany, France, and England on his way back from Europe in the late 1870's. This led to his extremely popular Saturday morning lectures to the school teachers of Boston in 1880. From this point on, pedagogy was one of his consuming concerns.

His thesis regarding education of the young was two-fold: First, there was a natural developmental process inherent in human growth that should be permitted to occur without disturbing it. In this regard he was in the great tradition of Rousseau and a precursor of Benjamin Spock who advised a whole generation of mothers to not be alarmed because most behavior problems would be outgrown (cf. Hall's theory of recapitulation). Second, education was the job of presenting the right material, in the right way, and at the right time.

The emphasis was on "the right time", as one might expect from Hall's epigenetic ideas. To present certain material too early would tend to confuse the child. To present it too late would be deprivation.

This leads us to the third of Hall's values, i.e. religion. It is here that we see the clearest application of his pedagogical method. It is well known that Hall originally trained for the Christian ministry and that the president of Union Seminary, where he studied, knelt in prayer for him after hearing his senior sermon. What he lacked in preaching skill he made up for in clear ideas about Christian education. The child, according to Hall, passes through various forms of religion in development (e.g. fetishism, nature worship, magic, idolatry, etc.). Only at adolescence is the person ready for the Christian faith which, of all the world's religions, alone leads individuals toward love and altruism—the true aims of life. The task of the Sunday School teacher is to guide the child through the preparatory stages of religious growth, neither precipitating premature piety and thus innoculating the individual against a deeper and more profoundly transforming interest nor delaying natural growth and transformation to a time when it will be more difficult to initiate and complete. (Wulff, in press)

Conversion, i.e. turning attention to one's highest and best potential, was considered by Hall to be a natural event during adolescence. The figure of Christ functions to call forth the racial soul and the deep seated potential for altruism in the adolescent. Jesus incarnates all the ideal tendencies of the human race. During adolescence, the presentation of Jesus can overcome the inertia in persons and awaken in them the desire to love and resist egotism. According to Hall, psychology's task was to reveal once again the profoundly transforming meaning of Jesus and to guide educators in the manner in which it was presented so that each individual would reach his/her potential and that there would be a "radical re-evolution and reconstruction of the world."

I began this section on Hall by suggesting that his prime contribution was not in his writing. This is indeed true in spite of the seminal quality of the above-mentioned ideas. Because if we agree with Pratt (1908) that the Clark brand of the psychology of religion should be described as thoroughly inductive, data based, and introspection grounded, then it is clear that Hall's successors did much more than Hall. But this is just the point. Hall's major contribution to the Clark School was to state the major issues, stimulate a group of young graduate students to become involved in them, and provide the facilities of a prestigious university for their pursuit. Nor should it be forgotten that Hall, through his proclivity for starting things, initiated two of the publications that provided outlets for his students' research for many years, i.e. the *American Journal of Psychology* and the *American Journal of Religious*

Psychology and Education. Without doubt much of the research that followed was but an explication of the themes Hall introduced and promoted.

EDWIN D. STARBUCK

Turning next to Edwin D. Starbuck: his publishing of the first full length book in the field, *The psychology of religion: An empirical study of the growth of religious consciousness,* in 1899 was said by some (e.g. Koepp, 1920) to be the event that gave the Clark School of religious psychology an identity. To be sure, another of Hall's students, A. H. Daniels, had published an article on conversion as early as 1893, but Starbuck's book marked the first thorough attempt to apply a rigorous scientific approach to the inner religious life via the questionnaire method. Although Starbuck acknowledged the "active sympathy and encouragement" of Hall is his preface, there is some evidence that Hall was not, in fact, enthusiastic about Starbuck's book. William James (1899) wrote in a preface to the book that he, too, declined to give support to Starbuck (then one of James students) when he wanted to use the questionnaire method to investigate religious ideas. It is probably more proper to say that Starbuck went beyond both his mentors in the method he used.

    Both Hall and James were to change their minds. Hall later even claimed credit for introducing the questionnaire method. He did, but not to measure religious ideas. Starbuck did that. Hall followed with his approval after the fact. James changed his mind, too. But, as distinct from Hall, James credited Starbuck for his tenacity and admitted his own error. To quote from James preface to Starbuck's book (1899): "Many years ago Dr. Starbuck, then a student at Harvard University, tried to enlist my sympathy in his statistical inquiry into the religious ideas and experiences of the population. I fear that to his mind I rather downed the whole project with my words of faint praise. The question-circular method of collecting information had already in America reached the proportion of an insipient nuisance in psychological and pedagogical matters... I have handled and read a large proportion of his raw material. I have just finished reading the revised proof of the book. I must say that the results amply justify his own confidence in his methods and that I feel somewhat ashamed at the littleness of my own faith (Starbuck, 1899, pp. VII-VIII, Preface), James utilized a number of Starbuck's cases in his 1904 Gifford lectures which were published as *The varieties of religious experience* (1903), without doubt the single most important book in the psychology of religion in this century.

    Hall even published the only wholy negative review of Starbuck's book in one of his journals. One might wonder why Hall, who avowedly espoused the application of scientific methods to human behavior, should have been ambivalent, even antagonistic, toward the use of these methods to study religion. Perhaps he was unconscious of a tendency toward thinking of religion as unique and thus unintentionally reserved the right to think deductively rather than inductively about it. Certainly Hall's *Jesus, the Christ in the light of psychology* owes little, if anything, to Starbuck's research.

Starbuck had passed out two questionnaires (circulars, they were called) at Harvard in 1893. He established what Hall hypothesized – that adolescence was the modal time for conversion. On the basis of 1265 questionnaires answered by 1011 males and 254 females. They reported on the age of their conversions, the age of their most rapid body growth, the age of their accession to puberty, their health before and after conversion, where the conversion occurred, the effect and its permanence, as well as when it happened. Most of the material James used came from 192 biographical essays written to such questions as "What religious customs did you observe in childhood and what was your childhood like?"; "What force led you to seek a higher life?"; "What were the circumstances surrounding the conversion?"; "How did relief come?"; "What unnatural sights, sounds, and feelings accompanied it?"; "Of what did the change consist?"; "What were your feelings after the crisis?"; "How easy has it been to follow the new life?"; etc.

On the basis of this material Starbuck inferred the distinction between gradual and sudden conversions. He also, as distinct from James, provided many important details about the more mundane religious experiences of average people.

Starbuck desired to bring some conciliation into the long-standing conflict between science and religion. Like most scholars in the Clark School he felt religion to be good for society and was not antagonistic toward it. Also, like most Clark scholars he was dedicated to science. He felt that inductive methods could be applied to religion without compromising science or destroying religion.

Starbuck was a describer, not a reductionist like Leuba. To him, religion could be described but not explained by science. He suggested: "Where is there room for beauty or for God in a world whose parts are all labeled and all of whose workings are understood? Such a feeling grows out of a mistaken notion of what science can do. Science really gives a final explanation of nothing whatsoever. All it can do is bring a little coherency and consistency into the midst of that which is constantly flowing, to explore a little into the ever enlarging region of the unknown. In applying the methods of science to the study of religion most of it will always remain out of our grasp" (1899, p. 10).

Staarbuck also intended to so apply the methods of science to that heretofore "sacred domain" (religion) that some order could be brought forth and the facts of the religious life be understood. He defined the psychology of religion as that science which had as its work the carrying of "the well established methods of science into the analysis and organization of the facts of the religious consciousness and to ascertain the laws which determine its growth and character" (1899, p. 1) His cardinal contribution in this regard was to establish conversion as part of the normal crises of adolescence rather than some mysterious, deviant, pathological event.

Finally, Starbuck intended that his research to have practical implications for religious life and the reputation of religion. He stated: "Psychology will contribute to religion by increasing our ... appreciation of spiritual things ... and by leading toward greater wisdom in religious education" (1899, p. 8-9). No doubt much religious education thinking during the next decades was indebted to Starbuck. In fact, Beit-Hallahmi (1976) noted that some authors have credited the enthusiastic approbation of the churches with the decline of the psychology of religion as science. Nevertheless, Starbuck went far in accomplishing all of his goals. A recent author (Wallace, 1975) went so far as to say that his seminal work in research on conversion had not been equaled up to the present time.

JAMES H. LEUBA

James H. Leuba who was by all standards the most prolific of the Clark scholars. Because of his writing he became known as the representative of the Clark School in the second decade of this century. As a testimony to his significance, he was invited to address the Hartford Seminary Foundation conference on "The possible contributions of modern psychology to the theory and practice of religion" and the session on the psychology of religion at the International Congress of Psychology in Germany. Both these events occurred in 1926,

His contributions came in the areas of method, theory, and subject matter. In regard to method, it is of note that in between Daniels' 1895 article and Starbuck's 1899 book on conversion Leuba published the first empirical research on conversion in 1896. He utilized published accounts, interviews, and questionnaires to study the psychological conditions leading up to conversion, the crisis itself and the effects. He proposed a psychological basis for faith, justification, and pardon that ruled out supernatural intervention. This was a precursor of his thorough naturalistic reductionism about which more will be said when theory is discussed.

Further, in terms of method, Leuba pioneered in using content analysis of myths, stories and sagas from many sources to ascertain the commonalities in psychological processes underlying all religious processes. Finally, he utilized survey techniques in assessing the incidence of belief and its concomitants within the population in general and imminent persons in particular.

In 1934 Leuba published *Religious beliefs of American scientists*. This was the first of numerous studies on the incidence of belief in God, immortality, and religious practices among academicians. He restated conclusions drawn from 1912 and 1916 research to the effect that he did not "see any way to avoid the conclusion that disbelief in a personal God and in personal immortality is directly proportional to qualities making for success in the sciences in question" (1916, p. 279). Although belief among the several scientific disciplines ranged from ten to thirty-eight percent, the more imminent and mature scientists were inclined to be the more disbelieving. In comparing disciplines, psychologists were the most skeptical, while physicists, astronomers, and chemists were the least.

Beit-Hallahmi (1971) suggests that religious psychologists are less productive, confirming Leuba's proposition. Moreover, Lehman and Shriver (1968) report data confirming the difference between psychologists and natural scientists which Leuba reported. Most recently, Ragan, Malony and Beit-Hallahmi (1976) have confirmed the continuing low overall level of belief and religiosity of psychologists in comparison to the general population. Certainly in the decision to study imminent scientists, Leuba began a lively tradition.

Finally, Leuba's contribution must be discussed in terms of theory. As noted, he was the earliest and most vocal among the reductionists. Unlike Starbuck, Leuba was concerned with beliefs as well as feelings in religious experience. More importantly, unlike James who considered religious experience to be uniquely based in the reality of the unseen, Leuba felt religion was completely explainable by the same psychological processes as any other human phenomenon. It did not require a supernatural assumption. He stated about his work:

> ... it represents an effort to remove that part of the inner life (i.e. religion) from the domain of the occult in which it has too long been permitted to remain in order to incorporate it in that body of facts of which psychology takes cognizance. ...we may at, least hope to have convinced the reader that there is in principle no satisfactory reason for leaving them outside of the range of scientific research and that on the contrary they are all explicable in the same sense, to the same extent and by the same general scientific principles as any other facts of conscience (1925, p.ix).

For Leuba faith was based on need to find relief from self-dissatisfaction and a yearning for a more improved consideration (1904-5, p. 73). The movement psychologically was from fear to sublime feelings through the process of suggestibility. Beliefs are confirmations, provided by culture, for the reality of the process. No transcendent cause or power is assumed or needed. The whole process is psychophysiologically based. In fact in]897 Leuba suggested the possibility of a psychophysiology "Ethics." His was a pure reduction-ism.

Leuba went beyond explanation, however. Since religion was based on need and grounded in suggestion, he proposed that it was a cultural artifact that needed to be outgrown by mature persons. In this regard, he was not unlike Freud, Comte, Feuerbach, and Nietzsche, among others. In one of his later books, *God and man* (1934) he suggested that mankind had asked the gods to do for them what could better be done through science, especially psychological science. He boldly suggested that psychology could better handle mankind than could religion. These ideas by no means died with Leuba. Leuba, as distinct from others in the Clark School, espoused a reductionism and an antipathy toward religion that still characterizes much modern psychology.

In conclusion, the school of religious psychology centered at Clark University between 1889 and 1930 was uniquely influential in setting the themes, procedures, and conclusions of the field from that day to this. In the persons of G. Stanley Hall and his students Edwin D. Starbuck (Stanford) and James H. Leuba (Bryn Mawr) the concerns for conversion, mysticism, belief, and faith/profession were pursued with rigorous methods and scientific assumptions. Although the psychology of religion went into moratorium between 1930 and 1950, we have seen in the last twenty-five years a revival of interests that are grounded in no small measure in their work and their approach. Appreciation for their endeavors is, therefore, both a privilege and an obligation.

REFERENCES

Beit-Hallahmi , B. Curiosity, doubt and devotion: The beliefs of psychologists and the psychology of religion. Paper presented at the meeting of the Society for the Scientific Study of Religion, Chicago, Illinois, October 1971-

Beit-Hallahmi, B. Psychology of religion 1880-1930: The rise and fall of a psychological movement. *Journal of the History of the Behavioral Sciences*, 1974, 19_, 84-90.

Betts, G. *The beliefs of 500 ministers*. New York: Abingdon, 1929.

Clark, E. T. *The psychology of religious awakening*. New York: The Mac-Millan Co., 1929-

Conklin, E. S. *The psychology of religious adjustment*. New York: The MacMillan Co., 1929-

Daniels, A. H. The new life: A study in regeneration. *American Journal of Psychology*, 1893, £, 61-103-

Hall, G. S. The moral and religious training of children. *The Princeton Review*, 1882, 9_, 26-48.

Hall, G. S. The contents of children's minds. *The Princeton Review*, 1883, JJ_, 272-294.

Hall, G. S. *Adolescence: Its psychology and its relations to physiology, anthropology, sociology, sex, crime, religion, and education.(2 vols.).* New York: D. Appleton, 1904.

Hall, G. S. *Jesus, the Christ, in the light of psychology (2 vols.).* London: George Allen & Unwin, Ltd., 1917.

Hiltner, S. The psychological understanding of religion. *Crozer Quarterly*, 1947, 24_, 3-36.

James, W. Preface. In E. D. Starbuck, *The psychology of religion: An empirical study of the growth of religious consciousness.* New York: Charles Scribners, 1899.

James, W. *The varieties of religious experience.* New York: Longmans, Green and Co., 1903-

Koepp, W. *Einfuhrung in das Studium der Religionspsychologie.* Tubingen: J. C. B. Mohr (Paul Siebeck), 1920.

Lehman, E. C., & Shriver, D. W., Jr. Academic discipline as predictive of faculty religiosity. *Social Forces*, 1968, 47, 171-182.

Leuba, J. H. The psychology of religious phenomena: Conversion. *American Journal of Psychology.* 1896, 7, 309~385.

Leuba, J. H. Faith. *American Journal of Religious Psychology and Education*, 1904, 1, 155-167."

Leuba, J. H. *A psychological study of religion: Its origins, function and future.* New York: The MacMillan Co., 1912.

Leuba, J. H. *The belief in God and immortality.* Chicago: Open Court, 1916.

Leuba, J. H. *The psychology of religious mysticism.* New York: Harcourt, Brace & Co., 1925-

Leuba, J. H. *God or man? A study of the value of God to man.* New York: Henry Holt, 1934.(a)

Leuba, J. H. The religious beliefs of American scientists. *Harpers*, 1934, 169. 291-300. (b)

Pratt, J. B. The psychology of religion. *Harvard Theological Review*, 1908, 1, 435-454.

Ragan, C. , Malony, H. N., & Beit-Hallahmi, B. Psychologists and religion: Professional factors related to personal religiosity. In Overcoming psychology's estrangement from religious phenomena. Symposium presented at the meeting of the American Psychological Association, Washington, D. C., September 1976.

Selbie, W. B. *The psychology of religion.* London: Oxford University Press, 1924.

Starbuck, E. D. *The psychology of religion: An empirical Study of the religious consciousness.* New York: Charles Scribner's Sons, 1899.

Strunk, O., Jr. *Readings in the psychology of religion.* New York: Abingdon Press, 1954.

Wallace, R. A. A model of change of religious affiliation. *Journal for the Scientific Study of Religion*, 1975, 4, 345-355.

Wilson, L. N. Bibliography of the published writings of President G. Stanley Hall. *American Journal of Psychology*, 1903, 14, 417-421.

Wulff, D. It. *Psychological perspectives on religion: An historical introduction.* Monterey, California: Brooks Cole Publishing Co., in press.

TWELVE

Conversion As Psycholinguistic Labeling: A New Model for Church Ministry

I write as a psychologist, not as a theologian or as a pastor. Yet, I would not want to be misunderstood. I strongly affirm the truth that "...in Christ, God was reconciling the world unto himself..." (2 Cor. 5:19, NRSV) and that the essence of Christian conversion can be summed up in Paul's conclusion that "... if anyone is in Christ, there is a new creation..." (2 Cor. 5: 17a, NRSV). However, I think it is very helpful for us to stand back and look more closely at the organism in whom conversion occurs, namely the *human being*. And that is where psychology comes in for psychology is the discipline that defines itself as *the study of human behavior*. And conversion is, at the least, a human behavior. So here goes.

My intent is to offer *psycholinguistic labeling* as a psychological definition of conversion. I claim that re-conceiving conversion from this point of view could possibly provide pastors a clearer understanding of what they seek when they engage in evangelism.

WORDS ARE IMPORTANT

When Paul asks in Romans 8:31a "What, then, are we to say about these things?" (NRSV) he was anticipating psychologist David Myers' statement that "The most tangible indication of our thinking power is language" (Myers, 1972, p. 242). Myers goes on to quote famous linguist Norm Chomsky's conclusion, shared by many, that "When we study human language we are approaching what some might call the 'human essence'." Words are important. *Labeling* (i.e. putting into *words*) the events of our lives is probably the most unique and decisive thing we human beings do. As far as we know we are the only creatures that have this ability to put our experiences into words.

Psycholinguistics is the study of how this labeling, these words, determine who we see ourselves to be (i.e. our *psyches*, our *self perceptions*). Words are important. In a essay I once wrote on religious experience (1981), I used the experience of Samuel (1 Sam 3:1ff) to illustrate this point. Samuel was tending the oil in the temple when he heard a voice call his name. Several times Samuel went to the priest thinking that it was Eli who had called him. Finally, Eli had the insight that it was God who was calling Samuel's name. He tells Samuel to say "Speak Lord, your servant hears," when next he hears a voice calling his name. After that encounter with God, Samuel's whole self-understanding changed. Under the authority of that experience, Samuel became the first great judge of Israel. He put words to the experience and it changed his life.

Whatever else we Christians sense is happening in conversion, at the very least, words have been put to the experience. As with Samuel, the words converts use to speak about what is happening changes their lives. In technical jargon, *psycholinguistic labeling* had occurred. This is the thesis I would like to develop.

I turn next to a clarification of the types of events that result in conversions. Distinguishing between "spirituality" and "religion" will be important when we consider further the ways converts speak about their experiences.

DEFINITIONS OF "SPIRITUALITY" AND "RELIGION"

We often hear people say they are spiritual but not religious. In my opinion, when they make such a statement, usually they are unclear about what they mean. Those who distinguish between spirituality and religion are making a valid discrimination, however, the difference is not apparent or easy to see. "Spirituality" is a human capacity or ability while "religion" is what results when that capacity is expressed. Let me explain what I mean.

It used to be said that "Everybody is religious." By this was meant that everybody put their faith in something. Whatever persons put their faith in was their religion – be it in the Los Angeles Dodgers, in the newest dress fashion, or in Jesus Christ. I think to call a baseball team or a current fashion a person's "religion" is insulting. To begin with, devotees to these interests would never *admit* that either of these was their religion. And in the second place, those of us who might find comfort in saying everybody had a religion would be demeaning the meaning of *religion.*

"Religion" is best defined as "the words we use to understand and explain *spiritual experiences* we have had." Religion has little to do with the interest we have in mundane affairs such as baseball games or clothes –no matter how strong such interests might be.

Of course, my definition italicized, but did not define, the words *spir-*

itual experiences. Therein lies the key to understanding "religion" as distinct from "spirituality." Spiritual experiences are those events during where we exercise our spirituality – the human capacity to relate to transempirical reality. "Transempirical reality" is that reality that exists above and beyond the reality human beings experience on a day-to-day basis through the five senses of touch, sight, smell, taste, and hearing. Personally, I well remember the event at age 16 when I experienced "transempirical reality" for the first time in my life. While walking away from a very moving service of evening worship at a summer camp, I suddenly had a sense that God was calling me into full time Christian service. Although goose pimples came over me, the experience was not accompanied by a an actual voice that I heard, Yet, the sense of reality was firm. I knew I had been summoned and I had to respond.

Many people would call this experience "supernatural" rather than "transempirical." I like the latter term because it clearly distinguishes the event from the reality of everyday where "empirical" describes the contact we experience through the five senses. While the experience might not be as vivid as mine, almost all the Christians I know would attest to some similar events in their lives.

This leads to my conviction that what is true of "religion" is likewise true of "spirituality." Not everybody is spiritual, just as not everybody is religious. Spirituality is a *capacity*; it is not an compelling instinct. Everybody is able to experience transempirical reality, but not everybody does. We call folk who never express their spirituality as "secular." We Christians would like every secular person to become a spiritual person. We will always work toward that through our evangelistic efforts. But we are never fully successful. This is what is meant by saying "spirituality is a capacity, or ability, but is not a compulsion nor is it an instinct that everybody expresses." Jesus spoke of this secular tendency in his parable of the seeds and the sower In Matthew 13 where the cares of the world block receipt of the Word. Jesus also noted how hard it was for the rich to enter the kingdom of God (Mark 10:24).

When people express their spirituality we say that they have *spiritual experiences*. They have related to transempirical reality. I agree with the psychologist, Benjamin BeithHallahmi (1995) in his contention that these transempirical experiences are the basic ingredients of what we will call "religion." When persons put words to their spiritual experiences, they have become *religious*. Religion could, therefore, be defined as "a set of words which explain spiritual experiences." It matters little whether these words are the words of Christian orthodoxy, the words of native Indian cosmology, the words of new age gurus, or the words of Buddhistic chants. Wherever words are put to better understand transempirical experiences, there you have a religion.

Religion has often been understood as that which binds life together into a meaningful whole. This understanding fits the function of religion as the words which explain spiritual (transempirical) experience because in almost every case these experiences bring order and wholeness to life. This brings us full-circle to my contention that *conversion is psycholinguistic labeling*. The words, or labels, that converts use to talk about their spiritual experiences, i.e. their religion, bring order and meaning to their self understandings, i.e. their psyches. Conversion could be conceived as life based on the religious language one has adopted to explain the transformation that occurred when one had a spiritual experience.

In the final section of this essay I will discuss the nature of the religious language that underlies conversion.

ALL SPEECH IS *PERSUASIVE*

In the past, it was thought that the words we speak were of two basic types: "descriptive" and "persuasive." Whereas persuasive speech was intended to influence or change the environment, descriptive speech was considered to be expressive of inner feelings and thoughts. Currently, most scholars think this distinction is incorrect. They think that all speech is *persuasive* – i.e. intended to modify or change reality. I agree.

In applying this contention about all speech being persuasive to religion, this means that the distinction often made between *confessional* language and *apologetic* language is not valid. Confessional language, such as when persons state "I have accepted Jesus as my Savior and Lord," is similar to what linguists formerly used to call "descriptive" speech – i.e. words simply telling what had occurred. Apologetic language, such as when persons assert "Accept the Lord Jesus Christ and you will be saved," is similar to what linguists call "persuasive" speech – i.e. words clearly intended to result in change in peoples' lives.

If my claim about all language being *persuasive* is correct, we should say that all religious speech is *apologetic*. But it might be asked, "How can this be? When a person confesses they have been converted, aren't they just *describing* an event? In what way can their words be construed as intending to change their environment.?" The issue is this: speaking about spiritual experience (i.e. becoming religious) is never simply an individual experience. It is always social. There is no such thing as *solitary* religion. When persons speak about what has happened to them in their spiritual experiences they do so expecting to be heard, accepted, confirmed and affirmed. The language of new converts is apologetic because converts claim they have new motives, new insights, new interests, and new behaviors that are to be acknowledged by others.

In his classic book *The Varieties of Religious Experience* (1902) one of the converts William James writes about claimed that all the world looked new to him; even his pigs and horses. This farmer expected that the farm animals would continue to look different and that other farmers would tolerate and understand his claims on the basis of what he said had happened to him. A friend of mine told me about a woman who fell down on the floor in response to being moved by the Holy Spirit in a worship service he was attending with his grandmother. He thought the woman had died and wondered why no one rushed to help her. Only later did he learn there was a set of expectations known to everyone about what had happened. The woman knew her fainting would be tolerated and that she would be allowed to experience God in this way without interference. She also knew that responding in this way would increase her status and acceptance in the group because it would indicate a significant depth to her religious experience.

This truth was clearly confirmed recently in the ruling of the Ninth Circuit Court of Appeals that a speech to be given to the graduating class of a high school in the San Francisco area was intended to proselytize in spite of the claim by the student that he was merely expressing his faith. The non-permitted speech included a lengthy quote from the Bible and the statement that eternal life through Jesus was a gift from God. The student later admitted he had a desire for fellow grads to develop a personal relationship with God through faith in Christ – a relationship he felt would better their lives.

These illustrations validate my claim that all religious speech is persuasive. It is never simply confessional; it is always apologetic. It is intended to have an effect on the environment as well as within the person. Religious speech is no different from language in general. It is always persuasive.

This assertion about the apologetic nature of religious speech is not meant to question the sincerity of those who claim otherwise. Nor is it meant to assert the true motive in our confessions of faith are not what we claim. It is to assert that human behavior is always social. It involves others. And speech is the way humans confirm their associations with those around them, receive support for their behavior, and adopt life meanings that determine their self perceptions.

That is why I claim that the words that result from conversion are *psycho*linguistic labelings. They are the words we speak to change our self understandings and to associate ourselves with others who are like minded. Our *psyches* or our *selves* are the results of the experiences we have and the words we use to confirm their impact on our lives. We may be born with a nature, but our *psyches* or *selves* are created through the events of our personal histories.

Conclusion

This essay has contended that a better understanding of what happens to human beings who are converted will provide new insights for those who engage in evangelism. From a psychological point of view, I claim that what we are hoping to attain in such efforts is to provide new words which will function within converts to change their lives. That is why I have reconceived conversion as *psycholinguistic labeling.*

In effect, what we do when we attempt to evangelize others is a twofold process: First, we would hope to induce persons to express their capacity to engage in spiritual experiences (i.e. relate to the transempirical reality; that reality we have called God Almighty, revealed to us in Jesus Christ); Second, we would stay with them in this experience and provide them the words to use to describe the impact of what has happened (i.e. Christ has saved you from your sin and given you a new way to live). Lastly, we confirm our own faith by seeking to include others in our associations. This, for the Christian evangel is *psycholinguistic labeling* at its best.

A final caution is in order. In the modern world, the Christian faith is not the only game in town. In modern culture, there are many marketers of alternative ways to for people to express their spiritual capacities. Spiritual experiences are available on every television screen. If we believe, as I think we do, that the Christian words we use are the BEST game in town, it behooves us to be as clear as we can be about the psychological dynamics involved in conversion and commit ourselves to apply these insights ruthlessly in the methods we use. We should never make the mistake of assuming that our gospel will sell itself. It won't. My hope would be that understanding conversion as *psycholinguistic labeling* will provide new insights for gospel task of evangelizing the world for Christ..

References

Beit-Hallahmi, B. (1995). Religion as art and identity. In H. N. Malony, Editor *Pspychology of religion: Personalities, problems, possibilities*, pp. 171-188. Pasadena, CA: Integration Press.

James, W. (1902). *Varieties of religious exerience.* NY: Longmans, Green.

Malony, H. N. (1985). An S-O-R model of religious experience. In E.B. Brown, Editor, *Advances in the psychology of religion*, pp. 113-126. Oxford, England: Pergamon Press.

Myers, D.G. (1993). *Exploring psychology, Second Edition.* NY: Worth Publishers.

THIRTEEN

Good, Better, Best: Varieties of Spiritual Expression in a Postmodern World

Shortly after the middle of the last century, Thomas Altizer proclaimed "God is Dead" (Altizer & Hamilton, 1966). Altizer was simply parroting the outcome that Sigmund Freud had predicted a quarter-century earlier in his *The Future of an Illusion* (1928). Yet in this new century, the book *Why God Won't Go Away* (Newberg & d'Auila, 2001) has been published. This newest volume concludes that, in the words of Mark Twain, the death of God has been "greatly exaggerated." Billed as a book on the "neuropsychology of belief," the authors of *Why God Won't Go Away* propose that human beings are hard-wired in their cerebellums to have spiritual experiences. They have identified the human brain's "spirituality circuit." When people are having spiritual experiences a bundle of neurons light up in the superior parietal lobe at the back of the brain.

Yes, God is here to stay because we are here to stay and we have been so created that spiritual experience is possible and probable. As Saint Augustine stated so truthfully long before the days of modern science, "Thou has made us for thyself, and our hearts are restless till they find their rest in thee." (Warren, 1963, 1.1). It is this conviction that provides the foundation for my address tonight entitled *Good, Better, Best: Varieties of Spiritual Expression in a Postmodern World.*

My intent is to build on the idea that there is a physiological base for spiritual experience in three ways.

First, I will attempt to expand a bit on this idea by comparing the terms *spiritual experience* and *spiritual expression*. It is my conviction that although spiritual *experiences* may be similar, spiritual *expressions* may differ widely from person to person.

Second, I will challenge Christians who are *associated in psychological studies* to consider the truths that our clients who live in this post modern world may come to us from a variety of spiritually *expressive* backgrounds.

Third, I will encourage us to become a *spiritual mechanics* who are pre-pared to work with all these other-than-traditional, even other-than-Christian, expressions of spirituality even though we may consider some of them deficient and even heretical. This is my solution to the problem clinicians have in deal-ing with the Good, the Better, and the Best religious faiths that our clients bring to us. This is my cryptic way of saying, most of the time it might be better for us to consider ourselves as "mechanics" who work with all types of cars rather than salesmen/or women who only represent one brand.

CONTRASTING SPIRITUAL *EXPERIENCE* WITH SPIRITUAL *EXPRESSION*

"I am spiritual but I am not religious." Would you not agree that this is a very common postmodern, 21st century, politically correct way of speaking these days? Yes, spirituality is in and religion is out. Note how the book titles have changed: Lovinger's (1984) *Working with Religious Issues in Therapy* has given way to Richard's and Bergin's (1997) *A Spiritual Strategy for Counseling and Psychotherapy*.

Of course, in itself, this discomfort with institutional religion is nothing new. Karl Barth contrasted *faith* with *religiousness* and Martin Luther com-pared the *visible* with the *invisible* church. And the respectable term *religiosity* evoked such disdain by the mid-20th century that Gordon Allport designed a scale to measure *Intrinsic* (individual, internal) over *Extrinsic* (church related, dogmatic) religious "orientation."

However, our preference for speaking of spirituality over religion may be based on every new generation's desire to tinker with the language and put its stamp on reality. Frank Sinatra put it well when he spoke of this urge in each of us when he said, "I did it my way!" Spirituality is just our way of talking.

I suspect there may be a serious insight into reality reflected in our use of the word *spirituality*. Surely, when we speak of spirituality it means more than simply putting a new twist on old ideas, although I must admit that sometimes I suspect this is all we are doing. I do think we need to be clear what we mean when we use the word, and I should like to offer my definition of the term. I confess that it may not satisfy some of you. It comes out of the theorizing Warren Brown, Nancey Murphy and I (1998) did in our book *Whatever Happened to the Soul? Scientific and Theological Portraits of Human Nature* and it is compatible with what I think is implied in the book entitled *Why God Won't Go Away*.

So, here goes a definition of spirituality: *Spirituality is the innate capac-ity of the human being to relate to transcendent reality.* Three of these words have a technical meaning: innate, capacity, and transcendent.

The first word: *Innate*. Spirituality is an *innate* capacity. The underlying idea has been labeled *non-reductive physicalism* (Brown, Murphy, & Malony, 1998). The human being is a body; not a body to which a soul is added. That is a fancy way of saying, we believe that spirituality is an inherent capacity of creaturehood. It comes with the physiological territory; it is not some ethereal, non-substantive, or supernatural addition to being human; it is there in the genes; it is part of the neuropsychology of the person.

Nothing has happened to what we use to call *the soul*; it is where it has always been – deep inside us as an innate capacity to relate to transcendent reality. Maybe we could finally say that the question of the soul's location has been answered – the soul is located in the brain. Theologically, I think this is what Augustine meant by *the restless heart*. Others have called it the *spark of the divine*. Spirituality is innate. It is built in.

This leads to the second word: *capacity*. Spirituality is an innate *capacity*. Spirituality is not an *instinct*, else we would all exercise it and express it in exactly the same way. Spirituality is not even a *basic drive* else everybody would have spiritual experiences, but they do not. It is not like hunger. Everybody must eat. They do not have to have spiritual experience. Spirituality is a capacity, an ability. Spirituality is a potentiality for everyone; although spirituality is not a guarantee for anyone. It lies dormant in us and in all our clients. Not our denial, nor our distraction, nor our depravity can annihilate spirituality. It remains deep within our brains as a muscle waiting to be exercised; like a computer program waiting for a mouse click.

Finally, the third word in my definition: *transcendent*. Spirituality is the innate capacity to relate to transcendent reality. Spirituality can become a skill and an interest, but it starts as a capacity or a possibility; a potential to relate to the *transcendent*. Just as each creature possesses the capacities to smell, hear, feel, taste, and see, they also possess the capacity to relate to the transcendent. It is a sixth sense.

Some have called the transcendent the *supernatural*—a reality above and beyond that which can be seen, heard, felt, tasted, and smelled. In their book, Newberg and d'Aquila (2001) say they have no way to determine whether the brain is *causing* the spiritual experiences or is *perceiving* a spiritual reality. Our faith affirms the latter; we are *perceiving* a spiritual reality – God who has come to us in Jesus Christ and who pursues us throughout the days of our lives. However, I admire their caution. That is all science can do: describe the experience of relating to transcendent reality. Science cannot, even with its most refined instruments, define that reality. Describing that reality is left to *faith* and that is where the difference between spiritual experience and spiritual expression comes in.

We have now arrived at the heart of this first part of what I have to say:

If spirituality is the innate capacity to relate to transcendent reality, then piritual *experience* is the act of doing that; *relating* to transcendent experience. And spiritual *expression* is, however, the act of labeling, conceptualizing, responding to that act of *relating* within some meaningful structure. Allow me to repeat my conviction that spiritual *experience* is the act of relating to transcendent reality while spiritual *expression* is the act of responding to that relationship with cognitive labels or linguistic structures.

Let me give you a biblical example of this difference between spiritual *experience* and spiritual *expression*. Consider the example of the boy Samuel who was a helper to Eli, priest in the temple at Jerusalem (1 Samuel 3: 1-10): Now the boy Samuel was ministering to the Lord under Eli. The word of the Lord was rare in those days; visions were not widespread.

At that time Eli, whose eyesight had begun to grow dim so that he could not see, was lying down in his room: that lamp of God had not yet gone out, and Samuel was lying down in the temple of the Lord, where the ark of God was. Then the Lord called, "Samuel! Samuel!" And he said, "Here I am!" And ran to Eli, and said, "Here I am, for you called me." But he said, "I did not call; lie down again." So he went and lay down. The Lord called again, "Samuel! Samuel!" Samuel got up and went to Eli, and said, "Here I am, for you called me." But he said, "I did not call you, my son; lie down again." Now Samuel did not yet know the Lord, and the word of the Lord had not yet been revealed to him. The Lord called Samuel a third time. And he got up and went to Eli and said, "Here I am, for a you called me." Then Eli perceived that the Lord was calling the boy. Therefore Eli said to Samuel, "Go, lie down; and if he calls you, you shall say, 'Speak, Lord, for your servant is listening.'" So Samuel went and lay down in his place.

Now the Lord came and stood there, calling as before, "Samuel! Samuel!" And Samuel said, "Speak, for your servant is listening."

Samuel had a spiritual *experience*. He heard a supernatural, transcendent sound. He heard something Eli did not hear. The sound of his name came from a transcendent, supernatural, trans-empirical reality. He did not realize it at first, but he acknowledged it at last. With Eli's direction, he returned to his bed, lay down, and waited for the next sound of his name. He exercised his capacity to relate to transcendent reality.

Then, Samuel engaged in spiritual *expression*. He followed Eli's recommendation of labeling who it was that was speaking his name. It was Almighty God. When the sound came again Samuel said, "Speak, Lord, your servant is listening." Out of all the possibilities he had, Samuel chose one – the God of Abraham, Isaac, Jacob and Hannah his mother. It was the sound of the voice of *that* God that Samuel heard and to which he responded, "Speak, Lord, I am listening."

The point is this: There is one spiritual *experience*; but there are can be a variety of spiritual *expressions*. Spiritual experience is the experience of relating to transcendent reality while spiritual expression is the conceiving or labeling of that experience within some meaningful cognitive structure. Spiritual *expression* can vary. Eli could have told Samuel that the sound he heard was a ghost of his dead grandfather or the gods of the Midianites. Instead he told him it was Jehovah, the God of the Hebrews, who was speaking.

From Samuel's day to the present there have always been a variety of spiritual expressions even though, from an innate physiological, cerebral point of view, there may be only one kind of spiritual experience. That is the reason, Kenneth Woodward (2001), the religion editor of *Newsweek*, which reported the publication of the book *Why God Won't Go Away*, correctly stated "Faith is more than feeling." Faith is *spiritual expression* the putting of words and ideas to the feelings associated with spiritual *experience*. Spiritual *experience* always leads to spiritual *expression*.

VARIETIES OF SPIRITUAL EXPRESSIONS

I want to challenge Christian counselors to at least consider the importance of this fact: Those who come to us for help may bring with them a variety of spiritual *expressions* – meaning a variety of interpretations of their spiritual experiences. Although William James knew this well when he wrote in 1904 his famous *Varieties of Religious Experience* the fact is written in spades by such contemporary authors as Princeton sociologist Robert Wuthnow. In his book After Heaven: Spirituality in America Since the 1950s, Wuthnow (1998) notes that today many people piece their faith together like a *patchwork quilt*. Of course, this has always been true, but we Christian counselors often forget this when we talk about integrating spirituality into our counseling. Not every body is Christian, not by a long shot. Consider the possibility that those who come for help might have interpreted their spiritual experience in the following expressive ways:

As *Astrologers*, they may read their horoscopes daily, assuming their lives are influenced by the transcendent reality of the movement of the stars;

As *Scientologists*, they may feel that "picking up the cans" in an Auditing session is their contact with the transcendent reality of their *clear*, or *free from contaminated* selves;

As *Reincarnationists*, they may seek insights into the transcendent reality of how their past lives are determining their daily experiences;

As *Charismatics*, they may express themselves daily in a glossolalic language that allows them to feel God is speaking through them in a prayer language;

As *Buddhists*, they may practice Zen rituals that reduce stress and tension and move them toward a transcendent experience of enlightenment;

As *Social Activists*, they may feel most alive and in touch with transcendent meaning when they are picketing for an increase in the minimum wage or fair trade practices;

As members of the *Church Universal and Triumphant*, they may engage in reading out-loud the dictations of their leader, Clare Prophet, as fast as they can in an effort to incorporate and digest the transcendent reality of the wise men whose ageless teachings have been given to her in trance;

As *Spiritualists*, they may seek weekly readings from a medium to keep in contact with the dead who live in a transcendent reality of wisdom and truth;

As *Deliverance believers*, they may claim healings and freedom from oppression as proof of the transcendent power available for daily life;

As *New Age devotees*, they may have had out-of-body and divine light experiences which have revealed to them the transcendent reality of wholeness;

As *Muslims*, they may kneel and pray five times daily in an effort to keep contact with the transcendent reality of Allah their God;

As *Catholics*, they may have attended Mass daily and felt in direct contact with divine transcendence as they imbibed the bread and wine;

As *Bible students* they may feel closest to God when they are reading and reflecting on scriptures which tell of a transcendent order and the acts of God.

The list could go on and on in an amazing "patchwork quilt" of combinations which might even incorporate several of these options. Wuthnow (1999) suggests that we live in an age of *seekers* where "Spirituality has become a vastly complex quest in which each person seeks his or her own way" (p. 4).

It could even be true of each of us, for as Carl Jung reportedly said, "People not only have their Gods, they make their Gods." It might even be said that spiritual *experience* compulsively results in spiritual *expression*. I am convinced this is even true of us who call ourselves *Christian*. The earliest creed symbolized by the fish is probably still the only creed which would unite us. We would likely all agree that we have faith in "Jesus, Son of God, Saviour," but that is about all. Likely, there are more differences within our individual churches than there are between our denominations. And even within those individual churches there may be a great variety of religious expressions.

So, this is the *Spiritual Expressive reality* of the postmodern world. It is a mix and match world of amazing pluralism. While variety in spiritual expressiveness is an ageless truth, it has become uniquely evident in a time when relativism and cultural diversity are touted as ideals. As Brenda Brasher (2001) confirms, the internet has made this truth an even more explosive reality. In her book, *Give Me That On-line Religion* she asserts that there is a new *cyber-spirituality* in which mix-and-match faiths have come into being at the click of a mouse.

As faithing Christians we may not like this and, definitely, we may think that some *expressions* are better than others. We even may be convinced that one *expression* is not only better but best. But in the workaday world of the average clinician we deal with the less-than-best again and again in the options we have for treatment and the skills of problem solving we find in our clients. The spiritual expressions we have to work with are no exception. While we may be firmly convinced that the *Christian interpretation* of spiritual experience is the best, it may turn out to be the exception to the rule in our day to day clinical work. What to do in the face of this fact is what I want to address in my final thoughts.

BEING A MECHANIC, RATHER THAN A SALES CLERK

I used to be a chaplain in a mental hospital. Again and again, whenever a patient said anything religious, the psychiatrists would refer them to me. As counselors who are known for their religious concerns, I suspect that this will happen to many of us, also. We will be known in our communities as those who know what to do with clients who claim to be spiritual or religious. As such, we will be increasingly exposed to all the varieties of religious expression I mentioned earlier and even more.

When you take a religious history – as I encourage you to do on every client – you may find an immense variety of spiritual expressions. Keeping in mind the distinction I have made between spiritual *experience* and religious *expression*, I predict we will wonder how to integrate our faith and our practice in the face of the amazing diversity we will observe.

I encourage you to become a *spiritual mechanic*. I have often advised my students that this is where most of us live. We are mechanics, not sales clerks. Our job is to get the car back on the road; the person back into reality; the marriage back into intimacy; the family back into relating. Our basic concern is similar to auto mechanics. They are not concerned about where the car has been or where it will be going once it leaves the shop. Nor do we. We are concerned with repair, not transformation; restoration, not conversion – as much as we would like to think otherwise. While we, like any salesperson who represents a given brand, may think that our Christian faith is the best, our basic task is to get the person back on the road of life utilizing the faith they bring with them. Our contract is to get the car to run again. Clients do not expect us to convince them of a new form of spiritual *expression* (i.e. the *Christian* faith). Similarly, they do not expect a car mechanic to sell them a new automobile. As the old saying goes, "If it ain't broke, don't fix it." That is what it means to be a mechanic.

I encourage you to become facile in dealing with religion in general and to become adept at handling the variety of spiritual expressions brought to you in counseling. In those days when most of the people who came to us were Christians, I used to tell my students to read *The Handbook of Denominations in the United States* (Mead, 1965). Today I recommend they read Harold Koenig's (1998) *Handbook of Religion and Mental Mealth* which has chapters on Jewish, Muslim, Buddhist, and Hindu points of view in addition to a variety of Christian alternatives. The variety you may face may be even greater.

You can become a *methodological* Jew, Muslin, Buddhist, Hindu, Spiritualist, Scientologist, Christian Scientist even if you do not become an *ontological* Jew, Muslin, Buddhist, Hindu, Spiritualist, Scientologist, or Christian Scientist—to name only a few of the alternatives that may present themselves to you. I once did this with exorcism or deliverance. A woman came to me for help in getting release from 12 demons she felt took possession of her body every afternoon. Personally, I had become convinced that most demons existed in people's minds not outside them. For many weeks I tried to help her reinterpret her symptoms in terms of past traumas, compulsive tendencies, environmental circumstances, family dynamics, etc. – all to no avail. She wanted to be exorcised. I decided to try it. I studied up on exorcist methods and put them into practice. They worked. One session, we had all twelve of demons out of her body about a foot above her head. I then instructed her to let the Holy Spirit fill her life. She tried but the demons slipped in and crowded out the Holy Spirit. I failed. Now before you conclude it was because I did not really believe, let me tell you the sequel to the story. I referred her to a deliverance counselor who did believe. He also failed to help her.

I think it is possible to practice methods in which you do not believe. In one of the classical studies of the effects of Christian counseling, Rebecca Propst (1988) compared cognitive behavior therapy that utilized Christian content with cognitive behavior therapy that did not. She found that even secular counselors who were not religious but agreed to use Christian resources had greater success than did those who did not use them. Of course, the greatest success was with those who believed in what they were doing, but the difference over the non-believing-but-methodologically-Christian counselors was not significant. It can be done.

I hope I have convinced you that there is a difference between spiritual *experience* and spiritual *expression*. I hope you agree that while the capacity for spiritual experience is written into our physiology, the expressions of spirituality are many and varied. As Kenneth Woodward (2001), the religion editor of *Newsweek* wrote, "faith is (indeed) more than feeling." I hope you will be committed to being a spiritual mechanic more than a sales clerk in your daily work with religious clients. Your time is limited and your prime goal should be helping persons make it in the social reality in which they choose to life. The therapeutic contract does not include converting clients to a spiritual expression; a faith – even a faith that you have found to be not only Good, but Better, and even Best.

A final caveat: Even if you fully agree with me, you should ask the question "What if my client has no faith at all or affirms a type of spiritual expression that is destructive or non-functional?" In a recent study of the role of religion among the persistently mentally ill, we found a small percent of persons reported their religious faith did not exist, or, if it did, did not sustain them in their illness and, even, deepened their pain (Tepper, Rogers, Coleman, & Malony, 2001). Here is where my model needs a ninety degree correction and perceptive re-reflection.

If you are convinced that your Christian faith and your form of spiritual expression would be healing and helpful, you have a therapeutic responsibility to suggest this to your client as quickly as you would suggest a possible change in new forms of self assertion, anxiety reduction, dynamic introspection, interpersonal reconciliation, or family system readjustment. If you did not offer this option of a new form of spiritual expression in a situation where faith does not function or does not exist, you would be therapeutically irresponsible.

It is in these conditions that I think the spiritual mechanic model must give way to the role of spiritual salesperson – without apology. But that is for another address, and I simply leave you with the possibility that such may be required. And I would not have you doubt that I remain fully convinced of the preeminent truth that God was in Christ reconciling the world unto himself (2 Cor. 5:19) and the value that such a *Christian* faith has for everyday life. There is a Good, a Better, and a Best!—and the *Christian* faith is best.

REFERENCES

Begley, S. (2001, May). Religion and the brain: How we are wired for Spirituality. *Newsweek*, 50-56.

Altizer, T. J. & Hamilton, W. (1966). *Radical theology and the death of God.* Indianapolis, IN: Bobbs Merrill.

Brasher, B. (2001). *Give me that online religion.* San Fransico: Jossey Bass.

Brown, W.S., Murphy, N. & Malony, H.N. (Eds.). (1998). *Whatever happened to the soul? Scientific and theological portraits of human nature.* Minneapolis, MN: Fortress Press.

Freud, S. (1928). *The future of an Illusion.* New York: Liveright Publishing Company.

Koenig, H.G. (1998). *Handbook of religion and mental health.* New York: Academia Press.

Lovinger, R. J. (1984). *Working with religious issues in therapy.* New York: Jason Aronson, Inc.

Mead, F. S. (1965). *Handbook of denominations in the United States.* Nashville, TN: Abingdon Press.

Newberg, A. & d'Aquila, E. (2001). *Why God won't go away.* New York: Ballantine.

Propst, L. R. (1988). *Psychotherapy in a religious framework: Spirituality in the emotional healing process.* New York: Human Sciences Press.

Richards, P.S. & Bergin, A. (1997). *A spiritual strategy for counseling and psychotherapy.* Washington, DC: The American Psychological Association.

Tepper, L., Rogers, S.A., Coleman, E.M., & Malony, H.N. (2001). The prevalence of religious coping among persons with persistent mental illness. *Psychiatric Services, 52(5),* 660-665.

Wodward, K.L. (2001, May). Faith is more than feeling. *Newsweek, 58.*

Wuthnow, R. (1998). *After heaven: Spirituality in America since the 1950s.* Berkeley, CA: University of California Press.

Wuthnow, R. (1999, March). Spirituality in American since the 1950s. *Theology News and Notes,* 4-6.

FOURTEEN

Religion as Interest, Rather than Instinct

(or, Why Religion Has Such Little Affect on Mental Health)

In a survey of the literature, Batson, Schroenrade, and Ventis (1993) analyzed 197 studies of the relationship between religion and mental health. Summarizing the data over seven definitions of mental health they concluded that the relationships appeared to be mixed but tending toward the negative. They stated, "Forty-seven findings are of a negative relationship; thirty-seven are of a positive relationship, and thirty-one show no clear relationship" (p. 240).

Noting that many of the associations were very weak, these reviewers concluded that religion was accounting for less than 5 percent of the variance in mental health either positively or negatively! Since their criteria included such variables as absence of mental illness, appropriate social behavior, freedom from worry and guilt, personal competence and control, self-acceptance or self-actualization, personality unification and organization, and open-mindedness and flexibility, it would seem that little, if any, aspect of mental health was being affected by religion.

Were religion a universal, instinctual life-response with survival value, one would expect more impact on life-adjustment than this, unless, as Beit-Hallahmi (1991) concluded, religion is not an instinct, but an interest. Thus, according to him, religion serves an aesthetic option rather than a instinctual necessity.

In agreement with Beit-Hallahlmi , the thesis of this essay, therefore, is that one of the ways the mixed nature of these data can be better understood is to reconceptualize religion as an social interest rather than an survival instinct. Once reconstrued in this manner, religion can then be studied as one among many options available to persons for handling the stress and boredom of life. This assumption avoids the problematic assumption that religion is the expression of humans' basic spiritual natures. Before discussing the "religion as interest" alternative, I will discuss the more traditional "religion as instinct" option.

RELIGION AS INSTINCT

St. Augustine' famous lines attest to the presumption that religion is instinctual. He said, "Thou hast made us for thyself, Oh Lord, and our hearts are restless until they find their rest in Thee." Of course, most have interpreted Augustine as making an apologetic claim that the Christian faith was the true answer to restless hearts, and that may well have been his intention. However, the syntax of his statement is a powerful affirmation that human beings are biologically created to seek God whether they know it or not. They are embodied with a basic impulse to be religious. They have a soul, as well as a body and a mind. Just as people have to eat so they have to seek God, according to Augustine. Their spiritual restlessness impels them toward the Almighty. The ritual of one major Protestant denomination confirms this position boldly by stating that the church "...is of God and will be preserved to the end of time...for the conversion of the world. All of every age and station, stand in need of the means of grace which it alone supplies" (The Methodist Church, 1965). Here again, what appears to be a straightforward affirmation turns out to be a claim that there is a fundamental human need for religion and that religious institutions, such as the church, are the means by which this need can be met. Churches will exist to the end of time because people will always have a need for the "grace" these institutions have to offer.

It should be noted that such a ritual statement does not claim that the church possesses grace. It says the church is a means of grace. People will instinctually seek to meet their religious needs and churches are to people what gas stations are to cars. They are the means or channels through which people can get their religious needs met. Only on the last day of existence, at the end of time, will churches go out of business because the last people on earth will be like the first people on earth; they will have spiritual needs that must be met. This is a bold claim for how the universal religious needs of human beings can be met.

Augustine and this denominations' ritual are not alone. Social-behavioral scientists have joined them in concluding that all humans have spiritual or religious needs. The English biologist, Alister Hardy even titled his survey of religious experiences in Great Britain *The Spiritual Nature of Man* (1979). The hundreds of accounts of trans-empirical, spiritual events sent in by mail, convinced Hardy that there was a universal genetic basis to spirituality. According to Hardy, scientific assertions that religion is dying out in the modern world are far too exaggerated.

In a similar vein, psychologist Theodore Sarbin (1970) described social identity as resulting from adjustment to five basic environments, one of which was transcendent reality. The underlying assumption underneath Sarbin's model was that humans not only had to interact with the transcendent, but were created so that they could.

The philosophical theologian Paul Tillich affirmed the universal necessity of religion by asserting that existence posed the questions to which faith was the answer (1957, p. 13). In a somewhat more positive restatement of this truth, consulting psychologist John Finch contended that humans were essentially "spirits" whose potential was only actualized when they were related to God as "Spirit" (Finch, p. 153ff). Thus, human ontology included a spiritual component which was as substantively real as flesh and blood. Humans are created to be religious.

Problems with the "Instinct" Idea

When applied to human being, the concept of "Instinct" has almost been abandoned. In the first part of this century, it became fashionable to claim that any behavior that was observed was based on an instinct. One sociologist reportedly compiled a list of 5769 human instincts. As social psychologist David Myers commented, "the instinct-naming fad collapsed under its own weight" (1993, p. 269).

More importantly however, it became apparent that almost no human behavior fit the definition of an instinct. Doyle (1987, p.135) identified four characteristics of instincts: "behavior that is stereotyped for the species; that is consists of fixed-action patterns; complex; performed correctly independent of practice on the first appropriate occasion when the sign stimulus appears; and is related to species survival." If religion were an "instinct" everybody would be religious in a clearly identified manner that could be seen in children as well as adults and such behavior would be clearly related to existence.

Although theorists such as Wilson (1978) and Lorenz (1966) have contended that some central aspects of human behavior are instinctive and heredity, there is wide agreement that, while humans may, indeed, have some basic NEEDS, the "ways of accomplishing these goals clearly involve learning and do not meet the definition of instinctive behavior." (Doyle, 1987, p. 135). Furthermore, few, if any, of these basic needs result in similar acts.

Religion as Basic Drive

If religion is not an instinct, then, perhaps, it is one of those "basic drives," or "biological needs" that psychologists Doyle (1987) and Myers (1993) suggest exist in all human beings. By calling religion a "basic need" rather than an "instinct," we might still be able to hold on to the idea that religion is generic or universal.

Such was the belief of the late philosophical theologian Paul Tillich. He concluded that "Gods" were those aspects of life about which persons were "ultimately concerned" (1957, p.14) or in which they put their basic trust. He postulated that everyone had an ultimate concern, a part of life in which they put most of their trust, therefore, everyone had their God. Further, if life cannot be lived without trusting in something, then everyone is religious. This would mean that all persons had a basic religious drive which they had to meet in some way.

This possibility could be an alternative way of stating that "all people are religious" or that "everyone has their God." The drive, or need, is the same; the behavior is different. Some people "live for God, some for country, and some for Yale," as the saying goes. But everyone lives for something; everyone is religious.

Returning to Doyle's (1987) statement that the ways in which humans meet their needs vary and involve learning, it could be said that while religion is a universal drive, religious behavior varies in terms of culture and personal learning histories. Just as preferences for food vary, so preferences for ways of being religious differ from person to person and culture to culture.

Conceiving of religion as the basic drive to have "basic trust" or be "ultimately concerned" about some aspect of life leads to the question, "Why be ultimately concerned about anything?" Milton Yinger (1970, p.7) offered an answer to this question by stating that "religion is the way persons handle the tragedies, the enigmas, and the mysteries of life." Tragedies are the unexpected disruptions of life due to deaths, accidents, physical forces, violence, and breakdowns in relationships. Enigmas are the injustices, lost opportunities, misfortunes and coincidences of fate and circumstance. Mysteries are the unfathomables, the unexplainables, the paradoxes, and the imponderables of experience. Yinger's presumption is that every person experiences these tragedies, enigmas, and mysteries and is driven to understand, or make sense, of them. Thus, everyone is religious, since the root meaning of the term "religion" is to "tie together, to bind-up, to unify."

Certainly, this is the presumption of many existential thinkers who presume that humans are "meaning seeking" beings (Fowler, May, 1958; Malony, 1986 Tillich, 1952). The meaning that is sought is relief from the anxiety humans feel when they experience tragedy, enigma, and mystery. Humans seeks answers to "Why?"

Why did this happen to me?

Why did something not happen to me?

Why am I here?
Where did I come from?
Where am I going?
What does it all mean?

At mid 20th century, the psychologist George A. Kelly (1953) contended that humans were strongly motivated toward consistency, logic, reasonableness, and predictability in their life experience. They wanted to make sense of life. Religion could be thought of as the extension of this "sense making" drive to those areas of life that defy logic and are beyond human capacity to explain or understand.

Religion is the Answer, more than the Question

But it should be noted that in such questioning the traditionally religious answers have an indirect connection to the basic drive. The motivation is to answer the questions of life rather than to be religious, per se. Two concerns about this observation are important to acknowledge:

First, not everybody seems to experience the kind of anxiety to which religious behavior is the answer, or so it seems. What has been presumed to be a universal, is for great numbers of persons non-existent. To contend that everyone is religious, that everyone has an "ultimate concern," may be a fantasy. If the thesis about concern over the meaning of life were explained to them, many would say they never had that need or felt that drive. Jesus' statement in Matthew 19:24 that it was easier for a camel to crawl through the eye of a needle than for a rich man to enter the kingdom of God attests to this truth. If persons are rich enough they can shield themselves for much of the injustice and tragedy of life. They can avoid the kind of need for meaning that others experience when they come up against the limits of life. Second, there appears to be great variety in what people do during traditional times of worship on Sunday morning. This suggests to even the most casual observer the possibility that either that there is an immense variety of ways of meeting the need for religious meaning or that many persons do not experience this kind of need in the first place.

As I was driving to church on a recent Sunday I observed people engaged in a wide variety of activities. They were:
- bicycle riding,
- soccer playing,
- jogging,
- car washing,
- leaf raking,

- window shopping,
- grocery buying,
- eating breakfast at a coffee shop, and
- dog walking.

My conclusions are: meaning seeking is a drive experienced by some persons, but not all and, for those who do seek meaning in their lives, religion is one, but not necessarily the only or dominant way they assuage the anxiety that is evoked by such concerns. As Voltaire reportedly stated, "There are truths which are not for all men, nor for all times." Such is religion; it is best understood as one "interest" or social incentive among many provided by culture to which persons can respond when they experience a need for meaning.

RELIGION IS AN "INTEREST" WHICH SOME PEOPLE HAVE

Religion is not even a basic drive and it, certainly, is not an instinct. In fact, I would propose that those who call religion a "biological need" or a "basic drive" have confusedly projected their own "want" into a "universal need"— a very well known process in Gestalt thinking. Their specific *is* has become a general *ought*.

Contending that everyone has a need for God or a spiritual drive may be comforting to those who are religious and who think others should be, but it is a delusion. Everyone is not religious by any stretch of the imagination. Many would reply as did LaPlace, "I have no need of that hypothesis," when asked by Napoleon, "Where is God in your thinking."

And even to the point, a significant portion of those who are religiously involved, do so out of an appreciation for the aesthetic experience of fantasy and transcendence which religion offers rather than a desperate need to find meaning in life. I well remember a member of the Church Universal and Triumphant, whose worship is far different from the average traditional church, who said to me, "I come and chant the words of Claire Prophet as fast as I can for an hour while sitting in a group because it gives me a kind of exhilaration I never experience in the rest of the week where I am having to deal with concrete reality every day." To the implications of this view of religion I now turn for a fuller discussion of its meaning and implications.

UNDERSTANDING INTERESTS

Interests are preferences for participation in one or more activities available in the environment. For example, the hunger need can be satisfied by an interest in eating fried chicken or eggplant—whichever one likes best or is in the refrigerator. Culture provides a variety of ways in which hunger can be assuaged. Preferences for one food or another are built up through learning and environmental conditions. It is unlikely that an adult New Yorker would prefer the taste of grasshoppers but equally unlikely that an Amazon River native would be interested in a hamburger.

As Myers (1993, p. 270) depicts it, the "internal pushes" (biology) are satisfied through the "external pulls" (culture and learning). Further, "...we are pulled by incentives—any stimulus that has positive or negative value in motivating our behavior" (p. 271). When we say we have "an interest in something" (like religion), we mean that some environmental incentive (like the church) is attractive to us. We feel motivated to participate in that activity as a means of satisfying a need we feel.

Beit-Hallahmi (1991) suggests that religion is like art; it is an "interest" that arises from the "capacity" for imagination. Earlier, I spoke of religion arising out of the stress and boredom of life. In both cases, there is yearning for the experience of fantasy—a type of event off to the side of the logic and rationality needed for pure physical survival. Being religious is an aesthetic experience that relieves tension, provides reverie, and furnishes an escape, according to Beit Hallahmi. Beit-Hallahmi states this thesis thusly:

> *"To put this claim in the strongest possible terms: religion is a work of art. It is (for believers, and even for non-believers) beautiful, harmonious, pleasing, and attractive. In a confused, confusing, and cruel world, where mankind feels helpless before nature and history, religion and art provide order and beauty. Religion and art are both comforting illusions in a world which makes such illusions necessary..."* (1991, p. 172).

LIKE ART, RELIGION IS TO BE APPRECIATED RATHER THAN USED

At best, religion, like music played by a famous musician, should result in a desire to go to another concert; nothing more, nothing less. Beit-Hallahmi contends that the reason religion predicts so few behaviors it that it was never intended to have a practical effect. It is stress reducing, not action inducing.

It is like a vacation; it simply refreshes one to return to daily existence. Religion's only expected effect is continued participation. Religion, like art, is an interest some have and some don't.

What are the implications of re-conceiving religion as an "interest" as opposed to an "instinct?" The first result of such a re-conception is to clarify why religion predicts so few behaviors. Interests predict behavior only if they are stronger than average. Interests are like hobbies; if a person has several in which he/she is interested, it will be impossible to know what they will be doing on a given day. So it is with religion. Just knowing whether persons belong to a group or say they are religious is insufficient information. It will predict little, if anything. Interest in religion will only predict behavior if it is strong; well above average. Our decade and a half long research into measures that will assess optimal religious functioning support this contention. Only when religious practice was well above average did it predict less stress, anxiety, and hostility. Average or below scores on our Religious Status Inventory predicted little or nothing (Malony, 1988).

Not only will religion be related to mental health if religion is very strong and important, knowing religion is an interest will change the way we communicate with one another in evangelism and/or counseling. Although we who are Christians may think that our faith is far superior and absolutely true (cf. Beit-Hallahmi, 1991, p. 178), we need to acknowledge that such claims are not self evident nor will they have any meaning to those who are not asking the questions to which faith is the answer.

Thus, while I think it is appropriate to raise the religious question in therapy, as well as in daily life, we must remember that, if religion is an interest, it is an answer to a felt need. Religion will not sell itself. We should avoid giving answers to questions nobody is asking. Our effort should be in helping persons become aware of the need to which religious faith is the answer. That is the reason the old time evangelists spent so much time bringing people "under conviction." They knew that interests are based on wants, and wants are based on needs. The process will not work in reverse.

This essay has attempted to re-construe the common assumption that people have a basic, instinctual need for religion. Religion is herein understood as an interest which must be awakened and which will only predict behavior once it is developed and has become strong. When this is understood, it opens up a whole new set of options both for stimulating the awareness of the need for which religion is an answer and for strengthening religious involvement so that it can validly be assumed to be related to mental health.

REFERENCES

_____ (1965). *The book of worship for church and home.* Nashville, TN: The Methodist Publishing House.

Beit-Hallahmi, B. (1991). Religion as art and identity. In H. N. Malony, ed. *Psychology of religion: Personalities, problems, possibilities,* 171-188 (Grand Rapids, MI: Baker Book House.

Batson, C.D., Schoenrade, P. & Ventis, W.L. (1993). *Religion and the individual: A social-psychological perspective.* New York: Oxford University Press.

Doyle, C.L. (1987). *Explorations in psychology.* Belmont, CA: Wadsworth.

Finch, J.G. (1980). The message of anxiety. In H. Newton Malony, ed. *A Christian existential psychology: The Contribution of John G. Finch*, 153-174. Lanham, MD: University Press of America.

Fowler, J.W. (1981). *Stages of faith: The psychology of human development and the quest for meaning*. San Fransico: Harper and Row.

Hardy, A. (1979). *The spiritual nature of man: A study of contemporary religious experience*. Oxford: Clarendon Press.

Kagan, J. & E. Havemann (1976). *Psychology: An introduction, 3rd edition*. New York: Harcourt, Brace, Jovanovich.

Kelly. G.A. (1953). *The psychology of personal constructs, Volume 1*. New York: W.W. Norton.

Lorenz, K. (1966). *On Agression* (M.K.Wilson, Trans.). New York: Harcourt, Brace.

Malony, H.N., ed. (1980). *A Christian existential psychology: The contributions of John G. Finch*. Lanham, MD: University Press of America.

Malony, H.N. (1986). Theology, social/behavioral science, philosophy, and natural science. In H. N. Malony *Integration musings: Thoughts on being a Christian professional*, 29-40. Pasadena, CA: Integration Press.

Malony, H.N. (1988). The clinical assessment of optimal religious functioning . *Review of Religious Research, 30*(1), 1-17.

May, R., ed. (1958). *Existence: A new dimension in psychiatry and psychology*. New York: Basic Books.

Myers, D.G. (1993). *Exploring psychology, 2nd edition*. New York: Worth Publishers.

Sarbin, T. (1970). A role theory perspective for community psychology: The structure of social identity. In *Community, psychology and mental health: Perspectives and challenges*, edited by D. Adelson and B.L. Kalis, 89-113. Scranton, PA: Chandler.

Tillich, P. (1957). *Systematic Theology, Volume 3*. Chicago: University of Chicago Press.

Tillich, P. (1952). *The courage to be*. New Haven, CT: Yale University Press.

Wilson, E.O. (1978). *On human nature*. Cambridge, MA: Harvard University Press.

FIFTEEN

Religion vs. Spiritual: The New Pluralism Reconsidered

The concluding chapter of Edward Shafranske's seminal volume Religion and the clinical practice of psychology reported the finding of the National Survey of Religion Identification that 90% of Americans identify with a religion (Shafranske and Malony, 1996, p. 565).

You can believe this if you want to. If such a statistic as this provides you with some feeling of comfort that the "God is Dead" movement of the 1960s is, itself, dead and that, in some fashion, the great majority of the population believes in (or is on its way to believing in) the Christian God of our fathers and mothers, then so be it. But before you get too comfortable, don't forget that "it ain't necessarily so."

As Dean Hoge stated in the first chapter of Shafranske's volume +"Religion in America is alive and well, but it is diversifying" (Hoge, 1996, p. 38). No doubt Hoge is correct in the type of religious diversity, the intensity of religious diversity, and the substance of religious diversity. A consideration of these issues would seem important for Christian counselors who deal daily with clients who present themselves as spiritual or religion.

TYPE OF RELIGIOUS DIVERSITY

Look at this summary of religious affiliation among the Muslims, Jews, and Christians in America in the mid 1990s.

Muslims	4,500,000
Jews	8,350,000
Christians	
Baptists	27,800,000
Methodists	19,900,000
Presbyterians	4,000,000
Roman Catholics	58,200,000

Lutherans	9, 400,000
Pentecostals	4,300,000
Episcopalians	2,500,000
Disciples of Christ	1,250,000
Latter Day Saints (Mormons)	4,800,000
United Church of Christ	1,500,000
Orthodox	2,900,000
Reform (RCA and CR)	2,000,000

And this list does not even include the mega-churches or emergent churches found in many urban areas—most of whom would identify themselves as "none of the above." Nor does it include the array of new religious movements such as Ramptha, The Church Universal and Triumphant and Scientology which alone claims 10 million members worldwide. Yes, diversity is, indeed, the name of the game as far as type of religion is concerned.

INTENSITY OF RELIGIOUS DIVERSITY

The same is true of intensity of religious diversity. Not everybody who calls themselves Christian, Muslim, or Jew is on the same page religiously. I have a friend who is a psychologist in Jedda, Saudi Arabia. He completed his doctoral dissertation on the topic "Adult converts to Islam in Saudi Arabia" Would you not have thought that everyone who lived in the near east, especially those who called Jedda (the sacred center of the Islamic world) home, would be faithful Muslims. But it just isn't so! There are non-practicing Muslims in Saudi Arabia as well as in Iraq where a secular political party made a significant presence in the last election. The culture may be Muslim in Saudi Arabia but the population is very diverse in their religious intensity.

Cultural anthropologist Alan Tippett suggested that conversion was a process that led from (1) a period of awareness, to (2) a period of decision, to (3) a period of incorporation (1992, p. 195). These periods of time, according to Tippet, were interspersed by a critical point of "realization" (between periods 1 and 2) and a critical point of "encounter" (between periods 2 and 3). In the ideal case, involvement and intensity increase over time, but even casual observers know that most persons stagnate at some place in the process. And as far as traditional, institutional, organized, creedal, reflective religion is concerned, conversion often never gets started or is sidetracked along the way.

SUBSTANCE OF RELIGIOUS DIVERSITY

Turning next to the substance of religion, Carl Jung reportedly said, "People not only have their gods, they make their gods." Robert Wuthnow (1998), the Princeton scholar, concluded that much of American religion has become a mix-and-match of various extant options. The National Study of Youth and Religion reached the same conclusion (Smith and Denton, 2005). Smith and Denton (2005) wrote about these results in the provocative volume Soul searching: The religious and spiritual lives of American teenagers. While eighty-five percent of American teenagers described themselves as Christian, they did not affirm many of the essential convictions of the Christian faith such as the God's loving presence, the divinity of Christ, salvation by grace, the reality of sin, the nature of absolute truth, the resurrection of Jesus. In these matters they seem to be very unorthodox. Smith and Denton stated that in the adolescents they studied "Christianity is either degenerating into a pathetic version of itself, or, more significantly, Christianity is actively being colonized and displaced by a quite different religious faith" (Vitagliano, 2005, p.1).

Smith and Denton labeled this brand of faith as *Moralistic Therapeutic Deism* (MTD). While teenagers report that they are enthusiastic about faith and consider faith very important for daily living, they consider all religions as worshipping the same God and that God's chief function is to help people remain good and happy. Barna summed up this permissive attitude by called teenage religion "Whatever' faith (Vitagliano, 2005, p.1). Youth accept the opinions held by other people. "Whatever works for them" is their pervasive super-tolerant, non-judgmental attitude. And, disturbingly, Smith and Denton suggest that the faith of youth is a mirror image of the faith of their parents.

All of this is to say that the religion that clients bring to us differs widely in type, intensity, and substance. Sensitive to these issues of religious diversity Richards and Bergin (2000) edited a volume entitled Handbook of psychotherapy and religious diversity. They made the presumption, however, that Christian meant Christian, Buddhist meant Buddhist, Native American meant Native American, Orthodox Jew meant Orthodox Jew—i.e. that labels for religious traditions meant something. I doubt this is true anymore, just as I doubt we can revel in the meaning of the report that over ninety percent of Americans believe in God. We are dealing with a hodge-podge, a type of diversity unlike any in our history.

RELIGION AND COUNSELING

Unfortunately, I fear that what is true of our clients is also true of us – those who claim to be part of a Christian Association for Psychological Studies. If they truth be known, I suspicion that we, too, tend to be advocates of a kind of Moralistic Therapeutic Deism or some other heretical variety of the Christian tradition.

Our own lack of consensus as to the meaning of our faith is the reason we have joined our politically correct secular colleagues in saying we will, by no means, impose our faith on those we counsel because we knew that the religiosity they brought to us was as varied as our own. We tended to deny this was true of us by identifying with the liberal teachings about missions and evangelism that religion was either culturally pervasive (all Israelis are Jews) or that each person had an ultimate concern (everybody has a religion).

In counseling, this meant we affirmed the politically correct position that neither a culture nor an individual were to be disturbed until and unless they brought up the "religious" issue. And then, the task was to listen to the culture, understand the individual, and/or affirm whatever spiritual or religious issues they brought up. By no means were we to become evangelists because religion was a private, very personal part of life that should not be disturbed. When we marketed ourselves as Christian, religious, or spiritual counselors we basically meant we would treat religion seriously and not automatically consider it as regressive or pathological. And this is ALL we meant, nothing more, nothing less. In no instance did it mean we would proselytize—share our own faith or promote a given religious tradition contrary to what was presumed to be the individual's religious background or personal history.

We now know this politically correct theory was based on an incorrect foundation. Instead of the 90% of individuals who believe in God bringing traditional religious beliefs to counseling, they bring a hodge-podge, mix-and-max diversity of type, intensity, and substance. We are probably ill-prepared to deal with them because of our own religious and spiritual diversity. Probably we will, thereby, do more harm than good when we try. What I think we need is counselors who espouse and know well thought-out religious traditions to overtly counsel from those points of view.

Several years ago when I was the editor of the International Journal for the Psychology of Religion we published an article entitled (13) "Third force therapy" (Jahangir, 1995). It was the account of an Islamic psychologist on study leave at the University of Glasgow. She was asked to consult on the treatment of two Iranian students diagnosed as suffering from clinical depression. All efforts to counsel these students by Scottish mental health workers had failed. The Islamic psychologist successfully counseled these students using religious constructs. The students responded to the presence of Allah and the Islamic approach used by the psychologist. This article illustrates what I recommend. But note that the treatment was explicitly religious tradition based. It was forthright and proactive in its utilization. It did not wait for the students to bring up the religious issue nor did it depend on their providing the content of their faith.

In a chapter in Marty and Greenspahn's book Pushing the faith:

Proselytism and civility in a pluralistic world (1988), I tried, somewhat timidly, to counter this tendency to disparage proselytism (i.e. overt evangelism) by normalizing the influence process that surrounds us in the modern world and insisting that everyone is a proselytizer – be they a religious evangelist, a used car salesman, a college teacher, a mother, a US president, or a mental health counselor. It has been said that all communication is rhetoric (influence directed); descriptive communication (simple reporting) is very, very rare. Practically no one is free from imposing on others their clients a point of view. There may still be a few client-centered, non-directive or eclectic professionals who claim they are simply mid-wives who stand by and let those who come to them for counseling heal themselves – but I sincerely hope they are a dying breed.

All counseling is impositional, advisory, proselytizing – be it family systems, object relations, cognitive behavioral, psychoanalytic, transcendental meditative, or even religious. Yes, I said religious. Religion is not sacrosanct; off to the side of public discourse, qualitatively different of those other theories that appear in general psychology textbooks where supposedly empirically verified models of health, healing and the good life appear under the guise of modern social/behavioral science. As Browning and Cooper state convincingly in their book Religious Thought & Modern Psychologies , 2nd Edition (2004) all contemporary, secular theories of counseling include implicit, if not explicit, religious-like presumptions about the nature of reality and ultimate values.

SPIRITUALITY AND RELIGION

These comments provide a seque into the thesis I would like to propose that a proper understanding of the meaning of terms like spirituality and religion will provide the foundation for boldly claiming that explicit CHRISTIAN COUNSELING (identified on marquees, in brochures, and in assumptions and methodologies) has a place in the mental health marketplace. In the post-modern world, (15) where no theory can be definitively declared absolutely true or false, explicitly religious counseling approaches have the right to sit at the table and market their wares. And as Lilienfeld, et. al. (2005, p.205-6) noted no theory should be discounted until it has the chance to demonstrate its social usefulness. I contend that the Christian faith is one among many counseling theories that should be tried and tested for its effectiveness .

In surveying religious diversity I failed to deal with the significant number of persons who claim to be spiritual but not religious. Often the distinction they are making is between private and organized religion. However, I would like to propose a most essential distinction between the two terms that I believe will be helpful in considering Christian counseling to be a legitimate option in a post-modern cultural environment. I would like to suggest that spirituality is a prelude to religion. Spirituality could be defined as "the human capacity to experience essential and/or transcendent reality." Religion is "a conceptual framework that provides a structure for understanding, enhancing, and replication of spiritual experience." In short, spirituality is the experience, religion is the explanation. Spirituality precedes religion and religion makes spirituality more likely to reoccur. Since spirituality is always unlike everyday empirical experience, it is always mysterious and demands understanding of what happens. That is where religion comes in. It labels and provides words to explain the event.

The experience of Samuel (1 Samuel 3:1ff) and the description of the singer in Psalm 8 are biblical examples of the experiences of transcendence and significance which are the core of spirituality. In the one case, Samuel hears a voice calling his name which he thinks is that of Eli but which Eli perceives as the voice of God. He gives Samuel religious words to put to the event. The next time you hear the voice answer "Speak Lord, your servant hears." And the "Lord" to which Eli is referring is the God of Abraham who has called the Israelites into covenant relationship with himself and whose temple Samuel was in when he heard the sound.

In the Psalmist case, an individual is outside looking up at the sky – perhaps at sunset just as the stars are coming out. He is awestruck at the beauty and immensity of it all. A sense of his place in the universe sweeps over him. He ponders the significance of being human. He proclaims, "When is see your heavens, the sun and the moon which thou has ordained, What is man that thou are mindful of him and the son of man that thou dost care for him."

In both the case of Samuel and the Psalmist we see the transition from spirituality to religion. Eli tells Samuel to respond "Speak Lord, thy servant hears" when next he experiences his name being called. The Psalmist moves from the sense of the immensity of the heavens to the concern of God for human beings. Words of understanding are provided which explain and personalize the event in a manner that gives meaning and provokes a means for re-experiencing it. In Rudolf Otto's terms, the sense of the numinous is given a constructive and comprehensive framework.

One humorist has described this distinction thusly: religion is when you go to church and day-dream about fishing while spirituality is when you go fishing and day-dream about God.

Seriously, I am convinced that spirituality is like a formless ameba unless and until it becomes a set of constructs which can be shared and used in both inducing and enhancing future events. Religious traditions serve this essential function. Unfortunately for contemporary America, there are many for whom spirituality remains so amorphous that attempts to relate to it or utilize it in counseling are doomed to failure. Or the labels people utilize are so convoluted, confused, and un-systemized that utilizing them becomes a formidable task. About all one can say about spirituality without religion or spirituality with mix-and-match religion is that one would expect to experience recurring spiritual emergencies (19) – a condition that led the psychiatrist David Lukoff to propose adding a new religious "V code" to The Diagnostic and Statistical Manual of Mental Disorders (cf. Malony, 2006b).

The Christian Religion

In my opinion, the Christian religion provides very valid and effective words to put to the spiritual experience. The Christian faith is a comprehensive set of ideas and words that can provide a context and content for counseling. The Christian faith is qualitatively different from other religions of the world. In comparing it to other faiths the following Christian distinctives should be noted:

- The Christian faith is, first of all, Mono-Theistic in that it affirms one God who exists apart from the natural world and human beings.
- Next, the Christian faith is Historical in that it affirms that this one God has acted in time to create the universe and all life within it. God continues to act in history by directing, supporting, and encouraging human beings.
- Then, the Christian faith asserts that God intends all creation to eventually fulfill a purpose he has determined for it. The life of creation does not move around in circles, getting no where. Life is intentional. God has a will; ; he wants life to go somewhere. Thus, Christianity is Teleological.
- The Christian faith is, subsequently, Revelational. God has made known his purpose for all of creation through inspired teachers, writers, prophets, and, especially scriptures (the Bible). Humans are not ignorant, they have been informed.
- The Christian faith, therefore, is Transactional in that the purpose of God for creation is that humans join Him in creating a world where people live together in mercy, in justice, in love, and in peace. Humans cannot fulfill God's purpose for their lives individually, without interacting with others. God intends that life be lived relationally.
- Unfortunately, the Christian faith is Realistic in its appraisal of whether the will of God has been actualized in creation. So far, it has not. Humans, created in the image of God, have fallen short of God's will for them. They have failed. They have sinned.
- Fortunately, however, God is busy in the Restorative process of renewing creation to its original purpose and
- Most importantly, the Christian faith is Incarnational in that God delib-

erately decided to appear on earth to reveal His purposes through Jesus of Nazareth – called the Christ, the Messiah, the Son of God. Everything humans need to know about God is seen through the life, the teachings, the death, and the resurrection of this one man Jesus. God has acted in history to Reclaim all creation through Jesus.

- It follows that Christianity is Salvific in that it provides a means, through faith, whereby persons can rededicate their lives to God's purposes, can be forgiven for their past lives, can experience freedom from their addictions, can be consoled when they fail, can find courage to face stress and tragedy, and can be strengthened to rededicate themselves to God's will and way.

- Among all the world's religions, the Christian faith is Communal in that those who experience salvation from sin and commit themselves to God's way do not act alone. They become part of the people of God moving across history as a body, the church. They covenant together to support one another, be open to the guidance of God's Holy Spirit, and to work together for good.

- Finally, the Christian faith is Eschatalogical by which is meant that in the final analysis God holds all of history within His creative/redemptive power. At the end of time God will achieve his purposes for all of creation – in nature as well as in humans alike. Revelation 11:15 states what Christianity believes, the day will come when "...the kingdoms of this world will become the kingdoms of the Lord and of His Christ." (Malony & Augsburger, 2006, in press).

No other faith contains all these unique features. While not exhaustive, this list is clearly comprehensive of classical Christian convictions. It is meant to be a descriptive categorization of the faith once delivered and affirmed throughout the centuries. It is this faith against which amorphous spirituality, mix-and-match religion, Moralistic Therapeutic Deism, and Whatever faith should be compared. It is these basic assumptions that should provide the foundation for anyone who is bold enough to claim to be a Christian counselor.

These are the ultimate realities and the explanatory words that should both explain as well as guide the spiritual experiences of clients who come for Christian counseling. It is these presumptions that can provide a counter to the diversity of type, intensity, and substance that is common today. Counseling grounded in these Christian affirmations can take its place around the table of alternative theories and legitimately request a hearing.

CHRISTIAN COUNSELING

Briefly noted, the Christian faith provides a basic context and a foundational content for what is essentially a cognitive/behavioral approach to counseling. By context is meant that Christian counseling takes place in the presence of Almighty God and the Risen Christ who provide ultimate acceptance and love as well as direction and encouragement. By content is meant that Christian counseling assumes that the interaction that takes place will always finally seek the will of God in solutions to the predicaments clients are facing.

While a more extensive discussion of these issues can be found in mine and David Augsburger's forthcoming book, Christian counseling: An introduction (2006), suffice it to say that the recent review in Time of Steven Hayes' Acceptance Commitment Therapy (2004) is a good example of a non-religious cognitive/behavioral approach that can be easily adapted for Christian counseling. Hayes is the former president of the distinguished Association for Behavioral and Cognitive Therapies and the author of Get out of your mind and into your life (2004)). He contends that The search for "happiness" in life is ill-advised and that, in most cases, people should learn to accept stress and suffering as normal. The solution to life's predicament is commitment to a higher set of values.

Christians seek "joy" in life, not "happiness." They know that Jesus was correct when He said, 'In this world, you will have much tribulation (persecution)" (John 16:33) and that Paul concluded that "
...suffering produces endurance, and endurance produces character, and character produces hope, and hope does not disappoint because God's love has been poured into our hearts through the Holy Spirit that has been given to us" (Romans 5:3b-5). These clearly fit into Hayes formula of acceptance of distress as normal in life coupled with commitment a higher set of values.

In conclusion, I have tried to counter religious diversity by presenting a case for tradition specific religious therapy. I firmly believe that the religious traditions of the world (in our Christian) have well thought out understandings of life's predicaments and ultimate solutions that can become legitimate bases for counseling approaches in our post modern world.

I close with one of Charles Schultz' classic Peanuts cartoons. Linus and Lucy were looking out at the rain. Lucy said, "If it doesn't stop raining everything will wash away." "Oh no," replied Linus, "Genesis chapter 9 says that never again will God wash everything away." "That is a great comfort," Lucy states, to which Linus replies "Sound theology will do that." And it will, I am convinced.

REFERENCES

_____ Time in Depth (2006). Happiness isn't normal. *Time, 167*(7), 59-67.

Barna, G. (2004) *Real teens: A contemporary snapshot of youth culture.* Ventura, CA: Regal.

Browning, D.S. & Cooper, T.D. (2004). *Religious thought and the modern psychologies, 2nd Edition.* Minneapolis: Fortress Press.

Hayes, S. (2004) *Get out of your mind and into your life.* Oakland, CA: New Harbinger Publications.

Hoge, D.R. (1996). Religion in America: The demographics of belief and affiiation. In E. Shafranske (editor) *Religion and the clinical practice of psychology* (21-42). Washington, D.C.: American Psychological Association.

Jahangir, S.F. (1995). Third force therapy and its impact on treatment outcome. *International Journal for the Psychology of Religion, 5*(2), 125-130.

Lilienfeld, S.O., Fowler, K.A., Lohr, J.M., & Lynn, S.J. (2005). Psuedoscience, non-science, and nonsense in clinical psychology: Dangers and remedied. In *Destructive trends in mental health: The well-intentioned path to harm1*, pp.87-219. New York: Routledge.

Malony, H.N. (1988). The psychology of proselytism. In M.E. Marty & F.E. Greenspahn, editors *Pushing the faith: Proselytism and civility in a pluralistic world* (pp. 125-142). New York: Crossroad.

Malony, H.N. (1998). Counseling body/soul persons. *International Journal for the Psychology of Religion, 8*(4), 221-242.

Malony, H.N. & Augsburger, D. W. (2006, in press). *Christian counseling: An introduction.* Nashville, TN: Abingdon.

Malony, H.N. (2006b). The V62.89 Code in the DSM-IV-R: Boon and bane for Christian psychologists. In *Theology News and Notes, 53*(1), 10-11, 25.

Richards, P.S. & Bergin, A.E. (2000). *Handbook of psychotherapy and religious diversity.* Washington, D.C.: American Psychological Association.

Shafranske, E. & Malony, H.N. (1996). Religion and the clinical practice of psychology: A case for inclusion. In E. Shafranske (editor) *Religion and the clinical practice of psychology* (561-567). Washington, D.C.: American Psychological Association.

Smith C. & Denton, M.L. (2005) *Soul searching: The religious and spiritual lives of American teenagers.* New York: Oxford University Press.

Tippett, A. R. (1992). The cultural anthropology of conversion. In H.N. Malony & Samuel Southard *Handbook of religious conversion* (pp.192-208). Birmingham, Alabama: Religious Education Press.

Vitagliano, Ed. (2005). God, Religion – Whatever –Are our church-going youth falling away from the faith. http.//headlines.agapepress.org/archive/1/132006a.asp

Wuthnow, R. (1998). *After heaven: Spirituality in America since the 1950s.* Berkeley, CA: University of California Press.

SIXTEEN

Taking a Step Back: A Proposal for a Psychology of Religious Expression

I have ceased to be interested in the "roots" of religion and intend to focus all my future attention on the "fruits." I have become disenchanted with psycho-analytic attempts to explore the origins of God representations (Rizzuto, 1981; McDargh, 1983) as well as with efforts to determine the Intrinsic or Extrinsic motives people have for being religious (Donahue, 1985). Further, I have become impatient with psycho-historical endeavors to understand the forces which shape individual faith (Erikson, 1958). I have even become bored with the types of out-of-the-blue experiences reported by William James (1902) in his library and David Hay (1990) in the Hardy survey in Great Britain. All of these seem to be ends in themselves and provoke only introspective ruminations about what was really happening. As a group, these ruminations ignore the results of such experiences.

When I declare my interest to be directed toward religion's "fruits," I mean something more than religion's consequences (Lenski, 1963) in pro-social or ethical behavior, however. Although I retain some interest in these uniquely western forms of religion-based ethics, I want to also to study religion's impact on such matters as coping styles (Pargament et al., 1988), and mental health (Malony, 1992).

RELIGION AS STATE RATHER THAN TRAIT

More specifically, I have become invested in studying religion as a state more than religion as a trait (Spielberger, 1966). States of mind are immediate, self-conscious, and intentional. Traits of behavior are preconscious, habitual, unpremeditated. For me, this concern for what eventuates from religious states, as opposed to religious traits, means that I have become much more interested in studying how people behave when they are trying to be religious rather than when they are just behaving in general.

Embree (1973) illustrates this distinction for me. He explored the difference in the way people behaved when they were told to be religious. On a word-association test he found a significant difference in the number of religious associations between administrations with and without instructions to see how many religious associations could be given to stimulus words. The intention to be religious in the task resulted in a significantly greater number of religious word associations.

Far too often, in my opinion, research in the psychology of religion has been undertaken with the presumption that a religious trait would be evident in general behavior. According to this approach, religion, like other cognitive determinants, would presumably become part of the covert, subconscious motivational mass and show up as one of significant influences on human action, a la Wundt's classic studies of the "apperceptive mass." Like a trace element in a chemical compound, religion was supposed to affect or color the mixture and reveal its impact.

In these trait, or trace, studies, typically religion has been assessed by ratings of activity, attendance, or importance of religion and correlated this with dependent measures of attitudes or actions. Using this general methodology of religion as sub-conscious influence or trait, it is not surprising that Batson, Ventis, and Schoenrade (1993), found that religion accounted for less than 5 % of the variance in predictions of mental health.

Rarely have associations between religion and behavior in such studies as these been explicit, in the sense that the participants in the studies were aware that the impact of their religion was being measured. An implicit, covert, or trait influence was assumed. Increasingly, I have become disillusioned with these presumed indirect associations with religion as some kind of pre-conscious trait and, instead, have become much more concerned with religion as a conscious, intentional, state of mind

I am convinced that if religion is, as Yinger (1970) and Fowler (1981) have surmised, a search for meaning in the midst of the enigmas, tragedies, and mysteries of life, then religion is, indeed, a cognitive, conscious, deliberate and premeditated act. When people are being religious, they know it and intend it. And they know when they experience it and they know when they apply it. Religion, if it has impact, does not slip down into the apperceptive mass. It is at the forefront of thought and, as Allport (1950) suggested, it is encompassing and heuristic—it unifies life around a common theme and it spreads its effect to every aspect of existence. This point of view perceives religious behavior as deliberate, calculated, and purposeful.

Such reasoning as this has led me to conclude that if we truly want to study the impact of religion on life, we should focus on what persons do when they are seriously trying to be religious. In support of this approach, some recent theorists have distinguished between moral states and traits (Rayburn, 1991). If one envisions religion, a la Kant, as the moral call, then it could be said that the essence of religion is that state of mind when one is most aware that they are acting morally. I agree with this approach, especially when we consider the word "moral" in a more general sense. If by "moral" we mean those ideals and values that pull thinking up toward the good and best, then to be religious means to try to live life in terms of these goals. And this only rarely occurs without conscious forethought and intention. Moral living can best be seen when one is in a moral state of mind. Only in saints does morality become habitual.

Morals function in yet another important way. The well-known maxim states, "There is nothing more practical than a good theory." In human behavior, morals function like a good theory. They exert a pull on behaviors and give them meaning. There is determination both upward to and downward. Behavior is judged upwards by moral ideals when one says, "What happened on those days was not right," or "I think we did what was just and good." Behavior is planned downward by moral ideals when one says, "I will not do that because it is not right," or "Because I believe in being forgiving, I will do this." In all these actions, a moral state of mind, rather than a moral trait, determines behavior. Morals function like a good theory that can best be utilized self-consciously and intentionally.

RELIGION AS INTEREST RATHER THAN INSTINCT

Taking this argument one step farther, I believe that religion should be perceived similarly to vocational interests. When vocational interests are strong and way above average, they will predict behavior. When vocational interests are weak or average, they will predict nothing. For example, if one is seeking to determine whether a person should become a biologist by scores on a vocational interest test, one should look for scores reflect interest in science that are one to two standards deviations above the average. Only such higher scores will predict that an individual will enjoy the work of a biologist enough to predict they will persist in the preparation such a vocation requires and, once in such a position, will continue to like the work after it become routine.

Religion is like that. Average belief, interest, and involvement in religion will predict nothing. In fact, one might question whether religion that predicts nothing should be called religion. It is this kind of average religion that has contaminated past research. Only the kind of religion that is way above average in strength and participation will predict behavior. If we want to study whether religion is a significant influence on behavior, we should look for the kind of scores that indicate relish for, satisfaction in, and passion toward religious activities that is in the top 20% of the population. It is here that we might expect to see the "fruits" of religious experience. That is my hypothesis.

In a recent presentation entitled "Religion as interest rather than instinct: Why religion has such little effect on mental health (Malony, 1995), I delineated this line of thinking and suggested that, while the urge to find meaning in life might be a universal "need," religious behavior could better be understood as a "culture-specific interest." It should be noted that religion is only one of the ways that persons assuage their need to find purpose and meaning. As Van der Lans (1991) has observed, in modern Europe, the religious option is only espoused by a small minority of people. Although there is much more overt participation in religious groups in the United States, there is still the possibility, even the probability, that a significant portion of the population handle their search for meaning and purpose in non-religious manners, just as they do in Europe. The presumption made by Fowler (1981), and others, that every one has a "religion" ignores the fact that most of those who meet their meaning and purpose needs in overtly non-, or a-, religious manners would strongly deny that they were "religious."

<h2>RELIGION AS SUBSTANCE RATHER THAN FUNCTION</h2>

In light of the above discussion, I think it best to define religious behavior in substantive, rather than functional, ways (Malony, 1977). Religion is something people believe and do that has cultural substance or content. It can be identified as "religious" by the general public; that is, by everyone, including the "man on the street." Berger (1974) contrasts this substantive viewpoint with a functional position which would emphasize the needs which prompt religious behavior. He noted that the functional point of view owed its origin to the thinking of the sociologist Emile Durkheim while the substantive point of view originated with Max Weber. Durkheim was interested in origins while Weber was concerned to study social realities. Fowler would be considered a functionalist; I would consider myself to be a substantivist.

The functional position emphasizes what religion does for persons, while the substantive position emphasizes what religion looks like out in the real world. Participating in overt religious activity, or giving an overt religious reason for one's behavior, is based on a substantive view of religion. Going into a church would be recognized by everyone as a religious act. Saying, "I feel good because I know there is a God," is a religious statement. These behaviors are distinctly religious. They are unlike interpretations that might assert that persons use baseball as their "religion" because they say, "I attend every baseball

game the LA Dodgers play and I know every player's batting average by heart."
A passion for baseball would not be considered religious by either baseball fans
or the public in general. I agree with Lemert (1975, p. 187), who asserted that
we should avoid labeling activities as religious "social phenomena that are not
perceived to be religious by their participants."

From a substantive point of view, "religion" becomes a meaningless term
is we say that everyone has a religion or that every passion, from baseball to
English literature, is a religion. Fowler (1981) makes this error by equating the
search for meaning with religion. I am not convinced that everyone has an
"ultimate concern," as Tillich (1951) proposed, and I think it more than obvious that not everyone expresses such a concern, if they have it, in religiously
recognizable ways. Thus, in stating that I want to focus on the fruits of religion,
I mean that I desire to study what people do that is acknowledged to be religious by their society and what they, themselves, claim to be religious acts.

I term this a "Substantive/Empirical" view of religion. In contrast to van
der Lans (1991) who opined that we would have to expand our understanding
of religion to a variety of non-traditional expressions of the search for meaning, this approach would narrow the psychology of religion to "the study of
personal and institutional behaviors which occur within the contexts of social
groups based on trans-empirical realities." A diagram of this model follows:

DIAGRAM 16-1

A Substantive/Empirical View of Religion

	COMPONENTS	
	Cosmic	Observable
Personal Expression	1	2
Institutional	3	4

The first panel, Personal Expression-Cosmic Level Idea, refers to all
those individual thoughts, feelings, and actions which are based upon and stem
from the basic transcendent conviction which is the essence of religion. Such
expressions as faith statements, prayers, deeds of compassion, political judgments, readings of scriptures, etc. would be examples.

The second panel, Personal Expression-Observable Social refers to individual involvement and identity with groups that reflect their corporate sense of faith in a cosmic level idea. Obviously, this refers to overt participation in worship in the mosque, the temple, or the church. It also reflects other outside-the-building identification with religious points of view espoused by the religious group of which one is a part.

The third panel, Institutional-Cosmic Level Idea, refers to statements, creeds, dogmas, published positions, etc. produced by religious groups which explicitly reflect the position that they are grounded in a conviction about transcendent reality. This would include all the publications presented to the public by denominations and religious traditions which explained or promoted their basic beliefs.

The fourth panel, Institutional-Observable Social Group refers to those gatherings of people which can be seen both on stated days of worship and at other times such as on pilgrimages and attendance at gatherings called to protest or support ideas central to the group's purpose.

Vivid examples could be given for each of the panels. It is crucial, however, to note how this model illustrates the substantive/empirical model of religion. Each of the four panels has substance; that is, the central cosmic-level idea. This is the sufficient nucleus that makes a religion a religion. This idea does not have to be theistic, although most religions include divine realities. Buddhism, however, is not theistic, but it is a religion because it's central idea is transcendental. This central idea is expressed both individually and institutionally. It is obvious by the bowing of the head in prayer and by the cross on the top of the steeple.

Then the model is empirical because it can be seen by all who have eyes to see. While individual persons are critical to religion, it is their coming together than makes religion recognizable. A one-person religion is a non-existent. The observable social group of like- minded persons is the necessary part of religion. It is only when two or more persons share a cosmic level idea and announce their conviction that a religion exists.

THE PSYCHOLOGY OF RELIGIOUS EXPRESSION

Thus, I propose we rename our discipline to "The Psychology of Religious Expression" and leave to history "The Psychology of Religious Experience."Really, however, I should admit that I am being a bit too narrow in my thinking. Religious "experience," as I have defined it in an article entitled "An S-O-R model of religious experience" (Malony, 1985), is an encompassing term that includes a Stimulus, Organismic processing, and a Response. Understood in this manner, I have self-limited my interest to the R (response) in the formula and intentionally leave preoccupations with "James/Hardy-like" events to those who want to still ruminate about the S (stimulus) component. In actuality, both are part of the facets of experience; one simply precedes the other. I confess I intend to focus on the behavior that follows the organismic processing—behavior that is confessed or can be observed in overt action. Expressive religion is, indeed, "responsive" in the sense that it is a self-conscious, willful reaction to that which one has come to know or that which one has seen or heard.

The above phrase "behavior that is confessed or can be observed in overt action" is a way of saying that behavior encompasses thoughts, words, and feelings as well as acts that can be seen. Such a phrase does, however, exclude inferences. On the one hand, it excludes the type of inference that might conclude that underneath a passion for dog breeding was a "religious" impulse. I have indicated throughout this essay that I have no interest in this or any other inference about the motive or origin of religion. On the other hand, this understanding of behavior also excludes inferences about the motives behind religious acts, such as can be seen in the intrinsic/extrinsic literature. My definition of religious behavior emphasizes what people say about themselves and what they do out in the public world, not what we infer or think about their actions.

In a volume entitled *The psychology of religion for ministry* (Malony, 1995), I have indicated what I think is the logical progression from thoughts to actions in religious behavior. I believe that religious behavior begins with insight about the nature of the gods and their action in the world. Philosophically, this involves some sense of cosmology, anthropology, soteriology, and epistemology. It is this "Ah-Ha" or insight about the nature of reality and the function of transcendent reality within it that is the beginning of expressive religious behavior. When a person is converted, this is the type of insight that has occurred. That it has occurred can be heard by the words in a person's confession and, often, can be seen in some symbolic act such as standing before a congregation in public worship.

The next step in expressive religious behavior is understanding. Understanding is the application of insight to the affairs of life. Understanding could be conceived as a pair of spectacles one puts on through which to perceive the inner meaning of life experiences. This is what Yinger (1970) meant when he said that religion is the way people handle enigmas, tragedies, and mysteries in life. Understanding is a way of looking at life through the eyes of faith. Enigmas, or fateful circumstance which one cannot change. Tragedies, or unplanned disruptions of wishes and plans, and mysteries, or yearnings to find purpose in the midst of chance and destiny. These are the life events to which faith understanding brings perspective and meaning. Faith understanding can be heard in confession and seen in the way people adjust to experience.

Understanding leads to feelings in this progression toward overt religious behavior. Feelings are those inward emotions that result from the practice of understanding. They are affections, inclinations, tendencies that build up at the subconscious level. They resemble the poise of the runner or the diver as they get set to race or dive. At choice points in life, feelings reflect the automatic bias to go one way or another. In the case of expressive religious behavior, religious feelings could be observed in the willingness of persons to look at life through faith eyes. Feelings can be observed in the quickness with which people respond or their confessions of satisfaction and attraction to faith involvement.

The final aspect of religious behavior is overt action. Of course, this is the behavior that is most commonly observed. Overt action is that which can be seen by all who are looking at what is happening. Here religious feelings lead to religious action. Whatever a given culture or tradition determines is religious is where religious action occurs. It can be readily observed and reported. Religious persons are involved in religious action—church worship, religious witness, private devotions, etc. The important thing, however, is to note that overt action is only one of four types of expressive religious behavior. As I stated, religious behavior is that which can be confessed or observed. What people think, feel, and say is just as important as that which they do. Any and all of these behaviors will be taken as their face value and no inferences will be made as to their "real" meaning or function.

A RELIGIOUS PSYCHOLOGY, NOT A PSYCHOLOGY OF RELIGION

I would like to conclude by asserting that I now see myself more as religious psychologist than a psychologist of religion. For many years, Benjamin Beit-Hallahmi (1974, 1991) has decried the infiltration into the psychology of religion of religious psychologists. I confess that I may be one of the worst offenders. Beit-Hallahmi and I are the best of friends. We have visited each other in Haifa, in Paris and in Pasadena. I respect his writing and have included him in both books of readings I have published (Malony, 1977, 1991). Nevertheless, I have long been convinced that only psychologists who are religious could ask the questions that made sense to the theologians and/or ultimately made sense to devotees (cf Pruyser, 1976). My opinion has not changed in spite of Beit-Hallahmi's observation that one of the prime reason the psychology of religion lost the respect of main-line psychology in the 1930s was that religious educators took over the field.

I have decided to forthrightly and boldly come out and assert that I am a religious psychologist. I claim this trademark less because I am an ordained clergy person within the Christian tradition and more because I have become strongly convinced that psychology must be recognizable to those it claims to study and that every religious tradition affirms an implicit, if not explicit, psychology embedded within it. I believe we owe it to religious traditions to study them from within in a manner that will be acknowledged and respected. I have become weary of having my colleagues in the theological seminary where I work discount my research as trivial. I agree with Spilka and Mullin that what we need is a "theological" psychology of religion. What I have decided to do in the future I will call what I do either "theo-psychology" or "psycho-theology."

As testimony to my "coming out," I confess that for the last decade-and-a-half my research has been directed toward the construction and validation of a scale to measure Christian religious maturity, or, better said "optimal religious functioning within the Christian tradition (Malony 1985b, 1988, 1990, 1991a, 1991b, 1992). The Religious Status Interview and Inventory are based the implications of Christian theology for daily living. They attempt to assess the religious expressive behavior that lies in between creeds and motivations. But, these measures go far beyond confessions of orthodoxy or simple worship attendance. They reflect my effort to produce a psychology of religion that can be respected both by the discipline of psychology and by theologians. I hope I am succeeding.

Conclusion

This essay has been my effort to step back and reflect on the psychology of religion. I has turned out to be a very personal document. While I did not intend its effect on me to be so pervasive, stating these ideas in print has helped me clarify what kind of psychologist of religion I want to be in the years ahead. I regret that this clarification has come as late as it has for I am near retirement age. However, "grey in the hair does not mean the loss of fire in the breast," as the old saying goes. I still have much to say and do. I hope that those who evaluate my work when all is said and done will find that I have been faithful to this diatribe about my focus and my intention.

References

Batson, C. D., Schoenrade, P., & Vends, W. L. (1993). *Religion and the individual: A social-psychological perspective.* New York: Oxford University Press.

Beit-Hallahmi, B. (1974). Psychology of religion 1880-1930: The rise and fall of a psychological movement. *Journal of the History of the Behavioral Sciences. 10,* 84-90.

Beit-Hallahmi, B. (1991). Goring the sacred ox: Towards a psychology of religion. In H. N. Malony (Ed.), *Psychology of religion: Personalities, problems, possibilities* (pp.169-194). Grand Rapids, MI: Baker Book House.

Berger, P. L. (1974). Second thoughts on defining religion. *Journal for the Scientific Studies of Religion, 13,* 125-133.

Donahue, M. (1985). Intrinsic and extrinsic religiosity: Review and meta-analysis. *Journal of Personality and Social Psychology. 48,* 400-419.

Embree, R. A. (1973). The Religious Association Scale: A preliminary validation study. *Journal for the Scientific Study of Religion, 12,* 223-226.

Erikson, E. H. (1958). *Young man Luther: A study in psychoanalysis and history.* New York: Norton.

Fowler, J. W. (1981). *Stases of faith: The psychology of human development and the quest for meaning.* San Francisco: Harper and Row.

Hay, D. (1990). *Religious experience today: Studies of the facts.* London: Mowbray.

James, W. (1902). *The varieties of religious experience.* New York: Longmans.

Lemert, C. C. (1975). Defining non-church religion. *Review of Religious Research. 16,* 186497.

Lenski, G. E. (1963). *The religious factor (Rev. ed.).* Garden City, NY: Doubleday.

Malony, H. N. (1977) The psychology of religion and the religion of psychology. Presented at the annual meeting of the Rocky Mountain Psychological Society, Albuquerque, NM.

Malony, H. N. (1985a). An S-O-R model of religious experience. In L. B. Brown (Ed.), *Advances in the psychology of religion.* New York: Pergamon Press.

Malony, H. N. (1985b). Assessing religious maturity. In E. M. Stern (ed.). *Psychotherapy and the religiously committed patient* (pp. 25-33). New York: Haworth.

Malony, H. N. (1988), The clinical assessent of optimal religious functioning. *Review of Religious Research, 30,* 1-15.

Malony, H. N. (1990). How counselors can help people become more spiritual through religious assessment. Paper presented at the conference on Religion, Mental Health, and Mental Pathology, Cracow, Poland.

Malony, H. N. (1991a). The uses of religious assessment in counseling. In L. B. Brown (Ed.), *Religion and mental health.* New York: Springer.

Malony, H. N. (1991b). *Psychology of religion: Personalities. problems. possibilities.* Grand Rapids, MI: Baker Book House (republished by Integration Press, Pasadena, CA.).

Malony, H. N. (1992). Religious diagnosis in evaluations of mental health. In J. F. Schumaker (Ed.), *Religion and mental health* (pp. 245-256). New York: Oxford University Press.

Malony, H.N. (1995). *The psychology of religion for ministry.* Mahwah, NJ: Paulist Press.

McDargh, J. (1983). *Psychoanalytic object relations theory and the study of religion.* Lanham, MD: University Press of America.

Pargament, K. I., Kennell, J, Hathaway, W., Grevengoed, N., Newman, J., & Jones, W. (1988). Religion and the problem solving process: Three styles of coping. *Journal for the Scientific Study of Religion 27*. 90-104.

Porter, III, Ross U., & Malony, H. N. (1995). Religious maturity and preferred mode of religious experience. Paper presented at the annual meeting of the American Psychological Association, New York, NY.

Pruyser, P.W. (1976). *A dynamic psychology of religion*. New York: Harper & Row.

Rayburn, C., Birk, S. M., & Richmond, L. J. (1991). Development of the State/Trait Morality Inventory. Paper presented at the Annual Meeting of the American Psychological Association, San Francisco, CA.

Rizutto, A. (1981). *The birth of the living God: A psychoanalytic study*. Chicago: University of Chicago Press.

Spielberger, C. D. (1966). *Anxiety and behavior*. New York: Academic Press.

Spilka, B., & Mullin, M. (1977). Personal religion and psychological : A research approach to a theological psychology of religion. *Character Potential, 8*, 57-66.

Tillich, P. (1951). *Systematic theology: Vol. 1*. Chicago: University of Chicago Press.

Ulanov, A., & Ulanov, B. (1975). *Religion and the unconscious*. Philadelphia: Westminster Press.

van der Lans, J. (1991/1995). What is the psychology of religion about? Some considerations concerning its subject matter. In H. N. Malony (Ed.). *Psychology of religion: Personalities, problems, possibilities* (pp. 313-322). Grand Rapids, MI: Baker Book House (republished Pasadena, CA: Integration Press).

Yinger, J. M. (1970). *The scientific study of religion*. London: Macmillan.

SEVENTEEN

The Psychology of Religion and the Religion of Psychology

This paper will review some of the dialogue about the meaning of the term religion. The value of a substantive/empirical definition will be detailed. Assuming such a point of view, the question of whether psychology is a religion will be considered. Finally, the essay will describe some of the research we have been doing in the psychology of substantive/empirical religion.

The importance of such an approach as this is that it will be a step toward making the psychology of religion more respectable in the eyes of the theologians and more acceptable to general psychologists. It is no secret that a significant segment of modern theology (cf., Karl Barth, 1960, Torrance, 1969) has made a radical distinction between religion (i.e. world view) and faith. In their proposals regarding revelation, these theologians insisted that the human sciences, psychology among them, are only tangentially related to either the content or the effects of faith.

On the other hand, it is apparent that while religion, as one of society's major institutions, has been of prime concern for sociology; it has only been revived as a significant interest in psychology in the last two decades. This resurgence is apparent from the establishment of Division 36 (Psychology of Religion) of American Psychological Association (APA) in 1976. There is, thus, still more dialoging that needs to be done between religionists (theologians) and psychologists. Definitional problems and research approaches are at the heart of the issues.

Spilka (1970) was addressing some of these concerns in his article entitled "Images of Man and Dimensions of Personal Religion: Values for an Empirical Psychology of Religion." He quite correctly notes that an important facet of the religion-science controversy has been psychology's emphasis on reductionistic mechanisms and reactive learning. This has led to an *adjustment view of life* in which religion functions as an oppressive and regressive power over persons.

Most of these evaluations have been of institutional religion, which psychologists have seen as an impenetrable, but explainable, pressure toward conformity. Understandably, theologians have been critical of this limiting of religion to its institutional expression. They decry the effort to understand faith through organizations and insist that "true religion" is (1) responsive in that it is more a reaction to the God who acts and less an adjustment to a culture or even the creation of an anxious/thoughtful philosopher; and (2) personal, in that it is more an individual/experience rather than a social phenomenon. Thus, religion is diluted through both dogmatizing and institutionalizing.

In this last viewpoint, they are in agreement With such humanistic psychologists as Gordon Allport (1950, 1967) who value intrinsic over extrinsic religion and deals with matters of ultimate significance rather than that which is instrumental, group centered, and provincial. Allport emphasized the personal over the institutional. James (1902) had made this point much earlier via his concern for the original experiences of religious geniuses as opposed to the second hand, hand-me-down religious life of ordinary believers.

It might well be asked, "Is there no way for psychology and religion to be related apart from focusing on the personal and private experience of individuals (which numerous theologians and humanistic psychologists would support) or the institutional and public expressions of groups (which numerous social and general psychologists would support)?" As Dittes (1971) so cogently noted, the preference for studying private over cultural events is "inspired by a concern to identify the purity of religion in a relatively primitive state... and to distinguish this purity from its contamination and dilution by non-religious elements of culture and of personality" (p. 376).

There is, thus, a constant temptation to prefer the prophetic (i.e. the intrinsic, the mystic, the sect) over the historical (i.e. the extrinsic, the church, the organizational) by both psychology and theology. Yet, these are value judgments and based more on the prejudgments of the investigators rather than on unquestioned reality. There is a paradox to historical religion that must not be overlooked in answering the question as to how psychology and religion are to be related. Dittes refers to this in stating,

> *these types seem to participate also in a dialectic tension fundamental in western religious outlook. Western religions pivot on a profound ambivalence between the transcendent and the immanent. The religions move by the rhythm of incarnation and purge. The Holy dwells in man... in history, in people... in visible sacraments and institutions and roles; indeed the Holy does not, perhaps even can not, dwell apart from these forms. Yet the dwelling places*

*must contaminate the Holy, and holiness is found in withdrawal
and purification from them. Holiness is in them; holiness is separation from them.* (1971, p. 377)

Thus, the problem of "what is religion?" for both religionists and psychologists must have a *both-and* rather than an *either-or* solution. It must
include both a personal and an objective, and individual and a cultural, a private and a public dimension. This seems to be synonymous with what Pruyser
called for in his *Dynamic Psychology of Religion* (1968; i.e. a concern for
church dogma and religious activity as well as individual experience). In one
sense, this is the approach suggested by Spilka (1967) in his call for a *theological psychology of religion*. Herein he details a transactional view of persons
whereby they are always acting upon the environment but are never absolutely free from it. He writes,

*The referent of normal gives way to ideal, and man the adjustor
and reactor is supplanted by man the actor. The search is for an
understanding of man in context; not in 'interaction' where he is
conceptualized as distinct and separate from all else, but in "trans-
action' where he is always part of something larger.* (p. 173)

The implications of religion for self-significance, social significance, and
ultimate significance are described by Spilka (1967). This is a suggestive model
which, however, emphasizes only the personal search for meaning. It is somewhat deficient in making other than a secondary place for corporate expressions of these experiences in creeds and institutions. There is thus, the continuing need for definitions which accord equal weight to both the individual and
the group.

A Substantive/Empirical Definition of Religion

The above prologue leads to a brief review of the contemporary definitions of
religion. Such a survey will, I believe, provide a basis for a
Substantive/Empirical definition that will include the *both-and* balance referred
to above. Berger (1974) suggests there have been two predominant definitions
of religion in recent thinking, the substantive and the functional. The *substantive* is grounded in the thinking of Max Weber and is embraced by sociologists
interested in the study of well-developed cultures which contain identifiable
units termed religious that can be described in terms of recognizable features.
The *functional* is grounded in the thinking of Emile Durkheim and is embraced
by psychologists and sociologists interested in the origins of religion in individual and social experience. In the former (i.e., the Substantive) the emphasis is

on what religion is while in the latter (i.e., the functional) the emphasis is on what religion does.

I tend to agree more with the Substantive. Lemert (1975) has suggested the two aspects of substance in regard to religion are (1) that it be manifested in some empirical social phenomenon such as a church and (2) that it includes an extra-empirical referent to some cosmic-level idea such as God (Lemert, 1975). Lemert suggests that the first, an observable social institution, is the necessary component while the second, the reference to a transcendent reality, is the sufficient component of such a definition.

THE RELIGION OF PSYCHOLOGY

The question next becomes "is psychology a religion?" Numerous functionalists (Bellah, 1967; Cox 1965; Luckman, 1967; Robertson, 1971; Tillich, 1952) would probably answer "If it is not *now*, it certainly can be." However, assuming a Substantive definition, the answer would be "No, psychology is not a religion." While it meets the necessary criterion of being an observable social entity (e.g. in its classes and in its articles, it does not claim that they are based on the belief in extra-empirical realities). To be more specific, while psychologists are always in danger of reifying their constructs (e.g. anxiety or cognitive imbalance) they would almost unanimously shy away from symbolic reification, such as the Christian religion engages in with the cross. Further, while social and behavioral scientists have, at times, assumed they had the answers for most human problems (e.g. during the Kennedy administration), they never present their recommendations as grounded in such a construct as *working toward the Kingdom of God*. No, psychology is not a religion in the crucial sense that it is not based on a transempirical cosmic idea.

But psychologists can be "religious" from this Substantive point of view. They can be religious both in substance (their belief in a transempirical reality) and in empirical reality (their participation in a group which affirms that reality). To be sure, Leuba, writing early in this century (1916), voiced the widely held opinion that religion and science did not go together. He stated, "I do not see any way to avoid the conclusion that disbelief in a personal God and in personal immortality is directly proportional to abilities making for success in the sciences" (p.279). The years have tempered this viewpoint more among natural than among social scientists.

Leuba, himself, in 1934 found this to be true and postulated that social scientists remained irreligious, on the whole, because religion, for them, was a topic to be studied scientifically. For natural scientists this is far less likely to be true. Interestingly enough, all studies of scientists in this century (e.g. Leuba, 1939; Lehman, 1974; Lehman & Witty, 1931; Lehman & Shriver, 1968) have found psychologists to be least religious among those studied. Therefore, it would appear that while we say from a Substantive/Empirical point of view that psychologists can be religious, characteristically they have not been religious as a group.

The most recent study of this phenomenon was undertaken by Ragan, Malony, and Beit-Hallahmi (1976) in a survey of a random sample of the members of the American Psychological Association. Once again, the findings showed that psychologists were less religious than the general academic population when compared with Lehman's (1972) sample of university faculty. This study did not compare psychologists to other scientists in the 1970s.

Four dimensions of religiosity were measured: ideology, ritual, experience, and cognition. In all four dimensions the figures are skewed in direction of psychologists being humanist rather than orthodox in ideology, being uninvolved in religious ritual, having fewer religious experiences, and having little religious knowledge. However, in each case there were psychologists who were overtly and traditionally religious to one degree or another. Psychologists can be religious if they so desire, but most are not.

The issue I intend to emphasize here is not so much the question of religion versus science as to indicate how a given type of definition (i.e. the Substantive/Empirical) can be used in answering the double questions of " Is psychology a religion?" and "Can psychologists be religious?" The answer to the first is "No" and to the second is "Yes."

Many will disagree with these conclusions but I suggest that the issue is definitional and that more than likely persons who disagree will be utilizing a functional approach that I believe confuses the issues. It would be inaccurate to claim psychology is a religion or that all psychologists are religious whether they know it or not. I will certainly agree that psychologists, like all persons, face the enigmas of life and have experiences of the numinous. But, some of them resolve those questions and interpret those experiences religiously, while others do not.

RESEARCH INTO SUBSTANTIVE/EMPIRICAL RELIGION

Included here is an illustration of how the Substantive/Empirical definition of religion in research has been utilized. I participated in an extended investigation of the Agasha Temple of Wisdom in Southern California (Malony and Miller, 1978). The Temple is a spiritualist church with a building, a membership, stated meetings, rituals of worship and study, written teachings, much transcendent beliefs and experiences, not to mention direct communications from Agasha, an ancient Egyptian seer living sometime before the birth of Christ. Without doubt, the most unique feature of the Temple was the pastor, Richard Zenor, who for over thirty years served as a medium, who, while in trance, makes contact with the dead, as well as with Agasha. The investigation was a participant observation study designed to understand, not explain, the varied meanings, motivations and styles of participation in such a religious organization. It is important to note why this group met the criteria for religious study. Most metropolitan areas have mediums, but persons seek them out as individuals and rarely do they come together as a church, nor does the leader organize them around the role as "pastor." The Temple of Agasha is unique in that it has transcendent substance and is an empirical reality. It is, thus, a religion.

Moreover, our method, of becoming participants and seeking to understand the religion from the inside, is consonant with our intent to be methodologically neutral and to let the religious consciousness speak for itself without judging the reality to which it attests. Berger (1974) strongly urges a return to looking at religious phenomena "from within." He suggests that phenomenology is probably the most appropriate method for such endeavors.

Interestingly enough, subjecting oneself to such a participant experience can have the effect of countering the social pressure most of us are well aware of to deny our transcendent experiences. I had such a thing happen at the Temple. One Sunday evening, when the pastor was in trance, he began to speak with the voice of Margie. To the Temple members, Margie is well known. She is a woman who died when she was two years old and has grown up on the other side, so to speak. Her special gift, according to the Temple belief system, is that she can help those who are dead make contact with the living. She does this by bringing these persons to talk with Pastor Zenor at the Temple meetings. He serves as a medium for their voices and, in turn, calls to persons present at the meeting to come talk with their deceased loved ones. They go up and stand close to him. He then talks with the voice of the deceased and the listener carries on a conversation. On the night of which I speak, numerous persons had been called forward.

"Mary, your mother is here and wants to talk with you?" "John, your wife is here and wants to talk with you;" "Bill, your uncle Harry is here and wants to talk with you;" etc. I had remained aloof from the process until a point where I became intrigued and began to wonder, "What would I do if he called my name?" I asked myself. At a point I decided, somewhat out of curiosity, "I will go and I will believe it if it happens." He did not call my name, but had he done so, I would have gone and cheerfully talked with my mother, father, or whoever wanted to talk with me. I have subsequently comfortably incorporated the possibility of such events into my own religious faith. It is an interesting testimony to openness in method that may or may not change one's own opinions. Suffice it to say, it is a method consistent with the Substantive definition of religion.

This essay has affirmed a preference for a Substantive/Empirical definition over a Functional understanding. This article then considered the question of whether psychology was a religion. It concluded with an example of how such a definition could be utilized in research.

REFERENCES

Allport, G.W. (1960). *The individual and his religion.* New York: Macmillan.

Allport, G.W. & Ross, J.M. (1967). Personal religious orientation and prejudice. *Journal of Personality and Social Psychology, 5,* 432-443.

Barth, K. (1960). *Church dogmatics (Vol.111).* Edinburgh: T & I Clark.

Bellah, R. (1967). Civil religion in America. *Daedalus, 96,* 1-21.

Berger, P.L. (1974). Second thoughts on defining religion. *Journal for the Scientific Study of Religion, 13,* 125-133.

Cox, H. (1965). The sociology of religion in a post-religious era. *Christian Scholar, 48,* 9-26.

Dittes, J.E. (1969). Secular religion: dilemma of churches and researchers. *Review of Religious Research, 10,* 65-81.

Dittes, J.W. (1971). Typing the typologies: some parallels in the career of church-sect and extrinsic-intrinsic. *Journal for the Scientific Study of Religion, 10,* 375-383.

James, W. (1961). *The Varieties of religious experience.* New York: The New American Library. (Original work published in 1902)

Jelsen, H.M., Everett, R.F., Mader, P.D., & Hamby, W.C. (1976). A test of Yinger's measure of non-doctrinal religion: implications fro invisible religion as a belief system. *Journal for the Scientific Study of Religion, 15,* 263-267.

Kalish, R.A. & Reynolds, D.K. (1973). Phenomenological reality and post death contact. *Journal for the Scientific Study of Religion, 12,* 209-221.

Lehman, E.C. (1972). The scholarly perspective and religious commitment. *Sociological Analysis, 33,* 199-216.

Lehman, E.C. (1974). Academic discipline and faculty religiosity in secular and church related colleges. *Journal for the Scientific Study of Religion, 13,* 205-220.

Lehman, E.C. & Shriver, D.W. (1968). Academic discipline as predictive of faculty religiosity. *Social Forces, 47,* 171-182.

Lehman, H.C. & Witty, P.A. (1931). Certain attitudes of present-day physicists and psychologists. *American Journal of Psychology, 43,* 664-678.

Lemert, C.C. (1975). Defining non-church religion. *Review of Religious Research, 16,* 186-197.

Leuba, J. H. (1916). *The belief in God and immortality.* Boston: Sherman & French.

Leuba, J.H. (1934). Religious beliefs of American scientists. *Harper's, 169,* 291-300.

Luckman, T. (1967). *The invisible religion.* New York: Macmillan.

Malony, H.N. & Miller, R.J. (1978). The Agasha Temple of Wisdom: Modern spiritualism reconsidered. *Journal of Altered States of Consciousness, 4(3)*, 277-290.

Pruyser, P.W. (1968). *A dynamic psychology of religion.* New York: Harper & Row Publishers.

Otto, R. (1956). *The sacred and the profane* (J. W. Harvey, trans.). New York: Oxford University Press.

Ragan, C., Malony, H. N., & Beit-Hallahmi, B. (1976, September). Psychologists and religion: Professional factors associated with personal belief. Paper presented at the annual meeting of the American Psychological Association, Washington, DC.

Robertson, R. (1971). *The sociological interpretation of religion.* New York: Schocken.

Spilka, B. (1970). Images of man and dimensions of personal religion: Values for an empirical psychology of religion. *Review of Religious Research, 11,*171-182.

Tillich, P. (1951). *Systematic theology (Vol. 1).* Chicago: University of Chicago Press.

Tillich, P. (1952). *The courage to be.* New Haven, CT: Yale University Press.

Torrance, T.F. (1969). *Theological science.* New York: Oxford University Press.

Yinger, J.M. (1977). A comparative study of the substructures of religion. *Journal for the Scientific Study of Religion, 16,* 67-86.

EIGHTEEN

John Wesley's Primitive Physick: An 18th Century Health Psychology

The 1980s have seen health psychology come of age. The Division of Health Psychology in the American Psychological Association, established in the late 1970s, has become one of the more active interest groups in the Association and both *The Health Psychologist* and *Psychology and Health: An International Journal* have become respected publications in the field. Although psychological interest in health issues is not new, it is only during this decade that these concerns have become focused in these explicit ways.

There have been, of course, many precursors to this increased interest in health among psychologists. Unexpectedly, among those who anticipated many current issues was the 18th century English divine, John Wesley. Although his professional identity was neither that of a psychologist nor that of a physician, out of a persistent concern for the plight of the poor Wesley became a leader in promoting both emotional and physical health in Great Britain. He wrote a volume entitled *Primitive Physick: Or an Easy and Natural Method of Curing Most Diseases* (1751). In this book, he advocated a number of surprisingly modern practices for healthy living and sickness prevention along with recommending a variety of simple cures for over 250 illnesses. In the 18th and early 19th century Wesley's book sold more than any other medical handbook and could be found in almost all British homes, particularly those of the poor.

Many of his admonitions could be placed in current textbooks of health psychology with little, or no, adaptation. In a noteworthy manner, Wesley dealt with every major area in the field as defined by Matarazzo (1982). This definition, given below, provides a set of topics under which Wesley's contributions can be considered. Such a discussion will afford contemporary health psychologists an awareness of how many of their issues are grounded in centuries-old concerns for the welfare of human beings. Matarazzo stated:

> *Health psychology is the aggregate of the specific educational, sci-*
> *entific and professional contributions of the discipline of psycholo-*
> *gy to (1) the promotion and maintenance of health, (2) the preven-*
> *tion and treatment of illness, (3) the identification of etiologic and*
> *diagnostic correlates of health, illness and related dysfunction, and*
> *(4) the analysis and improvement of the health care system and-*
> *health policy formation.* (1982, p. 4, numbers not in the original)

Prior to a consideration of his ideas and writings on each of these topics, some aspects of Wesley's background would seem appropriate to detail.

JOHN WESLEY'S INTEREST IN HEALTH

John Wesley (1704-1791) was an Anglican priest whose 87 years encompassed almost all of the 18th century. He is best-known as the founder of Methodism, a break-away movement of British Anglicanism which has continued to be a significant non-conformist religious movement in England and has become one of the larger Protestant churches in America. Originally begun as renewal movement among the poor and unchurched, Methodist distinctives have always included a strong concern for issues of social justice and welfare along-side a conviction that vital religion was grounded in personal religious experience.

The social and religious world of Great Britain during Wesley's time was a ripe field for concern about both social justice and human welfare. Wilder (1978) describes some of these conditions.

> *It was an age of immorality for England . . . Sir William*
> *Blackstone, the great jurist, went to hear every clergyman of note*
> *in London out of curiosity and "did not hear a single discourse*
> *which had more Christianity in it than the writings of Cicero;" and*
> *it would have been impossible for him to discover from what he*
> *heard "whether the preacher were a follower of Confucius, or*
> *Mohammed, or of Christ" . . . The court circles were characterized*
> *by open bribery and corruption . . . Adultery was the rule rather*
> *than the exception among the ruling and wealthy classes.*
> *Drunkenness was looked upon with tolerance, almost with admira-*
> *tion. It was even worse with the poorer classes. Every sixth house*
> *in London was a gin shop . . . Human life was cheap; law was*
> *severe. Over two hundred crimes, including petty theft, called for*
> *the death penalty . . . Women, for some crimes, were "publicly*
> *burned." The slave trade, brutal and horrible, reached its zenith*
> *during this period. Over four thousand men were imprisoned each*

year. (pp. 39-40)

In 17th century England, public hygiene was abominable. Open sewage and excrement from horses cluttered many streets. Sanitary conditions for personal toileting were very primitive. Food was often contaminated. Diet was poor and was weighted with fat. Epidemics were common. Medical treatment was expensive and rare. There was great disparity among the social classes. The industrial revolution was surging and working conditions were harsh. Child labor was rampant. Hopelessness among the common people was the order of the day. In fact, depression, known abroad as the "British Malady," was widespread.

It is noteworthy that although Wesley was privileged, in the sense that he was able to enjoy an Oxford education, his personal desire to be a holy person coupled with his concern to preach to the masses after his May 23, 1738 heartwarming religious experience, propelled him into compulsive action in behalf of the physical, as well as the spiritual and emotional, health of the average citizen. Wesley "forsook the seclusion of Oxford Halls to bear to the miners and fishermen, to the common people in general, a new religious life" (Barager, 1928, p. 59).

And this "new religious life, included a life free from physical illness; a life lived in conditions of cleanliness, justice, and emotional well-being. His success in these endeavors is attested in the "The Oxford Story," a well-known tourist attraction portraying the accomplishments of graduates over the 700 years of the university's history. John Wesley is pictured as the one outstanding light in what otherwise was a dull and mundane century of Oxford achievements. Although he lived through two revolutions, that of France and America, some have credited Wesley's influence on the social conscience of England with preventing that country from being involved in a similar upheaval.

In regard to health issues, Wesley is credited with originating the saying, "Cleanliness is next to Godliness." In an essay on the 19th century crusade against dirt, a professor of preventive medicine noted that a hundred years before, John Wesley had "fought his great fight for hygiene-he was *the greatest health educator of the eighteenth century in Britain*" (Hill, 1958, p. 117, underlining not in the original). Vanderpool (1986, p. 320) concurred with this assessment: "More than any other major figure in Christendom, John Wesley actively involved himself with the theory and practice of medicine and with the specific principles and practices of ideal physical and mental health."

A widespread health movement followed his work (Edwards, 1933) and many historians would agree with the statement that in matters of "hygiene and preventive medicine Wesley is an acknowledged pioneer, a voice crying in the wilderness . . . a voice of great power and penetration because of the enormous personal influence he came to have throughout the whole nation." (Turrell, 1938, p. 16) As an indication of his popularity, Wesley's book, *Primitive Physick* (1751) went through 38 English and 24 American editions before it took its place as a quaint artifact on library back shelves in the mid 19th century.

As a clergyperson, Wesley's involvement in medical matters might seem disturbing and inappropriate were it not for the fact that it was common in the 17th and 18th centuries for village parsons and lords-of-the-manor to act as healers for those under their care who were poor or far removed from physicians' offices (Rack, 1982). Moreover, Wesley was widely read in medical matters. He had always had a secret desire to be a doctor and had begun serious reading of medical texts in his spare time soon after entering Oxford as a student. The preface to his *Primitive Physick* is a thorough summary of the history of medicine and the cures he recommends, while quaint in light of modern procedures, are a respectable reflection of medical treatment in his day (Riddell, 1914).

Of greatest influence on his interest in healing, however, was his contention that most physicians, so-called "gentlemen of the faculty," were only interested in making money. He was convinced that they collaborated with the apothecaries in prescribing complicated drugs which often did little good. Wesley wrote two letters defending his practice of "physic" (i.e., healing) which negatively depict physicians. He stated:

Neither Jesus nor His disciples derived their authority from the national licensing corporation of their day . . . Licensing bodies may be set up as social safeguards or as protection for private interests . . . unrecognized authority may by-pass them or sweep them aside. (Hill, 1958, P. 15)

Further,

For more than twenty years I had numberless proofs that regular physicians do exceedingly little good. From a deep conviction of this I have believed it my duty within these four months last past to prescribe such medicines to 600-700 of the poor as I knew were proper for their several disorders. Within six weeks nine in ten of them who had taken these medicines were remarkably altered for the better and many were cured of diseases under which they had labored 10, 20, 40 years. Now, ought I have let one of these poor wretches perish because I was not a regular physician? to have said, 'I know what will cure you, but I am not of the College; You must send for Doctor Mead?' Before Dr. Mead had come in his chariot the man might have been in his coffin. (Hill, 1958, p. 15)

With this background in mind, I now turn to a discussion of Wesley's specific contributions under headings suggested by Matarazzo in his definition of health psychology noted above.

WESLEY'S IDEAS ABOUT THE PROMOTION AND MAINTENANCE OF HEALTH

Very early in his student days at Oxford, Wesley came under the influence of George Cheyne's book *An Essay on Health and Long Life* (1724). Cheyne (1671-1743) was a well known Bath physician whose popular medical writings "preached temperance to an intemperate generation" (Jeffrey, 1937, p. 61). Cheyne was a convert to his own teachings. After giving up preparing for the ministry and becoming a physician, Cheyne had set up practice in London where his habits exemplified Wesley's negative judgments about selfishness and greed. He eventually weighed over 350 pounds due to heavy drinking and rich eating. Even after strict abstention and "a course of waters at Bath," he slipped back into such obeseness that he could hardly breathe and could scarcely walk. He recovered by dieting on milk and vegetables. This led him to write his book, which was the first medical book written for popular consumption in England.

Wesley arranged his own life in accordance with Cheyne's prescriptions. He wrote his mother about his enthusiasm:

I suppose you have seen the famous Dr. Cheyne's book of Health and Long Life . . .

He refers almost everything to temperance and exercise and supports most things with physical reasons . . . He entirely condemns eating anything salty or highly seasoned, as also pork, fish, and stall-fed cattle and also recommends for drink two pints of water and one of wine in twenty-four hours . . . in consequence of Dr. Cheyne I chose to eat sparingly and to drink water. (Turrell, 1938, pp. 12-13)

Cheyne recommended six habits: breathe pure air, eat and drink temperately, sleep plentifully, exercise abundantly, evacuate and excrete without obstruction, and control the expression of the passions (i.e., emotions) (Rosseau, 1968). Wesley practiced these faithfully. He exercised daily, often went for a swim in the river, drank much water, and ate little. He even later advised the preachers in his movement to retire early and to "kill themselves a little each day" by eating less than they wanted.

Wesley devoted a chapter to each of Cheyne's six health habits in his *Primitive Physick,* These habits were known as the "non-naturals" for two reasons (Ott, 1980). In the first place, they were unnatural in the sense that they went against the natural inclination to gorge oneself and be intemperate in self-expression. Wesley even commented that people would likely pay little attention to Cheyne's book because it advised against eating and drinking. In the second place, they were, according to Wesley, the laws of health given by God for controlling the ways humans were intended to interact with and control nature. It was God's intention that humans fulfill their created potentials through long and healthy lives. Along with Plato, Wesley felt that health was a "secondary," not a "primary," virtue. Health was the means by which humans could do what God intended them to be and do.

Health was not an end in itself. Wesley took his cue from the biblical statement that "the body is the temple of the Holy Spirit," meaning that peoples, bodies were to be treated with great respect because they were like sacred buildings in which the spirit of God resided. Although perfect health was the state Adam and Eve enjoyed in the Garden of Eden, since the fall illness came and sensible regimen, based on the discipline of the "non-naturals," was the God-appointed pattern for healthy living, according to Wesley.

Wesley attributed most sickness to a violation of these six non-naturals. He came close to equating lack of care of the body with sin. The name "Methodist," a label of derision ascribed to him and his followers, was due, in no small measure, to the exactness in manner of living, i.e., the "method," which he recommended. Wesley, himself, perceived the name as quite appropriate since the label could be said to refer to an ancient sect of physicians called "Methodists,, who believed that most diseases could be cured by exercise and diet. Many would agree with the assessment that these rules for preventing illness and sustaining health "would serve as admirably now as then" (Barager, 1928, p. 63).

WESLEY IDEAS ABOUT THE PREVENTION AND TREATMENT OF ILLNESS

These comments about Wesley's concern for self-control, diet, and exercise lead naturally into a discussion of the second of Matarazzo's topics in his definition of health psychology, namely, the issues of prevention and treatment. Since prevention was related in the previous section to adherence to the non-naturals and will be considered in the section on the health care system, the present discussion will deal largely with treatment.

As noted earlier, Wesley was no stranger to medical matters. His interest in medical matters changed from a side interest to a central focus when he began preparing for a missionary assignment in Georgia in the early 1730s. He had hopes, as he wrote, of being "some service to those who had no regular physician among them." While in Georgia he participated in, at least, one autopsy and studied the healing practices of the Indians. He was convinced that native peoples were uncontaminated by the "theoretical medicine" of such cul-

tures as England and that they used tried and simple methods of healing which
could be rediscovered and applied by anyone willing to use them. Vanderpool
(1986) noted that Wesley asserted,

> *Ancient or primitive medical remedies have certain basic character-*
> *istics . . . They are efficacious and useful because they are founded*
> *upon trial-and-error experiments and experience. They are plain,*
> *simple, safe, and inexpensive, because they are readily found in*
> *ordinary plants, animals, and inorganic substances. These qualities*
> *paralleled the "plain and simple" Gospel proclaimed by Wesley, a*
> *Gospel unfettered by theological abstractions, available to all*
> *humans irrespective of wealth or station in life, curative for body*
> *and soul . . .* (p. 324)

This search for proven methods of healing became the guiding principle
in his book *Primitive Physick*. The title of this book portrays its content.
"Physick" is a synonym for "healing" and "Primitive" refers to its origins in
those ancient methods handed down from father to son. Wesley felt that cures
based on these methods were better for two reasons. First, they utilized procedures and materials that were accessible and available in the natural world.
Second, they had been pragmatically tried and demonstrated to be valid in
treating disease.

Wesley's chief complaint about physicians of his day was that they
depended on theory rather than proof for their treatments. He perceived, somewhat correctly, that 18th century medicine was still preoccupied with a
"humoral" theory of disease which concluded that illness was due to an imbalance of body humors. Humoral balance, in turn, could be restored by ingestion
of the many chemicals which were being concocted and stored at the apothecaries.

Although greatly concerned with these "theories" of disease and treatment, medicine at this time was not as unpragmatic as Wesley contended.
Physicians were functionally oriented and did continue to prescribe new drugs
when the old ones didn't work. Wesley's contention was that this process led to
great expense and danger for the patient. Wesley's recommendation would be
that physicians needed to attend to the tried and proven methods of folk medicine. Not only were these approaches cheaper, they had already gone through
generations of trial and error.

It is noteworthy that this approach by Wesley was almost atheoretical
in its pragmatism. He was not concerned with why a healing method worked;
only that it did. Some labeled him empiric;" he called himself "experimental."
In our contemporary understanding of these terms, empiric is probably far
more correct than experimental. In no way could Wesley be called experimen-

tal if, by that term, is meant an approach whereby conditions are controlled and the tenets of a theory are tested. At best, Wesley was a trial and error pragmatist, not an experimentalist.

Nevertheless, he recommended an approach that, in some ways, was very enlightened in that he provided in his book several cures for each of the 288 illnesses he described. He based these lists of possible treatments on the premise that not every cure works for every person. Nor do some cures work on every occasion. Wesley suggested that the ill person should try one of the recommendations and, if that did not work, try another. In a somewhat curious manner, he marked some of the 900 treatments "T" (Tried) and some "I" (Infallible) as if some of the unmarked treatments had not been subjected to "experiment" or as if some other treatments had been tried but worked only part of the time. At worse, these markings would seem a violation of his methodology while, at best, they would seem a humble admission that only a very few treatments work every time.

Turning to the recommended treatments themselves, judgments about their validity were, and are, mixed. It should come as no surprise that Wesley's negative criticism of physicians should be matched, among physicians, by equally negative reactions to his medical "dabbling." Hill (1958, p. 119) quotes the evaluation of one author who judged Wesley and his followers to be credulous, anti-intellectual, and dangerous to society. *Primitive Physick* was pictured as "a little book, on sale at all Methodist meeting houses; an absurd, fantastic compilation of uncritical folklore."

One humorous interaction occurred in the mid 1770s. William Hawes, a well-known physician to the London Dispensary, accused Wesley of being a quack and published a disparaging review of Wesley's book in a 1776 issue of *Lloyd's Evening Post*. Wesley replied by letter to wit:

> Dear Sir, My bookseller informs me that since you published your remarks on the Primitive Physick, there has been a greater demand than ever. If, therefore, you please to publish a few further remarks you would confer a favor upon your Humble Servant.

(Hill, 1958, p. 121)

The public's reaction to Hawes' criticism implies that Wesley was not the only one who distrusted the opinions of medical professionals!

Two evaluations in the early years of this century illustrate that, while some in the medical profession still retained a disdain for Wesley's ideas, others had come to see his treatment recommendations in less negative eyes. Thomas (1906, p. 198) writing in The American Physician concluded that " . . . there was something undignified in this preoccupation with bodily ailments and this meddling with their cure on the part of one capable of exercising so profound an influence on his generation as Wesley." He further opined, "There is nothing in the book of any value whatsoever, and, curiously nothing that might not have been written by a person with the slightest education and meanest intellect" (P. 198).

Yet, Riddell (1914, p. 68), writing in *The New York Medical Journal* only a few years later, reached a decidedly different conclusion. He stated,

> *It will be found that Wesley's treatment of diseases was at least as reconcilable with common sense as that of the contemporary regular practitioner, much more so in some cases. Of it, at least, it could be said . . . "It did no great harm."*

Riddell notes that, while Wesley was generally critical of physicians, he, nevertheless contended that his prescriptions were intended for those with chronic illnesses which had not been alleviated and that in the case of acute or life-threatening sickness one should seek the services of a "doctor who fears God."

Thus, it can be said, that while a number of Wesley's treatments did, indeed, rely on folklore, many of his treatments were in accord with the medicine of his day. Although they may seem quaint to us, they do not appear so when compared with much that was current in the 1700s. Rosseau (1968, p. 245) compared Wesley's recommendations to the writings Of six medical authorities of the same century and stated, "When discussed in this context, Wesley's treatise does not suffer." Of note is the fact that he disparaged some of the more radical treatments used by his contemporaries such as blood-letting and quicksilver.

Three examples of Wesley's prescriptions from *Primitive Physick* will serve to illustrate his approach. The 288 illnesses are arranged in alphabetical order like a dictionary. There are as few as 1 and as many as 10 prescriptions provided for each of the maladies:

> *A Chronical Head-ach*
> *Keep your feet in warm water, a quarter of hour before you go to bed; for two or three weeks; or*
> *Wear tender Hemlock-leaves, under the feet changing them daily; or Order a Tea-kettle of cold water to be poured on your head each morning in a slender stream; or*
> *Apply to the head bruised Cummuin-seed, fried with an egg; or Take a large tea-cup full of Cadinus Tea without sugar fasting for six or seven mornings; or*
> *Boil Wood-betony in new milk and strain it. Breakfast on this for five or six weeks.* (Wesley, 1751, p. 39)

Small Pox
Drink largely of Toast and Water; or
Let your constant drink be milk and water mixt; or
The best food is Milk and Apples; or
Bread dippled in Milk and water;
Take care to have a free, pure, and cool Air.
    Therefore open the casement every day, only do not let it chill the patient. If they strike in, and convulsions follows, drink a pint of cold water immediately. This instantly stops the convulsions, and drives out the pock. Lentils and Rape-weeds are a certain cure for small pox. (Wesley, 1751, p. 58)

A Stubbern Ulcer
Burn to ashes (but not too long) the gross stalks on which the red Coleworts grow.
    Make a plaister with this and fresh butter. Change it once a day; or,
    Aply a poultis of boilld Parsnips. This will cure even when the bone is foul. (Wesley, 1751, p. 71)

Primitive Physick is replete with remedies which would still be in vogue today. These include cold water bathing, poultices, hot and cold drinks, purges, and drugs made from ingredients found in most kitchens. Of course, there are other remedies, such as cow dung, ground up spider webs, and crushed up warts found on the inside of horses, legs, which appear curious and unusual.

The lists include amusing treatments such as those recommended for consumption and head cold. For the former Wesley recommends "Every morning cut a little turf of fresh earth, and, laying down, breathe in the hole for a quarter of an hour" (Dunlop, 1964, p. 70). For the latter Wesley recommends "pare very thin the yellow rind of an orange, roll it up inside out and thrust a roll into each nostril" (Dunlop, 1964, p. 70). An enticing recommendation for stomach ache was to lie with a live puppy resting on the stomach. He even included several treatments for aging which ended with "death—which is the final cure."

Of immense interest to modern health psychology are Wesley's prescriptions for nervous disorders. Here Wesley asserted that nervous disorders:

Are of two kinds: 1. Those which proceed from the Nerves being compressed by the swelling of the muscular flesh; Or, 2. When the Nerves themselves are disordered. In the former case, Temperance and Abstemiousness will generally cure; In the latter, when the Nerves perform their office too languidly, a GOOD AIR is the first

*requisite. The patients also should rise early, and as soon as the
Dew is off the ground, walk . . .*

Wesley follows these admonitions with several paragraphs concerning
diet and tincture made from Valerian-root and powder from Misletoe. He concludes with the following statement: "But I am firmly persuaded, there is no
remedy in Nature, for Nervous Disorders of every kind, comparable to the
proper and constant use of the Electrical Machine" (Wesley, 1751, P. 47).

This unexpected recommendation for shocking sick persons is likely the
least well-known and most controversial of Wesley's remedies. on the surface,
it would seem as if Wesley was anticipating the use of electroconvulsive shock
treatment in psychiatry by over 100 years. This is only partly true. More correct is the judgment by Hill (1957) that Wesley was one of the most outstanding general electrotherapists of the 18th century. He did, indeed, embrace the
general use of static electric shock when only a very few physicians had done
so but cautioned against the overly strong shocks which have come to characterize ECT today.

Wesley opined that electricity was the "elixir" which God had put into
all organisms to make them come to life. He felt that electric shocks were the
God-given answer to the need for a cheap and effective remedy for many illnesses. on the last page of *Primitive Physick* he lists 35 illnesses which
"Electrifying in a proper Manner, cures." This list is exceeded only by the 73
maladies which he says can be healed through "cold bathing." Wesley contended that such widely different conditions as blindness, gout, leprosy, rheuma-
tism, tooth-ache, lameness, cramps, and fits could be cured by "electrifying."
He evidenced some awareness of the underlying function by suggesting that
depressed persons needed to have electricity put into them while manic persons
needed to have electricity drawn from them. While his enthusiasm was likely
overstated, Wesley yet identified clearly the value of electrical stimulation in
nervous disorders, many of which we would term hysteric.

A man of broad interests, Wesley wrote over 200 books, mostly about
religious subjects. It is not realized, however, that he buttressed his opinions
about the healing power of electricity with study of almost all that was written
about the subject up to the 1750s. He summarized these theories and experiments in the first part of his book on the subject entitled, *The Desideratum: or
Electricity Made Plain and Useful by a Lover of Mankind and of Common
Sense* (1760). It is, indeed, noteworthy that he pioneered the application of a
thorough understanding of this phenomenon to the alleviation of human suffering and the cure of many diseases. In the preface to his book, Wesley stated
that he was aware that electricity would not cure all disorders. "Indeed," he
wrote, "there cannot be in Nature any such Thing as an absolute Panaccea . .

." (yet, he continued) "I doubt not, but more nervous Disorders would be cured in one Year, by this single Remedy, than the whole English Materia Medica will cure, by the End of the century" (Wesley, 1760, pp. 7,9). He could not resist buttressing his point with another dig at the medical profession!

WESLEY'S IDEAS ABOUT THE ETIOLOGY AND DIAGNOSIS OF HEALTH AND ILLNESS

The third aspect of Matarazzo's definition of health psychology pertains to the etiologic and diagnostic correlates of health and illness. Here, too, John Wesley had much to say that is relevant to the history of the field. On the one hand, he had an awareness of what would be termed today "psychosomatics." On the other hand, he had a deep appreciation for the part that the physical environment plays in both helping persons recover from illness and preventing their becoming sick again.

Wesley's awareness of psychosomatics is nowhere better exemplified than in a case report in his Journal reported by Hill (1958, p. 22):

> . . . *reflecting today on the case of a poor woman who had continual pain in her stomach. I could not but remark on the inexcusable negligence of most physicians in cases of this nature. They prescribe drug after drug, without knowing a jot of the matter about the root of the disorder, and without knowing this they cannot cure, though they can murder the patient. Whence came this woman's pain (which she would never have told had she been questioned about it)? From fretting for the death of her son. And what availed medicines while that fretting continued? Why then do not all physicians consider how far bodily disorders are caused or influenced by the mind, and in those cases which are utterly out of their sphere call in the assistance of the ministers; as ministers, when they find the mind disordered by the body, call in the assistance of the physicians?*

Toward the close of the preface to his book Wesley summed up his ideas regarding the relationship between the mind and the body; between the emotions, so called "passions," and health. He stated,

> *VI. 1. The Passions have a greater Influence on Health than most People are aware of. 2. All violent and sudden Passions dispose to, or actually throw People into Acute Diseases. 3. The slow and lasting Passions, such as Grief and hopeless Love, bring on Chronic Diseases. 4. Till the Passions which caused the Disease is calmed, medicine is applied in vain.* (Wesley, 1751, p. xx).

Wesley seems to have adopted a theory of maintenance and moderation. Ideally persons who experience strong emotions of any kind should do so infrequently and only for short periods of time if they would maintain their health. Sustained strong emotions work havoc on the body. Wesley offered no theory of how this happens but he definitely anticipates what is known today about stress reactions and the response of the parasympathetic nervous system to threat.

Subsequent to these comments on the emotions, Wesley adds a comment about the emotion, or passion, par excellence, namely "the love of God." Here he writing not about an emotion humans have toward God, but an emotion God has toward persons--to which humans can respond. He calls God's love the "Sovereign Remedy of all Miseries." His rationale is as follows:

> . . . for in particular it (the love of God) effectuallyprevents all the Bodily Disorders the Passions introduce, by keeping the Passions themselves within due Bounds. And by unspeakable Joy and perfect Calm, Serenity and Tranquility it gives the mind, it becomes the most powerful of all the Means of Health and Long Life. (Wesley, 1751, p. xx)

While Wesley's Christian presuppositions about the nature of the divine would, by no means, be shared by all contemporary health psychologists, the value of a philosophy of life which avails persons of inner strength over and beyond the exigencies of experience is a valid component of modern stress management and problem solving programs. Wesley, quite correctly, perceives that experiencing reassuring affirmation from a source beyond environmental stressors works toward "keeping the Passions within due Bounds," and provides "Calm, Serenity and Tranquility." The process he describes has been validated by modern approaches to the reduction of stress.

In addition to these ideas about psychosomatic relationships, Wesley had strong ideas about how the environment handicapped or enhanced treatment. He not only despaired about the unavailability of physicians for those who could not pay, but he also recognized that hospitals were often places where people became sicker rather than weller. It was very common for hospitalized patients to contract "hospital fever," a lethal form of typhus. Conditions were appalling. Sanitary conditions were crude. Smells were offensive. Nurses were ignorant about the spread of infection.

Taking his cues from the writing of Simone-Andre Tissot, a Swiss physician, on prevention and cure, Wesley detailed a set of conditions which would speed treatment and avoid complications. These recommendations included cautions about over-heating the room and keeping patients in closed rooms where the air would become foul "whereby so many diseases are heightened and prolonged and so many thousands of lives thrown away" (Hill, 1958, pp. 59-60). He opined that bad nursing often impeded healing. He was against forcing patients to eat, inducing vomiting, and sweating. He advocated fresh air, water, and leaving the stomach alone lest it become inflamed. He recommended plenty to drink, light food, and sleeping on a pallet--no feathers, covered only with sheets. He advised making the bed daily, changing the sheets every-other-day and eating a variety of fruits during the feverish stages. He cautioned against breathing near the face of those who were sick. By these simple methods he concluded that many acute diseases could be mitigated, if not cured.

Wesley even had advice for the regimen to follow in case of major illnesses such as pneumonia. In addition to seeking a "physician who fears God," he recommended:

> . . . drinking lukewarm barley water often, taking 10 ounces of oxymel of squills added to 50 ounces of elder flowers in fusion every two hours and applying a poultice of boiled bread, milk and hot water to the breast and throat. In extreme sickness he advised taking a spoonful of a mixture of 60 ounces of syrup of violets and 10 ounces of spirit of sulfur in barley water. (Hill, 1958, p. 75)

In regard to the living conditions which might cause illness, Wesley showed that he had done a thorough survey of typical working and living conditions. He advised against a persisting too long at fatiguing labor, resting in a cold place after becoming overheated, drinking cold water when one was very hot, and getting drunk or being intemperate in eating. He noted that changes in the weather, failing to air lodgings, having ditches too close to the window, eating bad grain or badly cooked bread, and constructing a house too close to the ground were all dangers to be avoided.

Wesley propagated these ideas in numerous pamphlets and in teachings at meetings of the Methodist Societies to which many people came. Hill (1958, p. 8) concluded that because of Wesley's influence, "thousands were so changed that, along with a spiritual renaissance, there was a desire for higher mental and physical standards." The leaders of the Societies were encouraged to be models of good health practices. Wesley quaintly advised one leader in Northern Ireland,

> If you regard your health, touch no supper but a little milk or water gruel. This will by the blessing of God secure you from nervous disorders . . . Avoid all familiarity with women. This is deadly poison both to them and you. You cannot be too wary in this respect . . . Avoid all nastiness, dirt, slovenliness . . . Do not stink above ground . . . Whatever clothes you have, let them be whole

. . . Let none ever see a ragged Methodist. Clean yourself of lice
. . . Do not cut off your hair, but clean it, and keep it clean. Cure
yourself and your family of the itch: a spoonful of brimstone will
cure you . . . Use no tobacco unless prescribed by a physician. It is
an uncleanly and unwholesome self-indulgence..... Use no snuff . . .
Touch no dram. It is liquid fire..... a sure though slow poison.
(Ayling, 1979, p. 166)

WESLEY'S ANALYSIS AND IMPROVEMENT OF THE HEALTH CARE SYSTEM

Wesley was an extremely socially sensitive person. Almost all aspects of life in 18th century England came under his scrutiny. Soon after his "heart-warming experience" in 1738 he returned to Oxford and preached sermons at St. Mary's church which became increasingly critical of the university's unconcern for the plight of the average person. Soon after examining some of Wesley's sermons, the chancellor caused invitations to preach at university chapels to cease. Pulpits of other dioceses also became closed when priests learned that Wesley wanted to carry worship to the streets.

Wherever Wesley went, he made statements about social injustice. At Stoke-on-Trent he spoke out against working conditions and corruption in the pottery industry. At Penzance he spoke out against smuggling among those citizens who moved the lighthouses and plundered ship-wrecks. The last letter he wrote, only a short time before his death, was to Wilberforce, encouraging him in his Parliamentary fight to rid England of American slavery which Wesley considered the greatest social evil of his day. He established a savings society which gave interest free loans to the poor. He became greatly concerned over prison conditions. Thus, it should come as no surprise that his protests should extend to the health-care system.

As we have noted earlier, he was very critical of physicians and druggists. After tracing the corruption of simple remedies by medical theories, Wesley states in the preface to *Primitive Physick*:

Is it inquired, But are there not Books enough already, on every
Part of the Art of Medicine? Yes, too many, ten Times over,
considering how little to the Purpose the far greater Part of them
speak. But beside this, they are so dear (expensive) for the poor
Men to buy, and too hard for plain Men to understand . . . In all
(the books) that have yet fallen into my Hands, I find many dear
and many farfetched Medicines; many of so dangerous a Kind, as
a Prudent Man would never meddle with. And against the greater
Part of those Medicines; there is a further Objection, They consist
of too many Ingredients. This Common Method of compounding

and decompounding Medicines, can never be reconciled to
Common Sense. Experience shows, That One Thing will cure
most Disorders, at least as well as Twenty put together. Then
why do you add the other Nineteen? only to swell the Apothecary
Bill: Nay, possibly, on Purpose to prolong the Distemper, that
the Doctor and he may divide the Spoil.
(Wesley, 1751, pp. xii-xiii)

To meet this need for cheaper and more available health care, Wesley wrote his book. He called himself both "God's steward for the poor" and "a lover of mankind." A more admirable motive for improving the social system would be hard to find. He went a step beyond writing about treatment and prevention, however. He made attending to the sick a central focus of the groups which he organized.

One of the chief duties of the leaders of Methodist Societies was to visit the sick. Wesley found, however, that this task for the "stewards" to attend to all who were sick was too big in addition to their other obligation. So he divided London into 23 districts and commissioned 64 leaders who he "judged to be of the most tender, loving spirit" to be official visitors of the sick. In his usual compulsive manner, Wesley mandated that each visitor would see the sick in his or her district three times a week. Their task was to "inquire into their disorders, and procure advice for them, and to do anything for them which might add to their comfort" (Marriot, 1846, p. 360). This plan was Wesley's own health-care system.

The system was only partially successful. It was more pallative than ameliorative. Wesley wrote:

I was still in pain for many of the poor that were sick; there was so
great expense. And, first, I resolved to try whether they might not
receive more benefit in the hospitals. Upon the trial, we found
there was indeed less expense, but no more good done than before.
I then asked the advice of several Physicians for them. But still it
profited not. I saw the poor people pining away, and several
families ruined, and that without remedy. (Marriot, 1846, p. 360)

In response to his own troubled reflections on the lack of treatment for the poor, Wesley set up free clinics in Bristol and London. His first dispensary for the poor was actually established in 1746, one year before the publication of *Primitive Physick*. He recorded his deliberations thusly:

At length I thought of a kind of desperate expedient: "I will
prepare and give them physic myself . . . and took unto my
assistance an Apothecary, and an experienced Surgeon; resolving,

at the same time, not to go out of my depth, but to leave all
difficult and complicated cases to such medical attendants as the
patient should choose." (Marriot, 1846, p. 360)

Dunlop described the first day the clinic opened in this account:
Thirty patients were waiting when the doors first opened.
William Kirman, an aged weaver, who lived on Old Nichol Street,
shuffled up to be treated.
"What complaint have you?" asked Wesley.
"Oh, sir, a cough, a very sore cough. I can get no rest night
or day."
"How long have you had it?"
"About three-score years; it began when I was 11 years old."
Wesley gave the old weaver a harmless drug. His first patient
was not likely to be a problem.
"Take this three or four times a day. If it does you no good, it
will do you no harm," he said.
The old man took the drug and later reported to Wesley that
he had been cured. (Dunlop, 1964, p. 23)

During the first month over 300 patients came. Over 500 came during
the first half-year. Expenses for medications were about 40 pounds. Eventually
Wesley established four clinics in London and one in Bristol. It is noteworthy
that Wesley earned over 150,000 pounds from his writings but spent almost all
of it on human welfare projects. He died with little money left. Although the
clinics did not survive his death, this effort to improve health care delivery is
significant testimony to his responsible involvement in human welfare.

CONCLUSION

Contemporary health psychologists can look with some appreciation on persons such as the 18th century divine, John Wesley, for focusing attention on
many issues with which they are still concerned. This essay detailed Wesley's
thoughts and actions in promoting health, preventing illness, identifying the
causes of disease, and in improving health care—each of which is an aspect of
health psychology according to the definition of Matarazzo (1982). One writer
summed up Wesley's contribution by stating,

He found the great masses without help in time of distress, and
failing a more satisfactory solution, he set himself with characteris-
tic energy and thoroughness to the task. He did much to direct the

attention of the public to the importance of health and he pointed to the source from which help must come. As a layman, he has earned, I think, an honored place in the history of medicine. (Barager, 1928, P. 65)

And we might add, "Wesley has earned an honored place in the history of health psychology, as well."

REFERENCES

Ayling, S. (1979). *John Wesley.* London: Collins.

Barager, C. A. (1928). John Wesley and medicine. *Annals of Medical History, 10,* 59-65.

Cheyne, G. (1724). An essay on health and long life. London. Dunlop, R. (1964). John Wesley: Medical missionary to the New World. *Today's Health, 42* (12), 20-23, 70-72.

Edwards, M. L. (1933). *John Wesley and the 18th century: A study of his social and political influence.* London: Allen and Unwin (New York: Abingdon Press).

Hill, A. (1958) John Wesley among the Physicians: A study in eighteen-century medicine. London: The Epworth Press. Hill, 0. (1951). J. P. Marat's use of electricity in the practice of medicine. *British Journal of Physical Medicine, 10* (5), 100-102.

Jeffrey, F. (1937). John Wesley's *Primitive Physick.*

Proceedinqs of the Wesley Historical Society, 21, 60-67. Marriot, T. (1846). Methodism in former days: medicine and medical advice. *Wesleyan Methodist magazine, 69,* 359-364. Matarazzo, J. D. (1982). Behavioral health's challenge to academic, scientific and professional psychology. *American Psychologist, 37* (i), 1-14.

Ott, P. W. (1980). A corner of history: John Wesley and the non-naturals. *Preventive Medicine, 9,* 578-584.

Rack, H. D. (1982). Doctors, demons and early Methodist history. In W. J. Sheils (Ed.), *The church and healing: Papers read at the twentieth summer meeting and the twenty-first winter meeting of the Ecclesiastical History Society—Studies in church history* (Vol. 19, pp. 137-152). Oxford, England: Blackwell's.

Riddell, W. R. (1914). Wesley's system of medicine. *New York Medical Journal, 99,* 64-68.

Rosseau, G. S. (1968). John Wesley's *Primitive Physick. Harvard Library Bulletin,* 16.

Thomas, B. G. (1906). John Wesley on the art of healing. *American Physician, 32,* 295-298.

Turrell, W. J. (1938). *John Wesley: Physician and electrotheravist.* Oxford: Basil Blackwell.

Vanderpool, H. Y. (1986). The Wesleyan-Methodist tradition. In R. L. Numbers & D. W. Amundsen (Eds.), *Caring and curing in the western religious traditions* (pp. 317-353). New York: Macmillan.

Wesley, J. (1751). *Primitive Physick: or an easy and natural method of curing most diseases.* London: J. Palmar.

Wesley, J. (1760). *The desideratum. or electricity made plain and useful by a lover of mankind and of common sense.* London: Bailliere, Tindall and Cox.

Wilder, F. (1978). *The remarkable world of John Wesley: Pioneer in mental health.* Hicksville, NY: Exposition Press.

NINETEEN

The Future Of An Illusion, The Illusion of a Future

An Historic Dialogue on the Value of Religion Between Oskar Pfister and Sigmund Freud

This is an account of the Freud-Pfister dialogue. Sigmund Freud was the well known Viennese neurologist who founded psychoanalysis. Oskar Pfister was a Reform Church pastor in Zurich, Switzerland. Pfister was the first religious professional to embrace psychoanalysis. Pfister began writing to Freud in 1908. They corresponded with each other until Freud's death in 1939. Pfister kept all his letters from Freud. Freud preserved a number of his letters from Pfister. They have been brought together in a book entitled Psychoanalysis and Faith (Meng and Freud, 1963).

In addition, in 1973, several organizations, including the Institutes of Religion and Health, sponsored a symposium to celebrate the centennial of Pfister's birth. Several of the presentations from this symposium have been published in the Journal of Religion and Health (cf. Stettner, 1973, Bonhoeffer, 1974, Irwin, 1973, Jager-Werth, 1974; and Stettner, 1974).

The issues are re-presented here in the form of quotations from the correspondence followed by concluding remarks. It is hoped that a reconsideration of this historic debate will enliven appreciation for the spirit of intellectual dialogue and evoke a new awareness of the major concerns. The points of view expressed by Pfister and Freud are by no means dead.

OVERVIEW

Both Freud and Pfister wrote many articles and books about psychoanalysis in general and about religion in particular. Pfister was influential in such clinical areas as the splitting off of the emotions and the question of lay analysis. In the area of religion they differed radically. Although Freud affirmed Pfister's use of psychoanalysis in pastoral work, he was a confirmed atheist who felt that religion was a collective neurosis without which society would be better off. Pfister, in turn, was a perennial optimist who was convinced of the value and the power of religion. He saw this exemplified in the love of Jesus. He thought that Jesus' love would one day bring all persons together in brotherhood and peace (cf. Pfister's book Christianity and Fear. 1944, 1948).

The two men remained friends to the end. This is more than can be said of many other colleagues of Freud (cf. Jung and Adler, for example). They debated civilly and openly. In 1927 Freud notified Pfister of his forthcoming book The Future of an Illusion and said he hoped that Pfister would not find it inappropriate. Pfister responded with an article entitled The Illusion of A Future (1928) and sent it to Freud for perusal before publication.

Freud was both more pessimistic and more optimistic than Pfister. Pfister was an old-line liberal who was convinced that the love of Jesus could conquer evil. Freud was pessimistic with regard to human nature and suggested that Pfister did not truly acknowledge evil in persons. Yet Freud had a naive faith in science and reason. According to Freud, persons needed no religious figure to follow. They could trust rationalistic science to lead them to nirvana. Pfister felt that Freud's trust in science was unproved and ill founded.

THE FREUD-PFISTER CORRESPONDENCE

The aforementioned issues are the heart of the letters between Freud and Pfister. Excerpts from this correspondence follow. Although their ideas about religion are of prime interest, references to many other historical events can be noted.

The correspondence is grouped into three periods: An Early Period of Cordiality from 1909 to 1922; The Era of Serious Debate from 1925 to 1928; and last, An Era of Reflections encompassing 1929 to 1939. Occasionally, due to the excerpting of and/or the loss of letters, two letters from the same source (Freud or Pfister) may appear in sequence.

EARLY PERIOD OF CORDIALITY 1909-1922

This section begins with Freud's first reply to a letter from Pfister, Pfister sent Freud one of his many articles. He was a prolific contributor to psychoanalytic literature. The reference in Freud's August, 1909 letter to the "journey across the barren waste of waters" is to his trip to the twentieth anniversary of Clark University in Massachusetts at the invitation of G. Stanley Hall. The death of Hermann Rorschach, a Swiss psychiatrist who invented the Rorschach Ink Blot Test, is referred to in the 1922 letters. This period is

marked by great cordiality and civility. It precedes the publication of Freud's
The Future of an Illusion in 1927.

Freud to Pfister January 18, 1909
Dear Dr. Pfister:
I cannot content myself with just thanking you for sending me your paper
Delusion, and Suicide among Youth.

I must also express my satisfaction that our psychiatric work has been
taken up by a minister of religion who has access to the minds of so many
young and healthy individuals.

. . . Your name has often been mentioned to me by our common friend
C. G. Jung, and I am glad now to be able to associate a more definite idea with
it . . .

Pfister to Freud February 18, 1909
Dear Professor:
Your letter has made the pleasure I take in the science initiated by you even
greater. It was a great satisfaction to me to gather from your remarks that basically I have correctly understood the application of psychoanalysis to pastoral
work. The (ethical) difference between your outlook and mine is perhaps not
so great as my calling might suggest.

Freud to Pfister August 16, 1909
Dear Dr. Pfister:
Yes, you can come and see me at any time, and I am delighted to hear from you
before undertaking the journey across the barren waste of waters. You always
make one cheerful, because you call into consciousness the things which
because of the unhappy human disposition are hidden behind small miseries
and fleeting cares. I do not know what promises you left behind with my children, because I keep hearing things like next year I'm going with Dr. Pfister, I'm
going climbing with him, and so on and so forth. I dare not mention your
10,000 foot climb with your son, because it would rouse my boys' blackest
envy, they would wish they had a father like you, who could still climb with
them instead of being tormented by his Conrad and picking strawberries in the
woods down below.

Freud to Pfister October 9, 1918
As for the possibility of sublimation to religion, therapeutically I can only envy
you. But the beauty of religion certainly does not belong to psychoanalysis. It
is natural that at this point in therapy our ways should part, and so it can
remain. Incidentally, why was it that none of all the pious ever discovered psy-

choanalysis? Why did it have to wait for a completely godless Jew
*[Footnote by Freud.] This personification of the body in Spitteler's Imago
impressed me greatly. (Imago was a novel published in 1906 by the Swiss writer
Carl Spitteler)*

Pfister to Freud October 29, 1918

. . . you ask why psycho-analysis was not discovered by any of the pious, but
by an atheist Jew. The answer obviously is that piety is not the same as genius
for discovery and that most of the pious did not have it in them to make such
discoveries. Moreover, in the first place you are no Jew, which to me, in view
of my unbounded admiration for Amos, Isaiah, Jeremiah, and the author of Job
and Ecclesiastes, is a matter of profound regret, and in the second place you are
not godless, for he who lives the truth lives in God, and he who strives for the
freeing of love 'dwelleth in God1 (First Epistle of John, 4:16). If you raised to
your consciousness and fully felt your place in the great design, . . . I should say
of you: A better Christian there never was. . . .

Pfister to. Freud April 3, 1922

Dear Professor Freud:
I had hoped to give you a little pleasure by sending you a new book, but now
the pleasure is overshadowed by a great sorrow. Yesterday we lost our ablest
analyst, Dr. Rorschach. . . . He had a wonderfully clear and original mind, was
devoted to analysis heart and soul, and threw in his lot with you down to the
smallest details. His 'diagnostic test,' which would perhaps better be called
analysis of form, was admirably worked out. . . . His intention was to become
a university teacher. He was a poor man all his life, and a proud, upright man
of great human kindness, and he is a great loss to us.

Freud to Pfister June 4, 1922

Rorschach's death is very sad. I shall write a few words to his widow today. My
impression is that perhaps you overrate him as an analyst; I note with pleasure
from your letter the high esteem in which you hold him as a man. Of course no
one but you shall write the tribute to him in the journal, and please write it
soon. . . .

ERA OF SERIOUS DEBATE 1925 TO 1928

This period begins with a letter to Freud from Pfister who is spending
Christmas in Bethlehem. He uses the occasion to suggest that Berggasse
(Freud's residence) had a holiness about it, too. The October 16, 1927 letter
from Freud is addressed to Pfister while he is on vacation in Scandinavia. Pfister

was a frequent traveler. The letter's importance is in its announcement that "a pamphlet of mine" would soon appear. This was the monumental The Future of an Illusion which was to become the focus of the serious dialogue between the two men. Note how the plot thickens but also note how the debate remains gentlemanly and cordial--Freud welcomes Pfister's review and critique in Imago, the journal which was the organ for the psychoanalytic movement. Pfister eventually wrote an article delineating his position in a 1928 article which turns a phrase on Freud's title, i.e. The Illusion of a Future.

Pfister to Freud December 23, 1925

One gladly takes refuge from the turmoil of Christmas in the quiet of Bethlehem to rest, reflect and meditate, free from dogma and science. ... There I derive gladness and strength, and science awakens memory, not of deprivation and hardship, but of germinating greatness, succour, and growth. You will smile, but in your neighborhood too I feel something of the clarity of the Lord, and in any case in thinking of you I am filled with an infinite gratitude and hope. Love is the greatest safeguard against intellectual envy, and after it realization of the blessing of humility and of the beauty of the honest labor of fetching and carrying, which in the case of your Titanic building is magnificent enough. . . .

Freud to Pfister October 16, 1927

Dear Dr. Pfister:

Thanks to your letters, I have been following with intelligible interest your triumphal progress through the Scandinavian countries. The very gratifying result must largely be attributed to your personality, because the resistance to analysis of these Scandinavians is particularly deep-rooted.

. . . In the next few weeks a pamphlet of mine will be appearing which has a great deal to do with you. I had been wanting to write it for a long time, and postponed it out of regard for you, but the impulse became too strong. The subject-matter--as you will easily guess--is my completely negative attitude to religion, in any form and however attenuated, and, though there can be nothing new to you in this, I feared, and still fear, that such a public profession of my attitude will be painful to you. When you have read it you must let me know what measure of toleration and understanding you are able to preserve for the hopeless pagan.

Always your cordially devoted, Freud

Pfister to Freud October 21, 1927

. . . As for your anti-religious pamphlet, there is nothing new to me in your rejection of religion. I look forward to it with pleasureable anticipation. A powerful-minded opponent of religion is certainly of more service to it than a thousand useless supporters. In music, philosophy, and religion I go different ways from you. I have been unable to imagine that a public profession of what you believe could be painful to me; I have always believed that every man should state his honest opinion aloud and plainly. You have always been toler-and towards me, and am I to be intolerant of your atheism? If I frankly air my differences from you, you will certainly not take it amiss. Meanwhile my attitude is one of eager curiosity.

Freud to Pfister October 21, 1927

Such is your magnanimity that I expected no other answer to my "declaration of war." The prospect of your making a public stand against my pamphlet gives me positive pleasure, it will be refreshing in the discordant critical chorus for which I am prepared. We know that by different routes we aspire to the same objectives for poor humanity.

Pfister to Freud November 24, 1927

Dear Professor Freud:

If I express my sincere thanks for the warmth of your dedication, please do not regard it merely as a conventional reaction to a friendly gift. That you care for me a little gives me uncommon pleasure and makes me almost a little proud. As for what I think of your work, it is exactly as I foresaw. If anything surprised me, it is that I was so little surprised. ...

What you say about the contradictions of religious and theological thought you yourself describe as a repetition, a repetition psychoanalytically developed in depth, of long familiar ideas. But what surprises me is that you pay no regard to the voices of those defenders of religion who bring out those contra- dictions just as sharply and resolve them in a higher philosophical-religious context. Let me mention von Euckan, and Brunstad, who concerns himself with conflicting values, and it is significant that deeply intelligent men have gone over from philosophy to theology. My friend Albert Schweitzer, the distinguished philosopher, professor of theology, organ virtuoso, etc., thinks just as pessimistically as you do about the optimistic-ethical interpretations of the world (*Civilization and Ethics*, 2, Introduction. p. xiii, 1932); but in his view that is only the beginning of the real problem, and he does not shut himself off from insight into the philosophy of life of those without a philosophy of life. (*Decay and Restoration of Civilization*, p. 53, 1932).

Your substitute for religion is basically the idea of the eighteenth century Enlightenment in proud modern guise. I must confess that, with all my pleasure in the advance of science and technique, I do not believe in the adequacy and sufficiency of that solution of the problem of life. It is very doubtful whether, taking everything into account, scientific progress has made men happier or better. According to the statistics, there are more criminals among scholars than in the intellectual middle class, and the hopes that were set' on universal education have turned out to be illusory. Nietzsche summed up your position in the words:

The reader will have realised my purport; namely that there is always a metaphysical belief on which our science rests--that we observers of today, atheists and anti-metaphysicians as we are, still draw our fires from the blaze lit by a belief thousands of years old, the Christian belief, which was also that of Plato, that God is truth and that the truth is divine. . . . But supposing that this grew less believable and nothing divine was left, save errors, blindness, lies?

I do not properly understand your outlook on life. It is impossible that what you reject as the end of an illusion and value as the sole truth can be all. A world without temples, the fine arts, poetry, religion, would in my view be a devil's island to which men could have been banished, not by blind chance, but only by Satan. In that case your pessimism about the wickedness of mankind would be much too mild; you would have to follow it through to its logical conclusion. If it were part of psychoanalytic treatment to present that despoiled universe to our patients as the truth, I should well understand it if the poor devils preferred remaining shut up in their illness to entering that dreadful icy desolation.

Have you as much tolerance for this frank profession of faith as I have for your long-familiar heresies? I hold it as a piece of good fortune that you had to deprive yourself of so much in order to do such tremendous work in your science (with which your faith or lack of faith has nothing whatever to do). But allow me to add two questions. Would you agree to my dealing with your views in Imago? Perhaps I might be able to offer a little aid to many who now, according to your own expectation, run the risk of rejecting the whole of psychoanalysis, and thus I might be doing a service to the psycho-analytic movement ?

. . . Well, I have come to the end of a long letter. In writing it I have had your picture in front of me, listening to what I said with indulgence and friendliness. I hope that speaking out like this has only strengthened our friendship. It has, has it not?

With cordial greetings, Yours, Pfister

P.S. As you quoted statements by a number of important men on our problem, you will certainly be interested in what Bleuler wrote to me:

I promptly devoured your Future of an Illusion and enjoyed it. Starting from quite different standpoints one comes to the identical conclusion, but your argument is not only particularly elegant, it of course goes to the heart of the matter. . . .

Freud to Pfister February 24, 1928
Dear Dr. Pfister,
It (your reply to me) has already gone to the editorial office. It was very necessary that my Illusion should be answered from within our own circle, and it is
very satisfactory that it should be done in such a worthy and friendly fashion.

What the effect on me was of what you have to say you have no need to
ask. What is to be expected if one is judge in one's own cause? Some of your
arguments seem to me to be poetical effusion, others, such as the enumeration
of great minds who have believed in God, too cheap. It is unreasonable to
expect science to produce a system of ethics—ethics are a kind of highway code
for traffic among mankind—and the fact that in physics atoms which were yesterday assumed to be square are now assumed to be round is exploited with
unjustified tendentiousness by all who are hungry for faith; so long as physics
extends our dominion over nature, these changes ought to be a matter of complete indifference to you. And finally—let me be impolite for once—how the
devil do you reconcile all that we experience and have to expect in this world
with your assumption of a moral world order? I am curious about that, but you
have no need to reply.

Freud to Pfister November 25, 1928
Dear Dr. Pfister,
In your otherwise delightful letter there is one point I cavil at, namely your find-
ing something surprising and gratifying in the attitude of the International
Journal (editor and staff) on the subject of the Illusion.

Such 'tolerance' is no merit.

In both works which have recently reached me from the publishing
house, one of which contains a reprint of your Discussion, I note with satisfaction what a long way we are able to go together in analysis. The rift, not in analytic, but in scientific thinking which one comes on when the subject of God
and Christ is touched on, I accept as one of the logically untenable but psychologically only too intelligible irrationalities of life. In general I attach no value
to the 'imitation of Christ.' In contrast to utterances as psychologically profound as 'Thy sins are forgiven thee; arise and walk" there are a large number
of others which are conditioned exclusively by the time, psychologically impossible, useless for our lives. Besides, the above statement calls for analysis. If the
sick man had asked: 'How knowest thou that my sins are forgiven?" the answer
could only have been: 'I, the Son of God, forgive thee.' In other words, a call
for unlimited transference. And now, just suppose I said to a patient: 'I,
Professor Sigmund Freud, forgive thee thy sins.' What a fool I should make of
myself. . . .

. . . You are quite right to point out that analysis leads to no new philosophy of life, but it has no need to, for it rests on the general scientific outlook, with which the religious outlook is incompatible. For the point of view of the latter it is immaterial whether Christ, Buddha, or Confucius is regarded as the ideal of human conduct and held up as an example to imitate. Its essence is the pious illusion of providence and a moral world order, which are in conflict with reason. But priests will remain bound to stand for them. It is of course possible to take advantage of the human right to be irrational and go some way with analysis and then stop, rather on the pattern of Charles Darwin, who used to go regularly to church on Sundays. I cannot honestly see that any difficulties are created by patients' demands for ethical values; ethics are not based on an external world order but on the inescapable exigencies of human cohabitation. I do not believe that I behave as if there were 'one life, one meaning in life,' that was an excessively friendly thought on your part,, and it always reminds me of the monk who insisted on regarding Nathan as a thoroughly good Christian. I am a long way from being Nathan, but of course I cannot help remaining 'good' towards you.

ERA OF REFLECTIONS 1929 TO 1939

In this period, we see Pfister beginning by espousing both lay analysis and lay ministry. He was an old line liberal who emphasized function over position. He also expresses his continued appreciation for Freud over and beyond their differences on the value of religion. Freud's seventy-third birthday is noted in an affectionate letter to Pfister dated May 26, 1929. The loss and rediscovery of the box containing Freud's letters is mentioned along with Pfister's remarriage after his first wife's death. Freud's chronic problem with cancer of the jaw and the beginning of his many operations is noted. Pfister also writes about the death of Ferenczi and the growing problems of Nazi rule in Germany. The section concludes with the touching letter to Mrs. Freud after Freud's death in 1939.

Pfister to Freud February 9, 1929

. . . Please allow me to return to your remark that the analysts you would like to see should not be priests. It seems to me that analysis as such must be a purely 'lay' affair. By its very nature it is essentially private and directly yields no higher values. In innumerable cases I have done nothing but this negative work, without ever mentioning a word about religion. The Good Samaritan also preached no sermons, and it would be tasteless to have a successful treatment paid for in retrospect by religious obligations. Just as Protestantism abolished the difference between laity and clergy, so must the cure of souls be laicised and secularised. Even the most bigoted must admit that the love of God is not limited by the whiff of incense.

. . . If no priest should analyze, neither should any Christian or any religious or morally deep-thinking individual, and you yourself emphasize that analysis is independent of philosophy of life. Disbelief is after all nothing but a negative belief. I do not believe that psychoanalysis eliminates art, philosophy, religion, but that it helps to purify and refine them. Forgive a long-standing enthusiast for art and humanitarianism and an old servant of God. Your marvelous life's work and your goodness and gentleness, which are somehow an incarnation of the meaning of existence, lead me to the deepest springs of life. I am not content to do scientific research on their banks, but have to drink and draw strength from them. . . . At school my cleverest master used to say that music was a pitiful row. I did not try to convert him, but took refuge in Beethoven and Schubert. At heart you serve exactly the same purpose as I, and act 'as if there were a purpose and meaning in life and the universe,' and with my feeble powers can only fit your brilliant analytical discoveries and healing powers into that gap. Do you really wish to exclude from analytical work a "priesthood" understood in this sense? I do not believe that that is what you mean . . .

Freud to Pfister May 26, 1929
Dear Dr. Pfister,
So far you are the only one whom I have not thanked for sending me birthday greetings. Now I do so, and I am glad that it is done. Life is in any case not easy, its value is doubtful, and having to be grateful for reaching the age of seventy-three seems to be one of those unfairnesses which my friend Pfister puts up with better than I. However, if you promise never to do it again, I shall once more forgive you, just as you seem to forgive me a lot of things, including The Future of an Illusion.

Freud to Pfistar February 7, 1930
I shall deal with only one point. If I doubt man's destiny to climb by way of civilization to a state of greater perfection, if I see in life a continual struggle between Eros and the death instinct, the outcome of which seems to me to be indeterminable, I do not believe that in coming to those conclusions I have been influenced by innate constitutional factors or acquired emotional attitudes. I am neither a self-tormenter nor am I cursed and, if I could, I should gladly do as others do and bestow upon mankind a rosy future, and I should find it much more beautiful and consoling if we could count on such a thing. But this seems to me to be yet another instance of illusion (wish fulfillment) in conflict with truth. The question is not what belief is more pleasing or more comfortable or

more advantageous to life, but of what may approximate more closely to the puzzling reality that lies outside us. The death instinct is not a requirement of my heart; it seems to me to be only an inevitable assumption on both biological and psychological grounds. The rest follows from that. Thus to me my-pessimism seems a conclusion, while the optimism of my opponents seems an _a priori assumption. I might also say that I have concluded a marriage of reason with my gloomy theories, while others live with theirs in a love-match. I hope they will gain greater happiness from this than I.

Pfister to Freud July 31, 1930

. . . I am writing a lecture for the psycho-analytical society in New York on 'The Origin and Conquest of Anxiety and Obsession in Judaeo-Christian Religious History.' It is a subject which has been in my mind for years, and it first attracted my attention because it provided such magnificent corroboration of your theories.

. . . It always gives me great pleasure to see the great stream that bears your name growing stronger, deepening its bed, and widening.

My wife had a piece of news for me on her arrival that gave me great pleasure. I had carefully preserved your letters since 1909 and kept them in a box in the attic. After my first wife's death I had a house-maid who inexcusably burnt some of my most valuable papers and robbed me dreadfully. After her departure I hunted for the box in vain and gave it up for lost. Now the letters have fortunately been found. I cannot tell you how much my correspondence with you has meant to me, and how much stimulus I have derived from it. I am greatly looking forward to seeing your kind and sagacious letters again when I return to Zurich in the middle of November. . . .

Freud to Pfister May 12, 1931

Dear Dr. Pfister,

After another major operation I am fit for little and un-cheerful but, if I have got back to some kind of synthesis again by the end of the month—that is what I have been promised—am I to miss the opportunity of seeing my old but by God's grace rejuvenated friend* here? Certainly not, I count on it.

* A reference to Pfister's remarriage.

Pfister to Freud May 24, 1933

Dear Professor Freud,

I heard the news of Ferenczi's death last night. I am deeply grieved at the loss of your distinguished champion, and I wish to share my sorrow with you. With Abraham he was the man who most thoroughly imbibed, not only your ideas, but also your spirit and, thus impelled and qualified, planted the banner of psychoanalysis in more and more new countries. In particular his brilliant discoveries about the psychology of philosophical thought, and metaphysical thought in particular, made me a grateful admirer of the modest man,

  ... I paid a brief visit to Germany last week, and it will be a long time before I am able to get rid of the feeling of disgust I got there. . . . Cowardly towards the-outside world, it wreaks its infantile rage on defenceless Jews, and even loots the libraries. Good luck to him who in the face of such crass idiocy still has the strength to be a doctor-of souls. . . .

Freud to Pfister June 13, 1934
Dear Dr. Pfister,
I congratulate you on your honorary degree, but cannot
agree your passing on to me the honour conferred on you; as the champion of religion against my Future of an Illusion you have the sole right to it. The fact that the Geneva theological faculty was not deterred by psychoanalysis is at least worthy of recognition.

Freud to Pfister March 2?, 193?
  ... My daughter will certainly gladly accept your report; she will hardly dispute that her files are incomplete. Actually I do not deserve your reproach for not writing anything. I have finished a sizeable piece about some significant matters,* but because of external considerations, or rather dangers, it cannot be published. It is again about religion, so again it will not be pleasing to you. So only a few short papers have been usable for the Almanac and Imago.
With cordial greetings, Yours, Freud
* Moses and Monotheism

Pfister to Frau Freud December 12, 1939
Last Saturday the Swiss Psycho-Analytic Society held a memorial meeting in honour of your great husband. ... The occasion was not for the purpose of doing homage to the dead man to whom we have such a tremendous amount to be grateful for, but a profession of loyalty to the living Freud, to whom we can pay off a small part of our debt of gratitude, not by expressing our admiration and veneration, but only by cultivating his work.

  In examining your husband's letters it was with both grief and pleasure that I was once again reminded of how infinitely much his family meant to him. I vividly remember his introducing me to you, his three fine sons, the vital Sophie, and the little mother of the lizards on April 25, 1909. I, who grew up fatherless and suffered for a life-time under a soft, one-sided bringing up, was dazzled by the beauty of that family life, which in spite of the almost superhuman greatness of the father of the house and his deep seriousness, breathed freedom and cheerfulness, thanks to his love and sparkling humour. In your house one felt as in a sunny spring garden, heard the gay song of larks and blackbirds, saw bright flower-beds, and had a premonition of the rich blessing of summer. To the visitor it was immediately evident that a large part of that blessing was to be attributed to you, and that you, with your gentle, kindly nature, kept putting fresh weapons into your husband's hands in the fierce battle of life. ... His letters show that his friends also meant much to him, and the fact that I had the privilege of counting among his closest friends cheered me in the sad business of paying him tribute. Now and in later years it must be a satisfaction to you and your children to remember how much you contributed to mitigating your husband's internal and also external sufferings and the tragedy of his old age by your goodness and piety.

From the letter of your daughter Anna to our president we learnt with pleasure how capable of enjoyment the great tolerator remained to the end. For that he was indebted to all of you.

. . . At any rate his wish for mental rest after dying in the royal harness of the thinker has now been fulfilled.

Your husband's letters are among my most cherished possessions. As long as I live I shall always have them by my side.

. . . With cordial greetings to you and your children, and especially Fraulein Anna and Dr. Martin.

With deep devotion, Yours, Pfister

CONCLUSION

Freud and Pfister continually interacted with one another over their views of religion and the significance of a religious experience to life. Three issues appear to be foremost in their interchanges.

The issue of religious experience was one of the focal points between them. Freud contended that there was only one "variety of religious experience," that being obsessionalism with its basis in totesnism. Pfister, on the other hand, was of the belief that the Judaeo-Christian religious experience removed the neuroses and created freedom for the individual. For him there was no room for obsessionalism in true religion.

Another issue was the testing of the reality of a religious experience. Freud contended that it was necessary to see with one's own eyes to accept something as reality. Religion had an incontrovertible lack of authentication due to the reliance of primal fathers' beliefs and the forbidding of raising questions concerning the belief of the fathers. Thus, it was impossible to test the reality in the here and now and "see" what the religious experience really was. Pfister's contention was that much of reality could not be validated directly, even such an accepted institution as the "family. He emphasized that "in practical questions on whose answers the structure of one's life depends, one must take a stand even where stringent proofs fail." Even so, there was also a need for trust in religion.

Finally there was the issue involved in Freud's Future of an Illusion and Pfister's Illusion of a Future. For Freud, religion was an illusion that had no future. 'Is it possible for mankind to endure the hardships of life without the consolations of religion?' Freud asked. Perhaps, but only if in the process of growth the religious phase is replaced by the higher order of science. His premise for hope in the future was science. He stated, "our science is no illusion. But an illusion it would be to suppose that what science cannot give us we can get elsewhere." Pfister opined that Freud "takes it as self-evident that we have only to do with the world of appearance." Citing his own experience with empirical criticism that proved unfulfilling, he stated, "In my opinion the world of spiritual order ... stands more securely ... than the whole deceptive world of the senses." Further "In my view there can be no such thing as a pure empiricist, and a man who sticks rigidly to the data is like a heart specialist who ignores the organism as a whole."

In conclusion, perhaps Pfister's comments to Freud best express the basis for their differing views on religion, "Our difference derives chiefly from the fact that you grew up in proximity to pathological forms of religion and regard these as religion; while I had the good fortune of being able to turn to a free form of religion which to you seems to be an emptying of Christianity of its contents, while I regard it as the core and substance of evangelism." (Meng and Freud, p. 122) It just could be that life experience, even more than well reasoned logic, led both men to their positions. Such an anti-Semitic milieu as that in which Freud existed must have contributed to his bitter anti-Christian feelings. He reportedly never forgot the insults of Christians to his father.

Moses became his prototype. This faithful, lonely, determined Jew who led his people out of slavery was an inspiration for Freud. Freud saw himself as a modern atheist Moses with a somewhat messianic mission. This atmosphere was quite distinct from the idyllic, pastoral, supportive upbringing of Pfister.

For whatever reason, nevertheless, the two men represented opposing views on the dynamics and values of religion that still persist. A reconsideration of their interaction is a testimony to scholarly dialogue and a crisp restatement of the concerns for contemporary discussion.

REFERENCES

Heinrich Meng and Ernest L. Freud, *Psychoanalysis and Faith: The Letters of Sigmund Freud and Oskar Pfister* (New York: Basic Books, Inc., 1963).

Thomas Bonhoeffer, "Christianity and Fear Revisited," *Journal of Religion and Health* 13:4 (1974):239-250.

Sigmund Freud, *The Future of an Illusion*. Translated by W. D. Robson-Scott (Garden City, N.Y.: Doubleday, 1958--published in German in 1927).

Sigmund Freud, *Moses and Monotheism* (New York: A. A. Knopf, 1939).

Oskar Pfister, "Delusion and Suicide among Youth" (Wahnvorstellungen und Schulerselbstmord), Schweizer Blotter fur Schulgesundheitspflege 1 (1909).

Oskar Pfister,"The Illusion of a Future" (Die Illusion einer Zukunft), *Imago 14* (1928):149-184.

Oskar Pfister, *Christianity and Fear; A Study in History and in the Psychology and Hygiene of Religion*. Translated by W. H. Johnston (London: G. Allen and Unwin, 1948—publ. in German in 1944).

John E. G. Irwin, "Pfister and Freud: The Rediscovery of a Dialogue," *Journal of Religion and Health* 12:4 (1973):315-324,

Albert Schweitzer,"Civilization and Ethics" (Kultur und Ethik) in *The Philosophy of Civilization* (London: Black, 1932, 1946).

Albert Schweitzer, "Decay and Restoration of Civilization" (Verfall und Wiederauffaau der Kultur) in *The Philosophy of Civilization* (London: Black, 1932, 1946).

John W. Stettner, "Pfister as Pastoral Theologian," *Journal of Religion and Health* 12:3 (1973):211-222.

John W. Stettner, "What to do with Visions," *Journal of Religion and Health* 13:4 (1974)-.229-238.

Hans Ulrich Jager-Werth, "Oskar Pfister and the Beginning of Religious Socialism." *Journal of Religion and Health* 13:1 (1974):53-61.

TWENTY

The Contribution of Gordon Allport (1897-1967) to the Psychology of Religion

G ordon Allport was a distinguished academician. He taught psychology at Harvard from 1824-1966 except for four years in which he was at Dartmouth. According to his autobiography he probably taught the first course on personality in the United States at Harvard in 1924. He became known as the dean of American personality theorists. He was chairman of Harvard's department of psychology for a time and was president of the American Psychological Association in 1939.

Little is known about Allport's own religious experience. He refers to his home as one characterized, by "plain Protestant piety and hard work." His mother brought to her sons "an eager sense of philosophical questioning and the importance of searching for ultimate religious answers" (1968,p. 379). He was very active in social service during college and perceived himself as replacing the doctrine of his childhood with "some sort of humanitarian religion" (1968, p. 380). He taught in Constantinople the year after receiving his bachelor's degree in the equivalent of today's Peace Corps.

Several years later he reacted to the "essentially Unitarian position" (1968, p. 380) because he perceived it exalted his own intelligence. He felt this was a "cheap" way out of the dilemma. Although we do not know where this insight led him, he does indicate the direction his faith took by writing, "Humility and some mysticism, I felt, were indispensable to me otherwise I would be victimized by my own arrogance" (1968, p. 380). Like William James before him, he appeared to embrace a most meaningful private faith. Although he does not report of himself, it is known that he was an active member of the Episcopal church.

In his autobiography he speaks of his persistent concern for studying "personality? which is composed chiefly of generic attitudes, values and sentiments. Therefore, "the prejudice-complex, the religious sentiment, the phenomenological ego, and one's philosophy of life are important subterritories to explore in individual lives" (1968, p. 402). As he said earlier,(1950)7 in the preface to The Individual and his Religion, "...I have undertaken the task of discovering the place of religion in the life economy of the individual" (p.vi). A final quote illustrates his viewpoint regarding the positive contribution of religion to personality development. He says "...I am seeking to trace the full course of religious development in the mature and productive personality. I am dealing with the psychology, not with the psychopathology of religion....Many personalities attain a religious view of life without suffering arrested development and without self-deception" (1950, p.viii).

With the above comments in mind, I propose to discuss the contribution of Allport to three areas of the psychology of religion. They are: 1) the growth and development of religion in the individual; 2) the definition of religious maturity; and 3) the measurement of religious dimensions.

THE GROWTH AND DEVELOMENT OF RELIGION IN THE INDIVIDUAL

Each person's religious faith is unique, according to Allport. In spite of the outside fact that certain people are called by the same denominational name and repeat the same creed, religion means something different to each one of them. Allport treats religion as he does personality traits. It is possible to call two people "sincere" just as it is possible to call two people "Christian" but the labels are conveniences which obscure uniqueness. Real events are idiographic (individual) rather than a nomothetic (group). In the final analysis proper study is of the individual. As Allport said, "...there are as many varieties of religions experience as there are religiously inclined mortals upon the earth" (1950, p.27). Therefore, it is more appropriate to examine diaries, listen to private prayers, read personal statements of faith than to compare persons by adding up answers to yes-no tests. Allport pioneered the use of "personal documents' (1942) for understanding persons.

With regard to development, Allport suggested each person's faith has been shaped by "his bodily needs, 2) his temperament by 3) his psychogenic interests and values, 4) his pursuit of rational explanation and 5) his response to surrounding culture" (1950, p.9). This is to say that each of these variables help determine the unique faith a person comes to have. These are the common roots of religion. Yet, as has been said, no two people's faith is alike—each is unique, idiographic, or individual. A person's faith is of his unique adjustment to life and his (sic) response to the various forces mentioned above. It has its own inner laws within the economy of his life. Pruyser (1960) suggested this emphasis on the ways religion functions in the individual life was the psycho-analytic contribution to the psychology of religion. He does not mention Allport' s theorizing. However, it is obvious that Allport's ideas parallel the psychoanalytic emphasis.

It may have been difficult for Pruyser to recognize Allport's value because of Allport's consistent criticism of the psychoanalytic model as based too much on unconscious motivations and infantile habit patterns. Allport preferred to think of man as determined by conscious thoughts and as outgrowing his childhood motives. To these we now turn in discussing Allport's contribution to a definition of Religious maturity.

A DEFINITION OF RELIGIOUS MATURITY

Religious maturity is based on two processes Allport suggests are inherent in normal development. The first is "functional autonomy" (1937). The second is "propriate striving" (1955). Both are integrally related to the above discussion of the roots of religion and conscious determination.

Allport insisted that adult motives could not be reduced to or explained in terms of childhood needs. While all behavior is dynamic (motivated, caused) it becomes free from its early sources in growth and maturation. Instead of being a habit that is carried over from childish dependency, the mature religious sentiment is motivated by adult, conscious values, He admits early conscience is a function of the fear of punishment. Further,childhood views of God resemble a projected father image.

Mature conscience is guilty not for the things it has done against parental wishes, but for things it ought to do for the sake of values it holds dear. Mature faith is seen as the search for meaning beyond all self-seeking. Thus, he suggests an attribute of mature religion is the "derivative yet dynamic nature of the mature sentiment" (Allport, 1950, p.63). As he states, "Immature religion, whether in adult or child, is largely concerned with magical thinking, self-justification, and creature comfort. This it betrays its sustaining motives still to be the drives and desires of the body. By contrast, mature religion is less of a servant, and more of a master, in the economy of the life. No longer goaded and steered exclusively by impulse, fear, wish, it tends rather to control and direct these motives toward a goal that is no longer determined by mere self interest" (Allport, 1950, p.63). This is functional autonomy .

"Propriate striving" is the ego-involved, intentional, conscious, self-actu-alizing basis for mature behavior. Mature behavior is "pulled" from the future, rather that "pushed" from the past. The character of the "pull" in mature behavior is what is referred to by the term "proprium." This is that integrating force of personality which orients behavior toward those events that make long range planning come true. Religion, of all human activities, gives dignity and value to man's strivings. It provides answers to man's deepest longings and solutions to life's enigmas.

Allport was aware that all human effort had its inadequacies. He implied that the values men strive for must be seen as coming from a transcendent source for them to be worthwhile. He likewise indicated that life required all men to go beyond verifiable evidence and seek solutions to the enigmas of life. Thus he does not see religion as "a prelogical prelude to empirical and scientific thinking" (1950, p.18). Rather it is a legitimate part of experience in all generations. Like C. Jung, Allport senses that at a certain point in life all men seek answers to questions regarding the meaning and destiny of life. Many men find these answers in religion. He suggested that "living in harmony with a unifying philosophy of life was a characteristic of the mature personality (Allport, 1961).

More that any of his predecessors in the field Allport made a place for reason. He acknowledged the positive contribution of doubt (1950) and indicated a characteristic of mature faith was that life was "well differentiated", i.e., critically articulated and conceived. He said the mature religious sentiment was "ordinarily fashioned in the workshop of doubt" (Allport, 1950, p.73). He even thought that the belief changes that occur during the college years (Allport, 1948) were part of necessary developmental process which led to maturity. Thus religion was much more than a feeling. It was a striving toward rational conceptualization of the crises of life in order that meaning might be found. As he states, "a mature individual knows with precision his attitude toward the chief phases of theoretical doctrine and the principal issues in the moral spheres..." (Allport, 1950, p. 58).

This self-actualizing dynamic makes religion serve self motives. Bertocci (1940) criticized this view of motivation because it did not allow for entirely new/motives (such as would come from revelation or insight) to become a part of man's behavior. Allport (1940) maintained that man's self-enhancing dynamics were continuous with past experience. At the same time they functioned free from these determinants and became directed toward the realization of one's self.

The critical issue for the psychology of religion remains the one toward which Bertocci (1940) wrote, namely, does man discover the self he wants to be? If so, how does this occur? If not, can he be given a new Self toward which to strive, as in revelation?

Suffice it to say, the mature religious sentiment for Allport becomes ego involving and the degree to which it becomes the "master motive" is a measure of its maturity. He suggests words like "integral", "comprehensive", and "hueristic" for this dimension. The more mature a person's faith the more his life and behavior will be subsumed under it and intepreted in light of it. Suffice it tm say, the mature religious sentiment for Allport becomes ego involving and the degree to which it becomes the "master motive" is a measure of its' maturity.

One of the areas Allport had most interest in has been the relationship between prejudice and religion (1954, 1966, 1967). He was puzzled by the research finding that there was a correlation between attending church and being racially prejudiced. He reasoned that religion's emphasis on the brotherhood of man should unmake, rather than cause, prejudice. He found that in reality those who attended with great frequency and those who did not attend at all were least prejudiced. Those who attended irregularly were the most prejudiced. The earlier reports obscured this curvilinear relationship. He and Ross (1967) began to search throughout for the experiential and motivational variables to explain this phenomenon. They conceived of differing religious maturity termed Extrinsic and Intrinsic. They reasoned that the more immature faith was Extrinsic in its orientation in that it used religion for its own ends and was directed toward security, status, and self justification. In addition, the Extrinsically oriented person took the creed lightly and never really gave selfish interests. Mature religion would be Intrinsic, they continued. This meant a faith n which the person internalized the creed, and lived his religion. Further, religion became the master motive for those initrinsically motivated. They did notuse religion. They lived it.

Among a sample of religious persons, Allport and Ross (1967) found that the more Extrinsic a person's religious orientation, the more prejudiced they were and the more Intrinsic was their orientation, the less prejudiced they were. Thus a measure of religious maturity helped to explain the relations between religion and prejudice.

THE MEASUREMENT OF RELIGION

The last major contribution Allport made to the psychology of religion was in constructing scales for measuring religion. Hall and Lmndzey (1957) feel that one of the weaknesses of Allport"s theorizing is that he generated little research. This may reject a prejudice against the subject of religion on their part because Allport has stimulated much research with his Study of Values (Allport, Vernon, Lindzey, 1960) and his Religious Orientation Scale (Allport and Ross, 1967).

The Study of Values was first published in 1931 with P.E.Vernon. A third edition in 1960 included revisions authored by G. Lindzey. This is a 45-item, forced choice scale in which a person's preferences for types of activity are measured. These preferences are theoretically related to six master motives or dominant values in life. The rationale for these Values come from E. Spranger's *Types of Men* (1928) with whom Allport studied in Germany in 1923. Spranger suggested there were types of men. They are described as follows:

Theoretical: Characterized by a dominant interest in the discovery of truth and by an empirical, critical, rational, "intellectual" approach.

Economic: Emphasizing useful and practical values; conforming closely to the prevailing stereotype of the "average American businessman."

Aesthetic: Placing the highest value on form and harmony; judging and enjoying each unique experience from the standpoint of its grace, symmetry, or fitness.

Social: Originally defined as love of people, this category has been more narrowly limited in later revisions of the test to cover only altruism and philanthropy.

Political: Primarily interested in personal power, influence, and renown; not necessarily limited to the field of politics.

Religious: Mystical, concerned with the unity of all experience, and seeking to comprehend the cosmos as a whole. (Anasta&i, 1968, p.488).

It has been said that the test is a beautiful blend of "American empiricism and European rationalism."

Of interest is the evidence that Allport agreed with Spranger who put the importance of striving to know God and to find a unified view of life alongside striving for knowledge, beatfty, power, riches, and service. His efforts to study religious values have resulted in a scale which has been widely used in research (Hundlely, 1965). The Study of Values (1931, 1951, I960) has been found to be related to occupational choice (Mawardi , 1952), college course of study (Sternberg, 1953), perceptual recognition of value oriented words (Postman, Bruner, McGinnies, 1943), denominational affiliation (Pyron, 1961), and longitudinal consistency of values (Bender, 1958; Kelly, 1955). According to Hunt (1968), the person who scores high on the "Religious" scale is an activist approaches religion intellectually and rationally. Further he endorses traditional forms of religious institutions and seeks to apply religious principles in daily life. That social science should consider this a positive value to be measured is due in large measure to the genius of Allport.

Of equal importance has been Allport's distinction of the Extrinsic-Intrinsic dimension in religion and his subsequent attempts to measure it via the Religious Orientation Scale (Allport and Ross, 1967). This distinction was previously noted in the discussion of religion and prejudice. Two of Allport's students (Wilson, 1960, and Feagin, 1964) developed scales to measure the Extrinsic-Intrinsic approaches to religion. Allport^s and Ross' 1967) Religious Orientation Scale was based on a larger norm group and is a refinement of these earlier measures. It is a set of twenty statements which measure the degree to which a person agrees with or believes certain ideas about religion because of what it does for him, or because of its worth in and of itself. The scale distinguishes between the utilitarian and the absolute value of one's faith. As may be remembered, Allport (1961) suggests that life is integrated and behavior is directed toward others by mature faith. This is intrinsic, as opposed to extrinsic religion. The latter is characterized by the fragmented selfish use of religion. It has been hypothesized and demonstrated that a relationship Exists between Extrinsic religion and the tendency to be prejudiced (Wilson, 1960; Feagin, 1964; Allport and Ross, 1967; Tisdale, 1966, and Tisdale, 1967).

While the Religious Orientation Scale has not been standardized, it has generated much research and has become an integral part of theorizing about the meaning of religious commitment (King, 1967; Gorsuch, 1966). Among similar distinctions now being discussed is that of consensual versus committed religious faith (Allen and Spilka, 1967).

Allport's contribution is important because it is grounded in a theory of personality which included a positive place for religion in its definition of Individual maturity. One of the incidental findings of the Allport and Ross (1967) research is interesting. It was not possible to tell by some subjects scores on Raligious Orientation Scale whether these persons had an Extrinsic or Intrinsic attitude toward their faith. The scale is constructed in such a manner that one is expected to agree with certain items and disagree with others. The relative number of Extrinsic or Instrinsic items with which one agrees supposedly measures the emphasis on one of the other orientations. However, certain subjects agreed with all the items. For example, they said they went to church because their neighbors would see them (an Extrinsic item) and because they found the meaning of their lives there (an intrinsic item). These people were called by Allport and Ross (1967) Indiscriminately Pro-Religious. They endorse religion for any and all reasons. This was perceived to be a cognitive style reflecting excessive width in categorizing and undifferentiated thinking. The Indiscriminately Pro-Religious were found to be more prejudiced than either Extrinsic or Intrinsic Religious persons. This phenomenon is now being researched as an Important variable in its own right.

CONCLUSION

Dittes (1969) suggests that the psychology of religion is still in a primitive stage of development. He calls for theory and research In four areas:
1) The definition of religion and a delineation of religious units and variables for study;
2) The relationship between religious behavior and social attitudes;
3) The Interrelation of religion and personality characteristics; and
4) The development and function of religious belief.

Gordon Allport made a contribution, to most, if not all, of these areas. Mention has been made of his theory about the unique growth of the religious sentiment in the individual that pertains to area four. Further, his delineation of the dimensions of religious maturity and its function in personality integration pertains to area three. Again, his studies of religion and prejudice pertain to area two. Only area one, the definition of religion has not been mentioned. Yet, even here, Allprt contributed to the field. He defined the religious sentiment as "a disposition, built up through experience, to respond favorably, and in certain habitual ways, to conceptual objects and principles that the individual regards of ultimate importance in his own life and having to do with what he regards as permanent or central in the nature of things (1950, p. 56). This definition is one of the most adequate contemporary statements of the William James (L902, 1958) tradition that emphasizes. It is consistent with Allport 's general emphases in personality theory.

Truly, Allport left a legacy which will stimulate the field for years to come. As Pettigrew said (1969, p.6),

> As a young science, American psychology has not had many men whose renown exceeds the confines of the dlscipline. But Gordon Allport was such a man to whom the profession can point with pride. For his professional colleagues, he widened the perceived alternatives open to the field. For the public he made psychology applicable to the problems of his time.... He was recognized in his lifetime as a great psychologist and will certainly be so remembered.

Few in the psychology of religion would disagree with this assessment.

REFERENCES

Anastasi, A. (1968). *Psychological testing*. New York : Macmillan.

Allen, R.O. & Spilka, B. (1967). Committed and consenu;al religion: A specification of religion-prejudice relationships. *Journal for the Scientific Study of Religion, 6*, 191-206.

Allport, G.W. (1937). *Personality: A psychological interpretation*. New York: Henry Holt.

Allport, G.W. (1942). *The uses of personal documents in psychological science*. New York: Social Science Research Council.

Allport, G.W. (1950). *The Individual and his religion: A psychological interpretation*. New York: Macmillan.

Allport, G.W. (1954). *The nature of prejudice*. Reading, Mass.: Addison-Wesley.

Allport, G.W. (1955). *Becoming: Basic Considerations for a psychology of personality*. New Have, Conn.: Yale University Press.

Allport, G.W. (1961). *Pattern and growth in personality*. New York: Holt, Rinehart and Winston.

Allport, G.W. (1966). The religious context of prejudice. *Journal for the Scientific Study of Zreligion, 5*, 447-457.

Allport, G.W. (1967). Autobiography. In E.G. Boring and G.Lindzey (Eds.) *A history of psychology in autobiography, Vol.5*, 1-25. New York: Appleton-Century-Crofts.

Allport, G.W. and Ross, J.M. (1967). Personal religious orientation and prejudice. *Journal of Personality and Social Psychology, 5*, 432-443.

Allport, G.W. (1968). *The person in psychology: Selected essays*. Boston: Beacon Press.

Allport, G.W., Vernon, P.E. & Lindzey, G. (1970). *Manual: Study of values: A scale for measuring the dominant interests in personality (revision of 3rd ed*. Boston: Houghton Mifflin.

Bertocci, P.A. (1940). Critique of G.W. Allport's theory of motivation. *Psychological Review, 47*, 501-532,

Dittes, J.E. (1969). Psychology of religion. In G. Lindzey and E. Aronson (Eds.) *The handbook of social psychology, Vol.5, (2nd ed)*, 602-659. Reading, Mass: Addison-Wesley

Feagin, J.R. (1964). Prejudice and religious types: A focused study of southern Fundamentalists. *Journal for the Scientific Study of Religion, 4*, 3-18.

Hall, C.S. & Lindzey, G. (1957). *Theories of personality*. New York: John Wiley & Sons.

Hunt, R.A. (1968). The interpretation of the Religious Scale of the Allport-Vernon-Lindzey Study of Values. *Journal for the Scientific Study of Religion, 11*, 65-77.

James, W. (1902, 1958). *The varieties of religious experience: A study of human nature*. New York: The New American Library of World Literature, Inc.

King, M. (1967). Measuring the religious variable : Nine proposed dimensions. *Journal for the Scientific Study of Religion, 6*, 173-190.

Postman, L.J., Bruner, J.S.& McGinnies, A. (1948). Personal values as a selective factor in perception. *Journal of Abnormal Psychology, 43*, 142-154.

Pruyser, P.W. (1960). Contributions to religion in the developing personality. (Proceedings of the Second Academy Symposium 1958, Academy of Religion and Mental Health). New York: New York University Press, 1960.

Spranger,E. (1914, 1928) *Lebensformen (Types of Men)*. Halle (Saale): Niemeyer. Translated by P.J.W. Pigors. New York: G.E. Shechort.

TWENTY-ONE

An S-O-R Model
of Religious Experience

In a recent article entitled "Religious experiencing: a phenomenological analysis of a unique behavioral event" (Malony, 1981), I suggested that religious experience could be subsumed under an S-o-R (or stimulus-response) paradigm. Although some may feel this model somewhat outdated, I feel that it captures the essence of religion as a behavioural response to a perceived stimulus and it both permits a focus on the uniqueness of that of which persons say they are aware, that is on the transcendent or the divine, and allows for interdisciplinary communication in that it corresponds to the terms theologians use to describe these events, i.e. revelation (stimulus), faith (organism) and work (response). This essay, therefore, uses this S-O-R paradigm as a foundation and attempts to relate it to several theories of religious motivation and demonstrate its utility in empirical research.

AN EXPANDED S-O-R MODEL

In the earlier essay, I suggested that the term "religious *experience*" encompasses all three components (stimulus, organism and response), not just one or two of them. By this, I did not mean to discount those moments in which persons sense they are in the presence of a transcendent reality, as did William James in his library that fateful evening. Nor did I intend to disparage thoughtful philosophizing about religion or action on behalf of social justice. What I did mean to do was to distinguish any and all of these isolated events from "religious *experience*" and to restrict the use of that term to those times when all three components were present. I think this aligns the model with the Judeo-Christian understanding of God/human interaction plus it avoids the danger of separating reality into small unrelated bits, as has been done in the past. The classical Hebrew-Christian model for religion has included a meeting between humans and God followed by a call to obedience and a response of commitment. Further, the psychological understanding of experience always includes elements of perception, conception and response blended into a unity or gestalt.

The experience of the prophet in Isaiah 6: 1-9 is illustrative. Isaiah was in the temple and "saw the Lord sitting upon a throne, high and lifted up" (v. 1). This is the initial sensation/perception response to the stimulus of the divine. The next several verses describe the event in terms of visual and auditory events. There are seraphims with wings; voices calling out "Holy, holy, holy is the Lord of hosts ... "; shaking resembling an earthquake; and smoke that fills the whole house. All this Isaiah sees, smells, hears and feels. Then he expresses his dismay. "Woe is me! For I am lost ... for my eyes have seen the King, the Lord of hosts" (v. 5). Next, there is an interaction between Isaiah and God. One of the seraphim touches his lips with a burning coal and declares that Isaiah's sins are forgiven. At this point God speaks and asks, "Whom shall I send, and who will go for us?." Isaiah responds with conviction, "Here I am! Send me." And God says, "Go!" This series of events includes all the parts of the S-O-R paradigm. God is the stimulus. Isaiah sees, perceives and reacts. This is the O or organism. God asks for help and Isaiah volunteers. This is the response. Religious experience is all of these put together and no one of them by itself.

This does not mean that an analysis of the several components (the S, the O and the R) is unimportant. It is to say that sensation, perception and behaviour go together and form a unity. To this unity we shall give the term EXPERIENCE. To the several components we shall give the term EVENT and suggest that several "events" go into an "experience." It is to a further consideration of these religious "events" that I now turn.

Table 1 illustrates the viewpoint expressed above, and depicts the several events from behavioural, theological and phenomenological perspectives. Keeping this paradigm in mind, I would next like to consider the several events one at a time.

TABLE 21-1

Perspectives on the three events in religious experience

Perspective	Event 1	Event 2	Event 3
Behavioral Perspective	Stimulus	Organism	Response
Theological Perspective	Revelation	Faith	Work
Phenomenological Perspective	Need	Perception/ Conception	Action

EVENT 1 IN RELIGIOUS EXPERIENCE

Event 1 has been labelled Stimulus, Revelation or Need. The underlying presumption of this event is that people are motionless unless prodded into action by some force from without or some impulse from within. The former, some force from without, was the thesis of Newtonian physics while the latter, some impulse from within, was the thesis of Thomistic philosophy. In both cases a somewhat passive organism is "stimulated" (cf. Stimulus) into action.

Although theologians following the Platonic/Aristotelian synthesis of insight and discovery proposed by Thomas Aquinas have defined Stimulus largely as "an inner impulse", a significant trend in Reform theology has defined it as a revelatory force from outside, namely God visiting or disclosing himself to persons. Theological differences in this regard have been complex and subtle and have even included combinations of these two emphases as can be seen in the concept of "prevenient grace" wherein what appears to be a search for God on the part of the individual was perceived as an example of power instilled in the individual by God. Augustine implied this in his famous prayer, "Thou hast made us for thyself, and our hearts are restless till they find their rest in thee."

A twentieth century illustration of these differences can be seen in the debate between Emil Brunner and Karl Barth in the volume Nature and grace (1946). Although both theologians agreed that there was a God who revealed himself to people, they disagreed as to how and when this occurred. The phrase "point of contact" became the point of contention between them. Brunner felt that God revealed himself by establishing a point of contact with persons' anxieties and that persons would not recognize God apart from His being an answer to the concerns they were experiencing. Barth, in contrast, felt that God needed no point of contact and that if God had to wait on persons to ask for His help He would be limited and, thus, the transformation which He worked in human life would never be radical. Barth felt that God revealed himself in a manner that revolutionized life rather than simply resolved it.

In developing a model for understanding Event 1, we shall call the first theological position "Revelation—Overwhelming" (cf. Reform point of view and Barth) and we shall call the second theological position "Revelation—Answering" (cf. Thomistic point of view and Brunner).

Since the issues in this essay are largely those of the psychology of religion, not theology, these subtleties will not be belaboured. Suffice it to say that these differences have important implications for both the design and interpretation of studies in this area, and while the psychology of religion cannot settle the validity question of whether there is a God or not, it should be well-informed regarding the assumptions that theologians have about the divine and the unique interpretations individuals make about the event.

Turning to the phenomenological perspective it can be seen that there are clear parallels to the theological positions noted above even though this perspective makes no presumptions about a transcendent reality and confines itself to a description of religious experience from within the confines of human psychological processes. For example, Wilber (1980) is one among many transpersonal psychologists who postulate a higher dimension to life than the mundane, and who perceive altered states of consciousness as indicative of this "religious" possibility. Although many such theorists take a passive or benign view regarding the induction of such events in the sense that they encourage persons to acknowledge them when they occur, others, such as Clark (1969), take a more active position and recommend the actual perpetuation of them. He shares the view of many that western society militates against such events with its overemphasis on the pragmatic and the positivistic.

The NEED which could be posited in this case would be a need to actualize one's potential for experience which goes beyond mundane sensationism. As a further construct in our development of Event 1, we shall call this "Need—Potential."

Custom refers to the manner in which persons are conditioned by culture to interpret events and to perceive the Gods via a given world view through certain types of language. Weber (1963) and others have commented on the tendency over time for religions to routinize religious events into rituals and theologies so that members of church-type groups come to envision reality in fairly common ways. Oden (1972) noted that there have been periodic attempts to break out of these traditions throughout religious history via pietistic revivals which have attempted to restore pristine religious experience. Nevertheless, most people continue to sense a need to repeat the type of religious event which has been handed down to them by their particular tradition. We shall label this "Need—Custom" and recognize that it functions as a stimulus towards perceiving reality in a given manner.

Comprehension is somewhat related to Custom. It refers to an impulse postulated by Proudfoot and Shaver (1975) wherein persons attempt to make sense of ambiguous situations in which they are hyper- or hypo-aroused. In such states persons interpret the meaning of events by referring to the environment and the actions of those around them. Proudfoot and Shaver suggested that religion should be no exception to this rule, and called for research to determine whether or not such aroused persons would interpret and experience a religious event more in the presence of religious, as opposed to neutral, cues. Imhoff and Malony (1979) attempted to test these hypotheses with only limited success. The study to be described later in this chapter is an extension of that

research. Suffice it to say at this juncture that an impulse to make sense of the
environment is postulated as a need and, thus, we label this aspect of the stimulus component of religious experience "Need—Comprehension." Although
"Need—Custom" also functions to assist persons in making sense of reality, the
emphasis in Comprehension is more on the Current environment than on an
ideological tradition.

The next alternative for defining the need component of religious experience is termed Resolution. Resolution refers to the "point of contact" assertion made by the theologian Emil Brunner. Religion has long been understood
to be the answer to the enigmas, tragedies, mysteries and injustices of life (cf.
Yinger, 1970). In a volume entitled *Understanding your faith* (1978), I affirmed
this position and suggested, along with the theologian Paul Tillich, that "life
poses the questions to which faith is the answer." I noted several basic anxieties
that seem to be common to all human existence and concluded that religion
provides resolutions to such concerns as suffering, death, tragedy, survival, and
injustice. As noted, this point of view has a long tradition (cf. religion as the
opiate of the people, Karl Marx) and it accords with the root meaning of religion as "binding things together." The label for this alternative is "Need—
Resolution."

Relationship is yet another possible definition of the need which impels
persons into religious experience. In an essay entitled "The therapeutic ingredients of religious and political philosophies" (1982), Edith Weisskopf Joelson
makes the point that there is a continuing nostalgia throughout life to re-estab-
lish the intimate and symbiotic relationships of childhood. Freud (1927/1961)
felt this to be the essence of religion. Numerous theoreticians (e.g. Erik Berne,
1965) have posited this need for intimacy in human relationships. Religion
could be conceived of as this urge on a transcendent scale. Sunden (1974), the
Swedish psychologist of religion, has constructed a total model of religious
experience on this foundation. Persons are impelled to relate personally to their
God and then adopt a style similar to the heroes of their faith. In a dramatic
manner they take on one of these traditional roles and imagine themselves to
be in communication with the divine. This aspect of the religious event will be
labelled "Need—Relationship" and will refer to this basic human impulse
which relates so integrally to religion.

The last alternative in this phenomenological perspective of Event 1 is
termed "meaning." This refers to the search for values or for understanding the
purpose of life. Gordon Allport (1961) termed this the impulse to find a unifying philosophy of life, while Daniel Batson called it the "quest" dimension of
religion (cf. Darley and Batson, 1973). Batson distinguished this from the traditional extrinsic (social comfort) and intrinsic (individual resolution) dimensions of religion. Herein one is compelled to seek religious events out of a need

to find meaning in life and a purpose for living. The impulse is perennial, and changes in format and content as life goes on and new situations arise as Jung (1963) and Erikson (1958) have noted. In this endeavour, doubt is not avoided but embraced as inspiring one to further discovery. This led Edgar Brightman (1940) to define religion as the search for values in life. This sense of and response to value implies something which supersedes one's egotistic impulse to survive. It functions to integrate life into a whole and provides a sense of groundedness or connectedness. This alternative is labelled "Need—Meaning." It functions as a basic stimulus for many religious persons.

It should be noted that there is an affinity between the Theological and Phenomenological perspectives when Revelation is understood as "answering" and Need is understood either as "resolution" or "relationship." Here, the divine stimulus to which persons respond seems to be acknowledged to be that which answers a person's search for a purpose in life, for intimate companionship and for a rejoinder to the crises of existence. This could be thought of as a CONFLICT model for religion.

Similarly, there is an affinity between Theological and Phenomenological Perspectives when Revelation is understood as "overwhelming" or "meaning" and Need is understood as "potential." The divine stimulus to which persons respond in this case seems to be an unexpected discovery of a dimension to existence which one had not anticipated or known was there. This could be thought of as a CAPACITY model for religion.

With this elaboration of the first religious event in our model of religious experience, I will now turn to a similar elaboration of Event 2—Organism, Faith, Perception/Conception. Hopefully, these elaborations will provide a basis for understanding the research to be reported later in this chapter. As an anticipation of that which is to come, let it be said at this juncture that the study to be reported was an attempt to ascertain which one of the several understandings of Need or Revelation best predicted the likelihood of persons having a religious experience.

EVENT 2—ORGANISM IN RELIGIOUS EXPERIENCE

Event 2 refers to those inner processes which occur in the mind of persons as they interpret Event 1. It is commonly assumed that most interactions with the environment by human beings involve thoughtful responses rather than the instinctual reactions characteristic of lower forms of life. Certainly this is true where the stimulus is trans-empirical, as is most often the case in religion. This is the rationale behind conceiving religious experience as Stimulus-ORGANISM-Response rather than Stimulus—Response. ORGANISM refers to those higher mental processes whereby humans take in sensations and interpret them.

This is analogous to the Need—Comprehension alternative discussed under Event 1. The outworking of that need is the way the mind works. As Kelly (1955) and others have suggested, there seems to be a practical compulsion in humans to make sense of the world in order that they may order reality and determine how to act within it. The point being made here is that there is nothing automatic or instinctual about that process. It involves "inside the head" thinking—especially in religious experience.

Two Biblical examples illustrate this process. The first was the experience of Moses and the burning bush (Exodus 3). Here Moses saw a bush that burned without burning up. He heard a voice calling his name from within the bush. He answered "Here I am." The voice told him to take off his shoes because the ground was holy. It also told him that the voice was that of the God of Abraham. Then Moses hid his face because he was afraid to look at God. It is noteworthy that while Moses' leaving the path to look at a burning bush may have been instinctual, his perceiving the voice as that of his God, his taking off his shoes and his hiding his face all involved thoughtful responses.

The second experience was that of Thomas (John 20:24-29) who doubted that Jesus has risen because he had not seen "in his hands the print of the nails" or placed his "hand in his side." Jesus appeared to him and encouraged him to touch his body. Thomas did and then proclaimed "My Lord and my God." This is a clear distinction between sensation and interpretation. Although the feel of Jesus' hand and side was a physical sensation, the faith which Thomas stated was evidence of a higher mental process which involved a thoughtful response.

There are two basic steps involved in this cognitive event—perception and conception. Perception is the term applied to the labelling of those messages sent to the brain by nerves which lead from the basic sense of touch, sight, hearing, smell and taste. Perception is the process by which the brain interprets sensations in terms that make sense to the person. Conception is the term applied to the organizing of these perceptions in the light of a larger context or a system. The perceptions are hereby incorporated either into another dimension of reality or into a pattern of meaning which serves as an answer to questions which one was asking. With minimal reflection persons can recognize these processes going on within themselves. This is the "phenomenological" perspective on Event 2.

The "theological" perspective terms this response FAITH. The eleventh chapter of the book of Hebrews is often called the "faith chapter" and provides us a framework for understanding what theologians often mean by the term "faith." As will be seen, faith is very similar to what social psychologists term "attitude" and includes at least two components: belief and feeling (cf. Fishbein and Raven, 1962). Belief has to do with whether something is true or not, while feeling has to do with whether one is attracted to that something or not. In faith one believes that the stimulus with which one is interacting is divine, and one feels strongly attracted to that relationship.

The theological words for belief and feeling are "assurance" and "conviction." Hebrews 11:1 puts it thus: "Now faith is the assurance of things hoped for, the conviction of things not seen." Of course, this is a statement within the Judeo-Christian tradition, but the format probably applies to religious experience in general. "Assurance of things hoped for" refers to the needs in Event 1 in the sense that it suggests that faith is the belief that one has found what one was looking for—be it an answer to problems or a higher dimension of life. What one "hoped to find" one has found! This is assurance.

The "conviction of things not seen" goes beyond assent or belief, however. What the social psychologists call "feeling" and what the theologians term "conviction" implies an intuition that one can commit oneself to this relationship with the divine and that things will work out to the good. This is often referred to as "trust"—which is the meaning of the Greek word for faith "pistis", interestingly enough! The result of this aspect of faith is to provide the person with a positive stance or set towards acting in response to whatever it is that one feels the divine is asking one to do. This process can be seen in the example of Isaiah 6:1~9. In the course of that interaction he experienced forgiveness and said with great conviction, "Here I am—send me!" This is conviction. A fuller discussion of these theological meanings of faith can be found in the volume Understanding your faith (Malony, 1978).

To summarize, the processes under Event 2 have been discussed in terms of phenomenological and theological perspectives. Combining these two, the organismic processes going on within persons as they interact with a transcendent stimulus include:

1) perception—the reception of the information from the senses and the labelling of these sensations as divine or supernatural;
2) conception—relating these perceptions to an understanding of the divine with which one is familiar and in terms of which the event has meaning;
3) belief—affirming the event as true and the self assurance that one is interacting with a person or a dimension that is real;
4) feeling—the emotion of positive attraction wherein one wants to continue the relationship and in which one is ready to act in response to the event.

EVENT 3—RESPONSE IN RELIGIOUS EXPERIENCE

The third and final event in religious experience is the response of the person.

In the second event the individual has perceived that he/she is in the presence of some transcendent reality and has conceived this reality in terms that make sense. Thereafter, the individual has passed judgement on the event to the point where he/she believes it to be true and is positively disposed to respond to it. It is at this point that the person acts. He/she does something in response to this interaction with the supernatural. According to William James, this IS religion. He stated that religion was "The feelings, acts, and experiences of individual men in their solitude, so far as they apprehend themselves to stand in relation to whatever they may consider the divine" (1902, p. 31).

James's emphasis, and the import of this third event in religious experience, is on the observable responses people make rather than on the inner processes detailed in Events 1 and 2. Certainly "responses" are what can be seen and what most people mean when they talk about religion. Religion is churchgoing, alms-giving, public praying, Bible-reading, creed-saying, choir-singing, etc. These are the observable RESULTS.

Berger (1974) termed this "substantive" as opposed to "functional" religion in the sense that religion defined as observable behaviour had a SUBSTANCE to it which is missing in religion when it is understood as processes within an individual. In the present chapter the functional processes are those referred to in Events 1 and 2 while the substantive processes are those which can be observed in Event 3. No one of the events, be they substantive or functional, are to be preferred or emphasized over another. As has been said, they ALL go together to compose religious experience. However, "responses", such as are being discussed here, are best termed "substantive" religion.

There are several types of responses which can be made to the perception/conception of a transcendent reality or faith. These are termed "actions" from a phenomenological and "work" from a theological perspective.

"Action" is a term applied to all intentional and self-conscious behaviour. As noted in the discussion of Event 2, they are thoughtful responses, not instinctual reactions. Stark and Glock (1969, pp. 28-39) have identified five dimensions of religion which are only one of several taxonomies for delineating religious action (e.g. King and Hunt, 1975). These five dimensions are:

1) ideological—referring to a religious response understood as the effort to work out and affirm doctrines or systematic beliefs;
2) ritualistic—referring to religious response understood as participation in organized worship or individual devotional activities;
3) experiential—referring to religious response understood as seeking out, entering into and labelling future events as interactions with transcendent reality;
4) intellectual—referring to religious response understood as the

attempt to acquire historical and theoretical knowledge about
religion;
5) consequential—referring to religious response understood as the
moral or idealistic acts and attitudes in which one engages.

*"Works" is the term theologians usually use to refer these responses to "faith"
(the term they use to denote Event 2, as noted earlier).* In fact these two, faith
and works, are often paired together and the presumption is made that one cannot exist without the other. In the Judeo-Christianreligion, at least, there is a
deep-seated conviction that mature religious experience always involves a
response to faith. It is not enough to believe. There MUST be action in response
to the new knowledge that one has obtained through interaction with the
divine, or religion is not complete.

The eighth-century prophets were most vocal about this connection
between faith and work. Amos, for example, cautioned the ancient Hebrews,
"Woe to those who are at ease in Zion ..." (6:1, RSV). By this he meant to warn
those who were satisfied with being God's chosen people without doing good.
In another place, Amos has God say:

I hate, I despise your feasts,
and I take no delight in your solemn assemblies ...
Take away from me the noise of your songs;
to the melody of your harps I will not listen.
But let justice roll down like waters,
and righteousness like an everflowing stream (Amos 5:21, 23-
24, RSV)

Righteousness, justice, neighbourliness, kindness, love—these are just a few of
the words used by the Biblical writers to refer to the "work" which those who
have met God are supposed to undertake. The New Testament writer of the
book of James spoke for the whole tradition in saying " ... faith by itself, ifit
has no works, is dead" (2: 17) and "Whoever knows what is right to do and
fails to do it, for him it is sin" (4: 17). All of this is to reassert how important
this aspect has been to theologians and how much emphasis has been put on
this dimension of religious experience.

Although the "consequential" dimension in the Glock and Stark taxonomy would seem most similar to "work" as understood by the theologians,
"response" as understood herein is much broader than that, and includes all of
the other dimensions in their paradigm. Although in the JudeoChristian faith a
concern for love and justice seems to take priority over the other responses
(such as worship), these other behaviours are of equal concern to social scientists in their endeavours to understand the total panorama of religion.

There may well be a sense in which the type of response that is given to the interaction between the individual and the divine (Event 2) is determined by the type of need which provoked the experience in the first place. For example, the "intellectual" response may be related to the search for "meaning." A list of the possible relationships between the other Glock and Stark dimensions and the needs mentioned in Event 1 follows:

Need: Potential may be related to Consequential responses;
Need: Comprehension may be related to Experiential responses;
Need: Resolution may be related to Ideological responses; and,
Need: Relationship may be related to Experiential responses.

In summary, this section has considered Event 3 in the S-O-R paradigm of religious experience. The Stark and Glock (1968) model of dimensions of religion was used as a helpful paradigm for conceptualizing the intentional and self-conscious responses persons make to encounters with the divine. A possible paradigm for understanding responses as related to needs was offered. It was noted that such responses are termed "work" by the theologians who integrally relate such behaviours to the "faith" which precedes them.

AN EXPERIMENTAL INVESTIGATION OF SOME S-O-R ISSUES

The above has been an extensive introduction to the following description of an experimental study. The discussion was intended to provide a paradigm in terms of which both the categories and the procedures would make sense. It was also hoped that such a foundation would provoke interpretations which would have meaning both for psychologists and for theologians. I am convinced that much work by both groups in the past has gone unnoticed because not enough attention has been paid to the ways in which their two disciplines interrelate .

In an effort to explore some of these S-O-R dimensions of religious experience we assessed the religious perceptions and behaviours of persons under conditions that controlled for the environmental setting and their predisposing states of mind (cf. Spradlin and Malony, 1981). This research was conceived as an attempt to investigate Events 1 and 2 in the S-O-R paradigm detailed above. A voluntary sample of 64 women participated in a visit to a local art museum. Half had been judged to be religious and half non-religious on the basis of prior questioning. They listened to a guided fantasy of flying which included all the dimensions of a classical mystical experience as they walked through either a religious or non-religious gallery of the museum. In addition, half of the women were induced through suggestion into an excited state of physiological arousal and half were induced into a relaxed state.

TABLE 21-2

Answers to the question "Was the event religious?"

Rated 1–5:
religious to non-religious

(Total *N*=64,
N in each subgroup=8)

			Religious Background			
			Religious		Non-religious	
Gallery setting	Religious	X	3.50	2.63	2.25	2.25
		SD	1.07	0.74	0.89	1.04
	Non-religious	X	2.88	2.63	1.63	2.00
		SD	1.64	0.92	0.74	1.07

After completing the gallery visit, participants rated the degree to which they had PERCEIVED the event to be religious and the degree to which they, personally, had had a religious EXPERIENCE. The data from this research are reported below. Table 2 reports the data on whether the event was religious while Table 3 includes the data on whether participants had a religious experience. We were interested in which of the three variables (religious environment of the setting, previous religiousness, and present mental state excited/relaxed) would most influence these results. The results were controlled for each participant's ability to go into an altered state of arousal and to enter into the taped fantasy.

Analyses of variance of the data in both these tables revealed that only "religious background" was significantly related to the dependent variables. Neither being in an excited or relaxed mental state nor visiting a religious or

TABLE 21-3

Answers to the question "Did you have a religious experience?"

Religious Episode Experience
Measure: Hood, 1975

(Total *N*=64,
N in each subgroup=8)

			Religious Background			
			Religious		Non-religious	
Gallery setting	Religious	X	41.00	49.25	29.88	28.50
		SD	17.94	17.33	11.73	12.82
	Non-religious	X	41.88	33.25	29.63	37.50
		SD	20.80	16.80	12.66	16.71

non-religious art gallery had any effect. Only women who were previously religious perceived the event as religious and had a religious experience. Neither differences in setting nor state of mind influenced the results. It should also be noted that there was no relationship between the number or type of life crisis events over the last six months reported by the women and either of the dependent variables.

Returning to the S-O-R model previously discussed, these results seem to support the Custom Need alternative in Event 1. The women who were religious-approached the situation with a history of involvement in organized religious activities. Their previous behaviour reflected an accommodation to culture although it should be noted that the questions asked did not assess their original motive for meeting their needs in such a manner. Nor did the research design provide for a comparison of all needs which were detailed in the discussion of Event 1.

At most the Comprehension Need and the Relationship Need alternatives could be inferred to be operative because in both cases the processes that occur in Event 2 are perceptual and experiential. In this regard, the two dependent variables of perceiving the event to be religious and having. a religious experience could be said to be biased toward some but not other need alternatives. Certainly, the interaction between a mystical fantasy and the viewing of art would seem to be more compatible with such alternatives as Potential, Comprehension, Relationship and Meaning. The Resolution of conflict would not seem to fit this paradigm as was demonstrated by the lack of a relationship between life crisis events during the previous six months.

It should also be noted that the use of the term "experience" in this research was non-technical. It was not used in the way that the S-O-R model applies it to the composite processes of Events 1, 2 and 3. It referred to the more typical use of the term in which a person reports a momentary contact with the spiritual dimension of life.

CONCLUSION

In conclusion, this chapter has presented an S-o-R model for understanding religious experience and it has illustrated how components within this model can be subjected to empirical investigation. The research which was reported did not include investigation of Event 3, the consequences or results of religious events, but future studies could be designed to include this component. The model presented here, coupled with the demonstration experiment which was reported, are intended to communicate a complex set of events which can only be simplified to the detriment of the experience. Religious experience has been denuded of its true complexity in much past research and this S-O-R paradigm is offered for its heuristic value for future investigations.

REFERENCES

Allport, G. W. The indiridual and his religion: A psychological interpretation. New York: Macmillan, 1961.

Berger, P. 1. Second thoughts on defining religion. Journalfor the Scientific Study of Religion, 1974; 13, 125-133.

Berne, E. Games people play. New York: Grove Press, 1965.

Brightman, E. S. The philosophy of religion. New York: Prentice Hall, 1940.

Brunner, E. M. and Barth, K. Nature and qrace. Translated by Peter Frankel. London: G. Bles—The Centenary Press, 1946.

Clark, W. H. Chemical ecstasy: psychedelic drugs and religion. New York: Sheed & Ward, 1969.

Darley, J. M. and Batson, C. D. "From Jerusalem to Jericho": A study of situational variables in helping behavior. Journal of Personality and Social Psychology, 1973; 27, 100-108. Erikson, E. Young man Luther: A study in psychoanalysis and history. New York: W. W. Norton, 1958.

Fishbein, M. and Raven, B. H. The A-B scales: an operational definition of belief and attitude. Human Relations, 1962; 15(1), 35-44.

Freud, S. The future of an illusion (1927). In Standard edition of the complete works of Sigmund Freud, vol. 21, pp. 3-56. London: Hogarth Press, 1961.

Hood, R. W., Jr. The construction and preliminary validation of a measure of reported mystical experience. Journal for the Scientific Study of Religion, 1975; 14, 29-41.

Imhoff, M. and Malony, H. N. Physiological arousal, environmental cues and the report of religious experience: a test of attributional theory. Paper presented at the annual meeting of the Society for the Scientific Study of Religion, Hartford, Connecticut, October, 1979.

James, W. The carieties of religious experience: a study of human nature. New York: Longmans, Green & Co., 1902.

Jung, C. Psychology and religion: West and East. New York: Bollingen Foundation, 1963. Kelly, G. A. The psychology of personal constructs: Volume 1—A theory of personality. New York: W. W. Norton, 1955.

King, M. B. and Hunt, R. A. Measuring the religious variable: national replication. Journal' for the Scientific Study of Religion, 1975; 14, 13-22.

Malony, H. N. Understanding your faith. Nashville: Abingdon Press, 1978.

Malony, H. N. Religious experiencing: a phenomenological analysis of a unique behavioral event. Journal of Psychology and Theology, 1981; 9(4), 326-334.

Oden, T. C. The intensite group experience: The new pietism. Philadelphia: Westminster Press, 1972.

Proudfoot, W. and Shaver, P. Attribution theory and the psychology of religion. Journal for the Scientific Study of Religion, 1975; 14(4), 317-330.

Spradlin, W. H. and Malony, H. N. Physiological state deviation, personal religiosity, setting variation and the report of religious experience. Paper presented at the annual meeting of the Society for the Scientific Study of Religion, Baltimore, Maryland, October, 1981.

Stark, R. and Glock, C. Y. American Piety. Berkeley: University of California Press, 1968.

Sunden, J. Religion psykoloqi: problem och methoder. Stockholm: Proprius, 1974.

Weber, M. The sociology of religion. Translated by Ephraim Fischoff. Boston: Beacon, 1963.

Weisskopf-Joelson, E. The therapeutic ingredients of religious and political philosophies. In Paul W. Sharkey (ed.), Philosophy, religion and psychotherapy. Washington, DC: University Press of America, 1982, pp. 187-210.

Wilber, K. A developmental model of consciousness. In R. N. Walsh and F. Vaughan (eds), Beyond ego: Transpersonal dimensions in psychology. Los Angeles: J. P. Tarcher, Inc., 1980.

Yinger, J. M. The scientific study of religion. New York: Macmillan, 1970.

Toward
a Christian
Clinical
Psychology

SECTION THREE

Personhood

TWENTY-TWO

Death Came Early for Me

Recently, I received a call from my youngest son. "I've got some bad news," he said, "Linda's grandfather in Detroit died in his sleep last night. I need some advice. Should I stay here in Kansas City with the boys or plan to go with her to the funeral? What's my role? I've never been to a funeral, you know."

"At 27 years of age you've never been to a funeral?" I replied, "I didn't realize that." He replied, "The closest I came was when we drove away from the hospital where Grandma Amie was dying on our move out to California almost 20 years ago. You remember I didn't go back to the funeral."

When I stopped to think, I did remember. I remembered that death had come early to me. My father died when I was about 6 years old. By the time I was the age of my youngest son, I had attended not only my father's funeral but those of a favorite uncle, a boyhood friend, several aunts, and a treasured pastor. And these did not include the funerals I had personally conducted in my time as the pastor of a church. Yes, death came early for me. At my son's age I was an old hand at dealing with death.

I was honored at my son's request for advice about what to do when his wife's grandfather died. I asked myself, "What are some of the lessons you have learned about how best to achieve wholeness and holiness through this the most inevitable of life's experiences?" As I considered this question I thought of upcoming Institute of Religion and Wholeness conference on Wholeness and Aging as well as past conferences on Growing through Loss. I saw this opportunity to add a bit to the wisdom that came, and will come, from these gatherings.

The first thought I had about what I had learned from the deaths in my life was that "time heals, but does not cure." The loss of a loved one is like a deep wound that scabs over but never completely disappears. After my father's death I cried each night; then every other night; then once a week; then once every two weeks; etc. When I think of him now, after 50 years, I still cry; I miss him. When I visit his grave I sob. Of course, I have gone on with my life; his loss has not severely handicapped me. Time has healed but it has not cured. I think it is healthy to still mourn him. I give myself permission to think of him and to wish I had known him better.

The second thought I had about what I learned from the deaths in my life was "talk is cheap, presence is expensive." I well remember the words of my mother as she sat with me on the bed where my father had died. She said, "Daddy has gone to be with God and we must so live that we will go and be with him some day. God will send his guardian angel to take care of us." These words were comforting. In fact, I can remember waking up startled a short time later and seeing a form in the room. I was frightened but almost immediately remembered her words and returned to sleep. The form was God's guardian angel to me. More important than her words to me, however, was her presence—then and throughout all the years of childhood and adolescence. She was there. She did not forget my loss. Although she rarely mentioned my father, she never failed to realize that I needed her support.

The final lesson I have learned from the deaths in my life is that "family is good, community is better." This may be an overstatement because there is likely no substitute for the support of family at the time of death. However, there is always the danger that families will turn in on themselves during these times and act as if they are entirely self sufficient. This can lead to denial and loneliness. Very soon after my father's death, my mother took me to church again. I have remained a regular part of that community up to the present day. It has nurtured and supported me throughout the years. It has been a "wider" family for me that surrounded me with love and encouragement.

In regard to the place of the community, I well remember the words of a man in a southern church where I was the assistant pastor in the late 1950s. He was extremely angry with the senior pastor over sermons he had preached encouraging brotherhood and racial justice. When asked why he did not try to fire the pastor, he replied, "Fire him? Never! He's my pastor. Why, the night my mother died, he was the first one to come to the house and the last one to leave." For me, this is a powerful illustration of the maxim that "family is good, community is better."

So, these are three of the lessons I have learned from deaths in my life. As you can see, they are grounded in what happened to me after the death of my father so many years ago. However, I think they apply to all of the deaths I have experienced since that time. While these three lessons are, by no means, exhaustive prescriptions for insuring that the experience of death leads to wholeness and holiness, I think others, including my youngest son, would not go wrong in following them.

TWENTY-THREE

A Psychotherapist's Confession of Faith: Part One

I title this a "psychotherapist's" rather that a "psychologist's" confession of faith because psychotherapy is one of the prime roles I play as a psychologist and because I want to indicate the manner in which faith affects this particular task.

I call this "Part 1" because I do not perceive it as exhaustive or complete. It is a beginning. Other parts are yet to come. There could conceivably be a part 10 or even a part 100. Nevertheless, I am willing to be judged on what I say here and will not take refuge in the more that is to come. These ideas are more than musings or random thoughts. They are developed even if they are not complete. Thus they are open for critique and for response.

I call this a confession but it could be preferably termed as a profession. It is not that I have been caught and apprehended. It is not that I am forced to admit that about which I would prefer to keep secret. No, I welcome the chance and covet this opportunity to profess my convictions. While I share my faith with some trepidation I nevertheless do so boldly confident that the God I worship is bigger than all my words about Him and that the community of which I am a part will accept me as I am even if it disagrees with what I say.

THE STRUCTURE OF FAITH

Turning next to the components of my faith, I would like to mention two. The first has to do with the structure of faith. This has to do with the ingredients of that in which I put my trust. This is parallel faith as "insight." What is the truth that I know? What is the good news that I have accepted? What has been revealed to me in Scripture and tradition?

Purely and simply stated it is this: Christ has come—Christ has died—Christ has risen—Christ is present. This is all I know; This is all I need to know. It is sufficient truth.

In the words of the hymn...
This is that great thing I know, This delights and stirs me so:
Faith in Him-who died to save. Him who triumphed over the grave, Jesus
Christ the Crucified.

The second component has to do with the "function" of my faith. This is parallel to the meaning of faith as response. What kind of action am I committed to? What types of behaviors do I engage in? What is this something I do? What is this process of faithing about which I spoke?

Initially I respond with a feeling or sense of being both chosen and called. As a person who has been chosen I like the children of Israel, the remnant of Judah, the disciples of Jesus, the saints of the church and my fore-parents throughout the ages have been selected to be among those whom God treasures and loves.

I am completely known and all forgiven, a child of the King, safe in the arms of the Lord.

Yes, I've been chosen, but I have also been called. With election comes obligation. I have a calling and a ministry. When I was a member of the church's youth fellowship as an adolescent they used to say to us "Where your talents or gifts meet the needs of the world, there your calling lies." I believed that. I still believe that.

I'm fairly certain that I have the talents to match people's three basic needs:

1) People have a need to hear words from God, i.e. good news that will answer the longings of their heart. I can proclaim the truth that God has come in Christ Jesus.

2) People have a need to respond to this good news and to recognize that they live in between Christ's coming and His return. I can help them prepare themselves for life that is life indeed—both now and in the world to came.

3) Finally people have a need to be needed, i.e. a need to be a part of God's bringing in His kingdom. They need to be able to use their power for good. I can assist them in becoming free enough to participate in the good work God is doing.

These, then, are my talents. This is my ministry. I am not afraid to proclaim "Joy to the world, the Lord is Come." Nor do I resist the task of guiding people in preparing to live abundant life. Further I welcome the chance to rid persons of whatever handicaps them in fully participating in the creating of God's good earth.

Proclamation, preparation, participation—these are my ministries this is my calling. Specifically, however, I function in several concrete ways to make these goals come about.

As a psychotherapist I spend long hours with individuals in an effort to help find themselves. For me, this means not only that they be rid of their worrisome habits or that they learn to fit into their environment. Finding themselves means that they come to know themselves as I know myself—a person chosen and called by God into ministry. Finding themselves is never complete until they are free to be good channels of God's blessings to others and thus enjoy life fully and abundantly.

To facilitate this process I engage in at least three specific therapeutic endeavors that, to me, are clear responses of faith. These are Potency, Permission and Protection.

In the parlance of Transactional Analysis, to which I am committed, troubled people are those who have weak Adult ego states because they have made early decisions to obtain happiness by giving in to others' wishes for their lives. At the time they seek help from psychotherapists like me they find themselves living entirely out of their Adapted Child ego states. Or, if compliance has failed to bring love, they have given into the rebellious part of their child. In both cases they live under the tyranny of their Critical Parent who relentlessly demands that which they are unwilling to give but who punishes them with guilt when they do not.

What a way to live! There is no happiness here—only games and tragic scripts.

Into this situation I come with power. My potency is my hopeful reassurance that this dilemma need not last. I am active with my strength and I side with the Adult part of them. I encourage, gently confront, and confidently offer help. I encourage dependency. I am there to be leaned on. I know that the only way they can break out of the trap is through their Adult Ego state which alone can stop the critical parent from persecuting the helpless child. Knowing that, the Adult feels dismayed and discouraged. I share my Nurturing Parent with them—and hook the Adult into an alliance with me. I say, "We can do it", and I will help you."

And the help I give is in the form of a Permission to their Child to disobey their Critical Parent. Most often Parental admonitions are in the form of prohibitions to enjoy or provocations to self-destruct. "Don't show feelings" is an example of the first. "All real men get drunk" is an example of the second.

The permission I give is to start or stop a behavior that their Adult knows is keeping their Child from being free. "You need permission to start laughing, stop drinking, stop trying to be perfect, start spending time at home. Take my permission. You've got it. I give it to you. Try it." That's what permission is.

In effect I become Parent for them. I take the place of their Critical Parent and become the Nurturing Parent they need.

But change is not easy. As Rachael Carson reportedly said about volcanic islands in the ocean, "Once they rear their heads above the surface of the waves all the forces of nature conspire to beat them back down again." And so it is with troubled people. They have become habituated with disturbance. Although they do not like their predicament, they do not know what to do instead. So, when they take my permission to disobey the parent voice within themselves, it is not surprising that they feel guilty, tense, or depressed right away.

It is at this point that I offer my Protection. I protect them against the harsh judgment of their Critical Parent who would like to shame or provoke them into conformity again. I assure them that they will not fade away simply because they feel uncomfortable or threatened.

Now you may be wondering what these techniques of Potency, Permission, and Protection have to do with the function of my faith. They have everything to do with it for, in the parlance of faith, troubled people are those who do not know that they have been chosen by God or that they have a ministry to fulfill their lives. The effect of my Potency, Permission, Protection regime is to free them to respond to Cod.

And I am convinced this is what it means for them to find themselves. This self that they find is the image of God that they lost through their decision to live life through neurotic games and tragic scripts. They can be free and find abundant life. They can become channels of blessing because they heard the proclamation of the good news, have prepared themselves to live the life of faith, and have become participants in the ministry of reconciliation.

FAITH: INTENTION MORE THAN PERFORMANCE

This is my confession of faith part one. I am aware that this confession is redundant with rhetoric and pretense. I humbly admit that I speak better than I do. As Fric Berne once said, "the real test is what you do when you are in that little room with nothing between you and a troubled person." He also said, "Heal the client first. We can talk about it later." I can talk better than I can act. I admit this with some chagrin.

Nevertheless, faith is, in the final analysis, more intention than performance. I, too, am a forgiven sinner saved by grace through faith (Ephesians 2:5). I have no need or right to boast. It is probably true that some persons get better in spite of me rather than because of me. Thank goodness God is bigger and better than my technique.

However, my biggest problem is not pretense but poor memory. I often forget who I am and as a result my therapy suffers. It is a sad but tragic truth that many times therapist and client sit out their hour together with neither one clear about what is going on. The therapist has forgotten and the client never knew.

I have long felt the need to remind myself of my intentions and presuppositions on a daily basis. Recently I got a cue from the style of a square dance caller with whom I am acquainted. He starts out every dance with a review and never presumes you remember from week to week. This is a bit insulting because the dancers should be able to recall the dances they learned just seven days before. But he is usually right—they have indeed forgotten.

So it is with faith. Jesus knew our proclivity for forgetfulness so he established the Lord's Supper. This do, He said. "in remembrance of me" (Corinthians11:24). So, the last part of my profession of faith is to admit to you that I have had to come to the place where I must remind myself daily of who I am and who I intend to be. Toward that end I have established the habit of reading a portion of the Holy Bible, praying for myself and those with whom I work in psychotherapy and receiving the Holy Communion at least once during every twenty four hour period.

This is part 1 of a psychotherapist's faith. I welcome your responses and reactions so that Part 2 may be more worthy.

TWENTY-FOUR

"Diaconal" Ministries of Service

I teach in a theological seminary. Our seminary catalogue states that we "train people for the multiple ministries of the Christian church." The great majority of our students are hoping to be pastors of churches or missionaries. As such they will preach the Gospel, teach the Bible, administer the Sacraments, call people to repentance, bury the dead, baptize converts, pray for the sick, and marry those in love. However, a minority of our students intend to do none of these things. They are training to become marriage/family/child therapists and clinical psychologists—in other words, "counselors."

These "counselors-to-be" will spend the great majority of their time outside the church—counseling individuals and families disturbed or in trouble. At best, they might teach some classes to church members, help those referred to them by pastors, or offer their services to those who desire a "Christian" counselor. But most of their time will not be directly related to the church. Are they, too, part of the "manifold ministries of the church?" Can we really say that we are preparing counselors for ministry when they don't do the things that most ministers do?

My answer is a firm, strong, unequivocal YES! It is not by accident that my seminary, Fuller, established a School of Psychology in the mid-1960s. It was a calculated effort to proclaim the "priesthood of all believers," as the 16th century reformer Martin Luther asserted. It was attempt to break-out of the traditional stereotype that only pastors were full-time Christian workers. When they established a "School of Psychology" the seminary leaders envisioned a "Christian University" where professions as different as space scientists and missionaries could be trained under the rubric of the "manifold ministries" of the church. We were the first of many institutions in the United States who now offer training in counseling—a vocation that was long thought to be "secular" vocation .

But are the counselors and psychologists trained in these institutions really ministers? Isn't it stretching the meaning of the word to claim that these vocations are part of the "multiple ministries of the church?" My answer to this is YES and NO. Yes, it is stretching the meaning of "ministry" to think that counselors and pastors are in the same kind of business. On the other hand, No, it is not stretching the meaning of "ministry" to think that counselors as well as pastors are doing the work of God in the world; work that God wants to have done; work that God intends to be done. This is God's good earth; the place where He is bringing in His kingdom. As Psalm 24 proclaims; "The earth is the Lord's and all that is in it, the world, and those who live in it; for he has founded it on the seas, and established it on the rivers." (vs. 1-2, NRSV)

God does not make the distinction between work done inside and work done outside the church. It is all one to Him; work is work and all work can be sacred. God has a will for the events of every day. Where God's will is done, persons are in ministry. 1 John 3:11 said it well:

"This is the message you heard from the beginning: We should love one another."

It would be presumptuous to think that the only times God's love could be seen were during a few hours on Sunday or a during-the-week meetings at church. In fact, many have thought that the question about ministry should be reversed. Instead of comparing them to pastors and asking "Are counselors real ministers?" maybe we should use counselors as the norm and ask "Are pastors real ministers?" After all, the church could be compared to a gas station. It prepares Christians to minister just as a gas station prepares cars to run. But neither the church nor gas stations are where the action takes place. Real driving takes place on the road, not at the station. Real Christian ministry takes place out in the world, on Mondays through Saturdays when the church doors are closed. That where the real, hard Christian "loving" is expressed.

Yet, in one sense, there is a clear difference between pastors and counselors that cannot be ignored. While counselors might teach a church school class or counsel someone referred to them by the pastor, they do not administer the sacraments or bury the dead or conduct worship. The work they do is different. Everyone would recognize that the work their pastors did was clearly ministerial, but they would have to think twice about whether the same was true of counselors.

I would like to invite you to "think twice" with me about the ministry of counselors. I have told my students, who are studying to be professional counselors, that they should look on themselves as DIACONAL ministers. By this I mean that they are "ministers of Word and Service." Pastors are "ministers of Word, Sacrament, and Order." There are distinctions of roles but there is one vocation—ministry.

In my church we call ministers of Word and Service "Deacons" and ministers of Word, Sacrament, and Order "Elders." Both are ordained. Both are considered "ministers." The work of deacons is out in the world; the work of elders is inside the church. In my church, United Methodist, both are ordained in a public service at our yearly conference. Our bishops lay their hands on both and commission them to meeting the needs of persons out in the world or to meeting the needs of God's people in the church. Both share the love of God. Two roles, one ministry.

Both types of ministers in my church are ordained to the ministry of the WORD. The WORD of God guides both deacons and elders in my church. All ministry is grounded in the WORD—the intent of God for life as revealed in the life, the teachings, the death, and the resurrection of Jesus Christ as well as in God's revelation of Himself in the history of the Jewish people. Not all Christians self-consciously base their daily work on this awareness about God's revelation, but all Christians can, if they are willing to pay the price.

This intentional grounding of one's life-work in the Word of God is not an after-thought for deacons and elders in my church. It is more than a commitment of oneself to Jesus as Lord and Savior, as important as that is for the Christian living. What is involved is a serious process of self-examination and training that goes beyond conversion and daily Christian witness.

Several steps are involved. First of all the process begins in the local church where one catches the vision of the call of God into ministry. While deacons will not live out their lives in church work, their sense that God wants them for His ministry always begins at church. The Christian life, be it in ministry or not, is always life in the church. To be Christian is to be a part of the church. The grace of God shed abroad in the world is first heard about "at church" for 999 out of 1000 believers. Being a solitary Christian is so rare as to be non-existent. To be in the church is to be part of the people of God walking across history. The church began with Abraham and continues with the church on the corner. The church is the means through which Christians first hear God's word. It is also the means through which Christians respond to that Word. It is the means by which Christians hear and respond to the call into ministry. And the church is the fellowship that confirms that call and declares that a given person is ready to go into ministry.

The second step after hearing the call is, thus, to announce one's call to ministry to the church and see if that call can be seen by others. If it can, persons in our church are referred to district committees that assign them a mentor who will lead them through a set of studies designed to determine whether they are truly called. These studies take candidates beyond being just a go-to-church-on-Sunday Christian. Becoming a minister is serious business and it is not a role to be undertaken lightly or without reflection.

The mentor guides these persons who are called through a set of studies that include intense reflection of what the Bible says about ministry. They read theology and seriously consider what it means to give oneself to full-time

Christian service. In addition, candidates undergo psychological evaluations that determine whether their vocational interests and personal adjustment are supportive of their desires to enter ministry.

These studies, which take up to a year of part-time effort, attempt to confirm or dis-confirm whether persons are truly called into ministry. And note, we require these studies of both candidates for deacons as well as elders; those intending to go into a ministry of service outside the church as well as those intending to work inside the church. After the studies are completed and the call into ministry is affirmed, the district committee helps the candidate decide the next steps to take to prepare for either a ministry of Word and Service or a ministry of Word and Sacrament and Order.

In the case of counselors, the next step might be to undertake the training that would lead them to be a skilled counselors in the eyes of the secular world. This might include, for example, entering Fuller Seminary's School of Psychology. But, note that the secular training is gounded in the WORD—a considered evaluation of one's talent and of one's call to serve God in this specific way.

Of course, counseling is only of many ways to serve God in service to the world. Teachers, nurses, physicians, social workers, policemen or women, politicians, lawyers, and business men or women are only a few of the many vocations in which service to others can become a ministry.

One alternative to these steps into ministry that is becoming much more common these days is the decision of persons to enter ministry who are already trained in the profession they now want to recons true as a ministry. We are seeing many second-career Christians enter into the kinds of studies I have described in an effort to become deliberate and dedicated ministers in the vocation in which they are already active. They still go through the process I have just described to determine whether their call into ministry is a good one. Counselors who begin to take their Christian faith seriously, often want to think of themselves as in ministry through the work that they already do.

While I feel that the process I have described in my denomination is a good well-thought out approach, it is not the only way to become a minister of service to the world. For example, most students who undertake study with us at Fuller School of Psychology have never been through the kind of candidacy studies that I have detailed above. But, our curriculum requires them to take a whole set of courses in Bible, theology, church history, ethics, and philosophy. When they graduate they have gone through much reflection on how their call to ministry is grounded in the Word of God. By describing the typical process. I only meant to illustrate how the decision should involve intentional and serious reflection. Although all Christians are called to follow Christ, becoming a minister, whether in the church pastoral role or in service to the world, should require sober and somber thinking. Like marriage, ministry is not to be entered into lightly or without earnest consideration. I only wish that every church would have the same kind of ordination celebration for ministries of service to the world that they have for church pastors.

I close by inviting you to "think twice" with me one final time. The question I should like us to consider is, "What might it mean to be a Diaconal Minister of Word and Service in the Christian practice of counseling?" Three answers to this question have been offered: Be explicit, Be implicit, Be intentional. While I prefer the last option, Be intentional, let me describe what it might mean to be explicit or implicit.

Be explicit: This would mean that counselors who are ministers would look for every chance to introduce their faith into their counseling. They would overtly, obviously, clearly, and explicitly bring up religious understandings of problems and religious answers to difficulties. Explicit minister-counselors would see it as their duty to talk about God every chance they could get. They would not hesitate to bring up spiritual issues.

Be implicit: This would mean that counselors who are ministers would not bring up religious issues unless, and until, the person they were trying to help did so. However, this approach would be based more on a conviction that their faith was communicated by the empathy and warmth that they showed than on the words that they spoke. They are concerned about imposing their religion on somebody else. These minister-counselors would be convinced that they incarnated God more by the way they related to others than on anything they might say. Just as Jesus showed God's grace by His actions, so these counselors would attempt to show God's love in the same way. Their actions would speak louder than words .

Be intentional: This would mean that counselors who are ministers would purposefully, playfully, and intentionally dedicate themselves to letting God lead them in what they said and did in counseling. The issue for these counselors would not be whether to use or not to use religious language. They would be relaxed about being explicit or implicit in their actions. In fact, they would be explicit or implicit as they felt led by God at specific times. These minister- counselors would be convinced that God was there with them in their work and that, if they listened, God would guide them as to how they might best be used to advance His kingdom. They would look on every counseling session as a holy hour in which God's good work could be done. They would be just as satisfied with those times when God's name was never mentioned as with those time when much "God talk" filled the session. These counselors would know that their chief job was to begin each day with a time of Bible reading and prayer in faith that God would use them in their work. They would not assume that they were perfect, nor would they fear that they could not be used by God. Each evening as they went to sleep, the would offer thanks for the way God had been present in their work and ask forgiveness for their best as well as their worst.

As I said, I prefer the "intentional" option and commend it to all of you who would yearn to become counselors who are Diaconal ministers of Word and Service.

ACKNOWLEDGEMENTS

Two friends made this volume possible: Louis Hoffman and Randall Cole.

Louis is one of those whose dissertation I chaired. We shared many priorities and interests. He has become a distinguished colleague in academia. He is a professor in the Executive Faculty of Saybrook Institute in San Francisco and has authored/edited several noteworthy volumes of his own. When we began discussions of the possible publishing of these articles, he eagerly took on the task of choosing, then closely editing, the corpus. I am honored by his trust that these thoughts deserve a wider audience. He is a true friend.

Randall (Randy) is the Director of Publications at Fuller Seminary whose skills and wisdom have brought these words to print. That he would undertake such a endeavor has always amazed me. But to do it with such winsomeness, availability, and skill has been even more impressive. I remain in his debt. Such new friends are not easy to find when one nears 80 years of age.

I have had one other writing companion: my wife of 57 years, Suzanna. She has never despaired of my long hours before a computer. However, she has been very incisive in her evaluations. My concerns have not always been synonymous with hers. I shall not forget two humbling comments she made—more than once): "Promise me this will be your last book," and "Read Newton's books and go to sleep." Nevertheless, her constant love and support has never wavered. As the saying on the street suggests, she has been "a keeper."

John Wesley, my spiritual hero, reportedly commented thusly on his prolific published writings, "Good Christians are reading Christians. I have made a little contribution toward that end. May others who have more time and talent, take up where I have left off." This is a statement with which I can identify.

Trinity Season 2010
H. Newton Malony

PUBLICATIONS

Books published

Malony, H.N. (in press). *The Amazing John Wesley: An Unusual Look at an Uncommon Life.* Colorado Springs, CO: Paternoster.

Hoffman, L. (in press). *Toward a Christian Clinical Psychology: The Contribution of H. Newton Malony.* Pasadena, CA: Fuller Theological Seminary Press.

Malony, H.N. & Augsburger, D.H. (2006). *Christian Counseling: An Introduction.* Nashville, TN: Abingdon 2007.

Malony, H.N (with M.D. Dunnam, Eds.). (2003) *Staying the Course: Support for the Church's Position on Homosexuality.* Nashville, TN: Abingdon Press.

Malony, H.N., Editor (2001). *Pastoral Care and Counseling in Sexual Diversity.* Binghamton, NY: The Haworth Pastoral Press.

Malony, H.N. (with N. Murphy & W.S. Brown, Eds.)(1998). *Whatever Happened to the Soul: Scientific and Theological Portraits of Human Nature.* Minneapolis, MN: Fortress Press.

Malony, H.N.(1998). *Living with Paradox: Religious Leadership and the Genius of Double Vision.* San Francisco, CA: Jossey-Bass.

Malony, H.N. (1998). *Brainwashing, Coercive Persuasion, Undue Influence, and Mind Control: A Psychologist's Point of View.* Pasadena, CA: Integration Press.

Malony, H.N. (1996). *Christ in the Heart of Psychology: The Early Years of Fuller Seminary's School of Psychology.* Pasadena, CA: Fuller Seminary Press.

Malony, H. N.(1995). *Win/Win Relationships: 9 Strategies for Settling Personal Conflict Without Going to War.* Nashville, TN: Broadman/Holman.

Malony, H. N., & Southard, S. (Eds.)(1992). *Handbook on Conversion.* Birmingham, AL: Religious Education Press.

Malony, H. N. (1992). *Relaxation for Christians.* New York, NY: Ballantine..

Malony, H. N. (Ed.) (1991, 1995). *Psychology of Religion: Personalities, Problems, Possibilities.* Grand Rapids, MI: Baker Book House, 1991 (Republished by Integration Press, Pasadena, CA in 1995).

Malony, H. N. & Spilka, B. (Eds.) (1991). *Religion in Psychodynamic Perspective: The Contributions of Paul W. Pruyser.* New York, NY: Oxford University Press.

Malony, H. N. (with R.A. Hunt) (1991). *The Psychology of Clergy.* Harrisburg, PA: Morehouse Publishers.

Malony, H. N. (1990).*When Getting Along Seems Impossible: Straightforward Help to Reduce Conflict and Stress at Home, at Work, and at Church.* Old Tappan, NJ: Fleming Revell Publishers..

Malony, H.N., Editor (1990). *A Christian Existential Psychology: The contributions of John G. Finch.* Pasadena, CA: Integration Press..

Malony, H. N. (with R. Hunter, L.O. Mills and J. Patton, Eds.) (1990). *Dictionary of Pastoral Care and Counseling.* New York, NY: Abingdon..

Malony, H.N., (with R.A.Hunt and J. E. Hinkle, Jr.), Editors (1990). *Clergy Assessment and Career Development.* Nashville, TN. Abingdon

Malony, H.N. (1986, 1995). *Integration Musings: Thoughts on being a Christian Professional.* Pasadena, CA. Integration Press

Malony, H.N., Editor (1986). *Is There a Shrink in the Lord's House: How Psychologists Can Help the Church.* Pasadena, CA: Integration Press.

Malony, H.N. (with C. Rosik), Editors (1983). *The Travis Papers in the Integration of Psychology and Theology.* Pasadena, CA: Integration Press.

Malony, H.N. (with C.B.Johnson) (1982). *Christian Conversion: Biblical and Psychological Perspectives.* Grand Rapids, MI: Zondervan.

Malony, H.N. & G.R.Collins (1981). *Psychology & Theology: Prospects for Integraation.* Nashville, TN: Abingdon Press.

Malony, H.N. (1979). *Living the Answers.* Nashville, TN: Abingdon Press.

Malony, H.N. (1978). *Understanding your faith: A Christian Psychologist Helps You Look at Your Religious Experience.* Nashville, TN: Abingdon Press..

Malony, H.N. (1978). *Ways People Meet God: Today's Religious Experience.* Nashville, TN: Discipleship Resources.

Malony, H.N., Editor (1977). *Current Perspectives in the Psychology of Religion.* Grand Rapids, MI: William B. Eerdmans Publishing Company.

Malony:H.N. & Gorsuch, R.L. (1976). *The Nature of Man: A Social Psychological Perspective.* Springfield, IL: Charles C. Thomas Publishers.

Malony, H.N., W.H. Clark, J. Daane, & A.R. Tippett (1973). *Religions Experience: Its Nature and Function in the Human Psyche.* Springfield, IL: Charles C. Thomas Publisher.

Other Recent Writings

Malony, H.N. (1995). John Wesley and the Eighteenth Century therapeutic uses of electricity. *Perspectives on Science and the Christian Faith,* 47(4), 244-254.

Malony, H.N.(1996). John Wesley's Primitiv Physick: An 18th Century Health Psychology. *Journal of Health Psychology,* 1(2), 147-159.

Malony, H.N. (1998). Counseling Body/Soul persons. *International Journal for the Psychology of Religion,* 8(4), 221-242.

Malony, H.N. (1998). Religion and Mental Health from the Protestant perspective. In H.G. Koenig (Editor) *Handbook of Religion and Mental Health* (pp.203-210). San Diego, CA: Academic Press.

Malony, H.N. (2000). The psychological evaluation of religious professionals. *Professional Psychology: Research and Practice, 31*(5), 1-5.

Tepper, L., Rogers, S.A., Coleman, E.M., & Malony, H.N. (2001). The prevalence of religious coping among persons with persistent mental illness. *Psychiatric Services, 52*(5), 660-665.

Rogers, S.A., Malony, H.N., Coleman, E.M., & Tepper, L. (2002). Changes in attitudes toward religion among those with mental illness. *Journal of Religion and Health, 41*(2), 167-178.

To request a complete vita from Dr. Newton Malony you may contact him directly at hnewtonm@yahoo.com

www.ingramcontent.com/pod-product-compliance
Lightning Source LLC
Chambersburg PA
CBHW071843270326

41929CB00013B/2085